Internet Governance in Transition

CRITICAL MEDIA STUDIES
INSTITUTIONS, POLITICS, AND CULTURE

Series Editor
Andrew Calabrese, University of Colorado

Advisory Board

Recent Titles in the Series
Global Media Governance: A Beginner's Guide,
Seán Ó Siochrú and Bruce Girard
*The Global and the National: Media and Communications in
Post-Communist Russia,*
Terhi Rantanen
Newsworkers Unite: Labor, Convergence, and North American Newspapers,
Catherine McKercher
Principles of Publicity and Press Freedom,
Slavko Splichal
Critical Communication Theory: Power, Media, Gender, and Technology
Sue Curry Jansen
Digital Disability: The Social Construction of Disability in New Media,
Gerard Goggin and Christopher Newell
Internet Governance in Transition: Who Is the Master of This Domain?
Daniel J. Paré

Forthcoming in the Series
Recovering a Public Vision for Public Television,
Glenda R. Balas
Herbert Schiller,
Richard Maxwell
The Party System and Public Service Broadcasting in Italy,
Cinzia Padovani
Contesting Media Power: Alternative Media in a Networked World,
edited by Nick Couldry and James Curran
Harold Innis,
Paul Heyer
Toward a Political Economy of Culture,
edited by Colin Sparks and Andrew Calabrese
The Blame Game: Why Television Is Not Our Fault,
Eileen R. Meehan
Film Industries and Cultures in Transition,
Dina Iordanova
Globalizing Political Communication,
Gerald Sussman
Elusive Autonomy: Brazilian Communications Policy,
Sergio Euclides de Souza

Internet Governance in Transition

Who Is the Master of This Domain?

DANIEL J. PARÉ

ROWMAN & LITTLEFIELD PUBLISHERS, INC.
Lanham • Boulder • New York • Oxford

ROWMAN & LITTLEFIELD PUBLISHERS, INC.

Published in the United States of America
by Rowman & Littlefield Publishers, Inc.
A Member of the Rowman & Littlefield Publishing Group
4720 Boston Way, Lanham, Maryland 20706
www.rowmanlittlefield.com

P.O. Box 317, Oxford OX2 9RU, United Kingdom

Copyright © 2003 by Rowman & Littlefield Publishers, Inc.

British Library Cataloguing in Publication Information Available

Library of Congress Cataloging-in-Publication Data

Paré, Daniel J.
    Internet governance in transition : who is the master of this domain? / Daniel J. Paré.
       p. cm. — (Critical media studies)
    Includes bibliographical references and index.
    ISBN 0-7425-1845-0 (cloth : alk. paper) — ISBN 0-7425-1846-9 (paper : alk. paper)
       1. Internet—Management. 2. Internet addresses—Government policy. 3.
Telecommunication policy. I. Title. II. Series.

TK5105.875. I57 P368 2003
004.67'8—dc 21

                                                                     2002073861

Printed in the United States of America

♾™ The paper used in this publication meets the minimum requirements of American
National Standard for Information Sciences—Permanence of Paper for Printed Library
Materials, ANSI/NISO Z39.48-1992.

For my parents, Claude and Suzanne Paré

Contents

Figures

Tables

Abbreviations

AIM	Association for Interactive Media
APNIC	Asia Pacific Network Information Center
ARIN	American Registry for Internet Numbers
ARPA	United States Department of Defense Advanced Research Projects Agency
ARPAnet	Advanced Research Projects Agency Network
ccTLD	Country-code Top-Level Domain
CCIC	United States National Science and Technology Council's Committee on Computing, Information and Communications
CIX	Commercial Internet Exchange
CORE	gTLD-MoU Council of Registrars
DARPA	Defense Advanced Research Projects Agency *(known as ARPA prior to 1972)*
DDN	Defense Data Network
DISA	United States Defense Information System Agency
DNS	Domain Name System
DOC	United States Department of Commerce
DTI	United Kingdom Department of Trade and Industry
EU	European Union
EuroISPA	European Internet Service Providers Association
FNC	United States Federal Networking Council
gTLD	Generic Top-Level Domain
gTLD-MoU	Generic Top-Level Domain Memorandum of Understanding
IAB	Internet Architecture Board
IAHC	Internet International Ad Hoc Committee
IANA	Internet Assigned Numbers Authority
ICANN	Internet Corporation for Assigned Names and Numbers
IESG	Internet Engineering Steering Group
IETF	Internet Engineering Task Force
IFWP	International Forum on the White Paper
INTA	International Trademark Association
InterNIC	Internet Network Information Center
IP	Internet Protocol
IPv4	Internet Protocol version 4
IPv6	Internet Protocol version 6
ISI	Information Sciences Institute, University of Southern California
ISOC	Internet Society
ISP	Internet Service Provider
ITU	International Telecommunication Union
JAnet	United Kingdom Joint Academic Network

JNT	United Kingdom Joint Network Team
LINX	London Internet Exchange
MoD	United Kingdom Ministry of Defence
NIC	Network Information Center
NRS	United Kingdom Name Registration Scheme
NSF	United States National Science Foundation
NSFnet	United States National Science Foundation Network
NSI	Network Solutions Incorporated
NTIA	United States National Telecommunications and Information Administration
POC	gTLD-MoU Policy Oversight Committee
RFC	Request for Comments
RIPE NCC	Réseaux IP Européens
SRI	Stanford Research Institute
SRI-NIC	Stanford Research Institute Network Information Center
TCP/IP	Transfer Control Protocol/Internet Protocol
TLD	Top-Level Domain
UCL	University College London
UKERNA	United Kingdom Education and Research Networking Association
UUCP	Unix-to-Unix Copy Protocol
VLSI	Very Large Scale Integration
WIPO	World Intellectual Property Organization
WTO	World Trade Organization

Acknowledgments

The greater part of the investigation into the restructuring of the Internet domain name system which forms the core of this study is based upon research conducted while I was working toward the completion of my DPhil at SPRU—Science and Technology Policy Research, University of Sussex.

While at SPRU I benefited immensely from the fascinating and inspiring environment its faculty offers to young researchers. My first thanks, and an extended one, must go to Robin Mansell who was my supervisor. Her ideas, suggestions, and criticisms greatly strengthened the research and writing that went into this study. It was a privilege to have worked with her, and I am the richer as a result of everything I learned from her. I also would like to thank my immediate peers at SPRU and various members of the research faculty who contributed their enthusiasm, support and, when necessary, skepticism. Although it is not possible to name everyone, special mention goes to the following people: Grové Steyn, David Neice, Ammon Salter, Jonathan Sapsed, Tiago Santos-Perieira, Steffen Bayer, Stefano and Eugenia Brusoni, Pablo D'Este Cukierman, Amal-Lee Amin, Richard Torbett, Jenny Gristock, Jane Calvert, Puay Tang, Jordi Molas-Gallart, Cynthia Little, who contributed enormously with the editing of this book, Ed Steinmueller, Martin Bell, Keith Pavitt, and, of course, the ever inspirational Christopher Freeman.

After completing my degree, I had the good fortune to obtain a post as a Research Fellow at Media@LSE, London School of Economics and Political Science. It is here that most of the work involved in transforming my dissertation into book form took place. Colleagues at the LSE commented on earlier drafts and contributed their insights. I am particularly grateful to Saskia Sassen, who was the first to suggest transforming the dissertation into a book, and to Andrew Murray, whose interest and research in this subject area has made him an ideal conversation partner.

An immense debt of gratitude is owed to my parents and to my sister for their endless support and encouragement. They never doubted that this work would be completed and their fortitude provided much of the motivation to make sure that it was.

Finally and most importantly, I would like to thank my partner, Ingrid Schenk. Her lively spirit and humor consistently inspires me.

Chapter 1

Introduction

As we move into the first decade of a new century the evolving capabilities of information and communication technologies are increasingly central features of the way business and everyday life are organized. The rapid spread of inter-networking infrastructures and the enormous growth in the range of related applications means that the manner in which these technologies are coordinated and regulated has major consequences for a growing number of people. Controversies have erupted at international, national, regional, and local levels over the appropriate forms of governance for the Internet and its applications. This book offers an in-depth examination of two such controversies and their resolution.

The issues that have given rise to controversy over the restructuring of the Internet domain name system (DNS) have provided a focal point for discussions about appropriate forms of governance for the Internet and its applications. Prior to the mid-1990s the issue of Internet addressing was widely perceived as being primarily a technical matter. However, as the 1990s drew to a close the issue of domain naming had become the principal locus for political and legal controversies associated with the Internet and its governance. The legal and political wrangling about the manner in which the domain name system is coordinated and administered is directly related to the economic significance of the technology involved and reflects different actors' perceptions of both the goals of this infrastructure and how these goals might best be achieved. Simply put, the fundamental question(s) focus on the management of value allocations and choice alternatives.

At the international level, four years of protracted debate culminated, in the autumn of 1998, with the formation of the Internet Corporation for Assigned Names and Numbers (ICANN). This entity is a private nonprofit organization that is responsible for developing and implementing global domain naming policy. It was not the product of a pre-ordained plan. Rather, it emerged from a period of institutional flux and was shaped by formal and informal processes of interest mediation between social actors. However, a number of factors relating to the manner in which ICANN was formed, the way in which it operates, and the scope of its powers have resulted in a situation wherein the legitimacy of its authority for overseeing the administration of the DNS remains steeped in controversy.

Some of the conflicts that have coincided with efforts to restructure the global Internet addressing regime were also visible in the disputes underpinning the transformation and reorganization of the Internet addressing regime in the United Kingdom. The conflicts associated with the management and administration of the *.uk* domain were not restricted to the technical features of the UK registry system. They too encompassed a reconfiguration of the institutional framework of Internet governance, albeit at a national level. Disputes about the management and administration of the *.uk* name space fostered the emergence, in August 1996, of a new registry organization—Nominet UK. This organization has since grown from a membership base consisting of approximately 100 providers of Internet services into an organization composed of more than 1,000 members. In contrast to ICANN, however, the processes of interest mediation associated with the emergence of Nominet coalesced in a manner that legitimated the outcome of this period of institutional flux.

In both the ICANN and Nominet cases, the outcomes of collective exercises in decision making affected the perceived legitimacy and efficacy of these organizations as intermediaries between those who manage and administer the technical aspects of the architecture for Internet addressing and those who seek to use it. The controversies associated with these, and other related, events have given rise to an emerging discourse about the Internet and its governance. Within this growing dialogue, the notion of "governance" has become an imprecise catch-phrase that often is used interchangeably in reference to the perpetuation of the "Internet paradigm" and to the creation of more hierarchical regulatory oriented architectures. For example, in some contexts the term "governance" has been used to denote the informal and formal coordinating processes that make network based interactions, and transactions, possible on the Internet and the World Wide Web. In other contexts the hierarchical aspects of "governance" have been emphasized by those actors who point to the necessity of establishing rule sets, or regulations, vis-à-vis such issues as: the protection of intellectual property rights, freedom of speech, information flows, privacy, and content.

In addition to these two approaches, the scope of the "governance" concept also includes politically charged questions pertaining to who, or what, in the electronic realm has the right to make authoritative decisions, and on what basis such authority rests. In terms of Internet addressing, the semantic ambiguity characterizing the use of the term "governance" reflects, in part, the fact that the controversies associated with domain naming form only one aspect of a complex "governance" picture involving a multitude of different issues and actors.

Despite the somewhat ambiguous application of the notion of governance, the bulk of the Internet governance literature may be divided into two schools of thought, each of which offers conflicting visions about the means, and necessity, of constraining various dimensions of cyberspace or virtual society.[1] Perspectives rooted in the first, or commons school of thought, argue that the Internet encompasses numerous technical and nontechnical elements which, when taken together, constitute a conceptual whole. Supporters of this view have tended to advocate the implementation of top down, or hierarchical, governance frameworks to ensure the well-being of the conceptual whole. In contrast, approaches rooted in the second, or decentralized school of thought assert that there is no conceptual "whole" and have tended to favor more laissez-faire-oriented policy frameworks.

In terms of Internet addressing, it should be borne in mind that many of the proponents of these contending schools of thought were writing as the events leading up to the formation of ICANN were unfolding. It is not particularly surprising to find, therefore, that the greater part of what was written about this subject during the mid- to late 1990s consisted primarily of commentaries and/or appraisals of various formal and informal governance framework proposals, and/or specific aspects of such proposals. Consequently, the normative evaluations set forth by many commentators generally did not account for the emergent or changing structures of Internet regulatory and coordinating bodies, nor do they offer much insight into the dynamic relationship between regulatory change and the technical characteristics of networks.

During the same period, a parallel line of theorizing about the Internet and its governance which incorporated elements of both the commons and decentralized schools also emerged. The emphasis of these third, or process-oriented, approaches has been on the procedures that give rise to various outcomes in the electronic realm. For example, Johnson and Post (1996a, 1996b) maintained that, since the legitimacy of rule sets governing online activities could not be traced to any geographically based polity, the various dimensions of internetworking, including Internet addressing, were likely to be governed by privately produced rules that would lead to the emergence of common standards for mutual coordination. In contrast, Reidenberg (1996, 1998) suggests that the hardware and software constituting the electronic realm imposes a set of default rules or *Lex Informatica* on communication networks. He argues that, whereas political governance processes usually establish the substantive laws of nation-states, in the cyber-realm the primary sources of default rule making are the technology developer(s) and the social processes through which customary uses of the technology evolve. Similarly, Lawrence Lessig (1998d, 1999b) argues that the architecture, or code,[2] of cyberspace establishes conditions of entry and participation in the electronic realm and reflects a distinct philosophy of social ordering. He claims that since architecture is underpinned by specific values, the potential exists for government encroachment into the virtual realm as well as for the private sector to embed its values within the "code" of cyberspace.

Consequently, there is a need to ensure that the architectures of cyberspace protect values such as liberty, free speech, privacy, and access.

Unfortunately, the perspectives outlined above appear to underestimate the significance of the sociopolitical dynamics of governance processes. Consequently, they yield relatively little insight into how regulatory initiatives establish social, political, and cognitive[3] legitimacy within cyberspace. This highlights the need for empirical analysis of what social actors *actually* do rather than prescriptive, ideologically laden speculations about what they *should* do.

The argument presented in this book takes as its starting point that the software and hardware comprising the Internet should not be viewed simply as technologies that limit or enhance the ability of the state and/or commerce to limit freedom in cyberspace. There is also a need to recognize that the interplay between social actors influences, in a multitude of ways, the manner and extent to which the values embedded in the architecture manifest themselves. These interactive processes involve multifaceted power relations that give rise to the authoritative allocation of values. Therefore, insofar as specific design features of a system establish the patterns and boundaries of interaction, the choices and decisions that are implemented by social actors may be regarded as a political phenomenon.

Focusing on the way in which politicking and power relations between social agents influences the architectures underpinning internetworking offers an alternative basis for thinking and theorizing about the Internet and its governance and has important implications for understanding the nature of regulation in the electronic realm. First, it provides a richer and more dynamic picture of Internet politics that does not fall prey to ideologically motivated positions. Second, it offers a means of coupling investigations of the determinants of the technical architecture of the Internet and the way the social and political interests of its designers and users become embedded in the various layers of that architecture.[4] Third, it suggests that other features of the evolution of the Internet and its governance can best be understood by examining the manner in which new configurations of power constellations are influencing the emergence of the policies and institutions responsible for managing and administering the Internet's core functions.

In developing my argument I adopt a social constructivist approach to illustrate how the collective and individual actions of industry players, Internet and non-Internet organizations, governmental authorities, and specific individuals have influenced the scope and direction of change for a key dimension of the architecture supporting internetworking. Examining the role that power relations and politicking have played in shaping the policies and institutions that have emerged from attempts to reconfigure the Internet domain name system, and in influencing the degree of legitimacy attained by these innovations, provides an empirical basis for critically assessing the normative evaluations underpinning much of the contemporary theorizing about the Internet and its governance.

My hope is that understanding how emergent and established Internet regulatory and coordinating bodies are constituted will enable us to hypothesize about their behavior and effect on the governance trajectory of internetworking. Therefore, my purpose here is not to develop specific policy prescriptions about how the Internet domain name system should be managed or coordinated per se. Rather, my goal is analytical in nature and reflects an attempt to develop a more nuanced view of Internet politics that will help to stimulate further discussion and debate about the nature of the Internet and its governance.

Notes

1. Gould (1996b) defines these terms as referring broadly to "human and computer interactions across open networks and without reference to geographical location (and therefore legal jurisdiction) or real-world social understanding."

2. Lessig (1998d:4) labels the architecture of cyberspace "code." It refers to the "software and hardware that constitutes cyberspace as it is—the set of protocols, the set of rules, implemented, or codified, in cyberspace itself, that determine how people interact, or exist in this space...It [code], like architecture, is not option."

3. In this context cognitive legitimacy refers to the extent to which new regulatory initiatives are taken for granted. See Hunt and Aldrich (1998).

4. The notion of layers in this context refers to the different layers within the architecture of internetworking that together make communications possible. See Benkler (2000), and Wu (1999).

Chapter 2

Fomenting Dissent:

A Brief History of the Domain Name Wars

We reject: kings, presidents and voting. We believe in rough consensus and running code.
—Zittrain and Clark (1997)

Prior to the mid-1990s the issue of Internet addressing was widely perceived as being primarily a technical matter. One of the consequences of the rapid growth of internetworking throughout the last decade was a concomitant emergence of numerous domain naming related controversies. In fact, as the 1990s drew to a close the issue of domain naming had become the principal locus for the political and legal controversies associated with the Internet and its governance. This was due, in part, to two interrelated factors. The first is the fact that domain names are unique, and their creation and registration are one of the "few centralized points of authority in the supposedly open, decentralized world of the Internet" (Mueller 1997c). The second factor relates to the fact that domain naming was the first aspect of internetworking within which the authority of the traditional governance structures of this technological infrastructure was challenged.

Before proceeding with a discussion of the factors influencing the evolution of the governance trajectory of internetworking, there is a need to become familiar with the addressing infrastructure of the Internet, and the sociopolitical institutions that coevolved with it. Given the nature of this subject matter, the discussion presented in this chapter is largely descriptive and is divided into three sections. The first provides the reader with a basic understanding of what the domain name system (DNS) is and how it works. In the second section the evolution of the DNS is examined to illustrate the extent to which a particular set of values and norms[1] influenced the way in which this technical infrastructure evolved and was administered prior to 1995. As the Internet became increasingly commercialized, these value constructs, combined with the ambiguities they fostered, gave rise to and perpetuated numerous political, economic, and legal controversies that are commonly referred to as the domain name wars.[2] The third section of the chapter focuses on attempts by the various Internet stakeholders to establish workable solutions to these controversies. The significance of these negotiation processes cannot be underestimated because, as Leiner et al. (1998) have pointed out, "The most pressing question for the future of the Internet is not how the technology will change, *but how the process of change and evolution itself will be managed*" [emphasis added].

Technical Features of Internet Addressing

The creation of an identity in cyberspace, or virtual society,[3] is contingent, in part, upon the establishment of a point of contact at which an entity may be located. Within the realm of internetworking, the process of identification is made possible through the mapping of alphanumeric character strings, or domains, to numeric addresses. The subsections below outline the manner in which these two complementary addressing parameters interoperate.

Internet Protocol (IP) Addresses

In order for a network, or an individual computer, to be connected to the multitude of networks comprising the Internet it must have a unique numeric identifier. This identifier is known as an Internet Protocol (IP) address. It is responsible for distinguishing individual computers directly connected to the Internet (Krol 1989; Mockapetris 1987b; Murphy 1997; Rony and Rony 1998; Semeria 1999). The established IP protocol, IP version 4 (IPv4), defines unique 32-bit address values by dividing this numeric address into four 8-bit segments that specify the value of each segment independently.[4]

At present, the majority of IP addresses consist of a string of four decimal numbers separated by periods (e.g., 139.184.14.18). Although this numeric address consists of four separate octets, the address structure itself consists of two parts: (i) the network prefix; and (ii) the host, or computer, number. The network prefix identifies a particular network where an individual computer is located. The host number, on the other hand, identifies a specific computer on a particular network. All the computers on a given network share the same network address but must have a unique host number. Likewise, computers on different networks must have differing network prefixes but may share the same host number.

IP addresses are differentiated primarily on the basis of three network classes—A, B, C—each reflecting different interpretations of the four 8-bit segments of the address.[5] As Krol (1989) points out, this classification scheme allows computer networks to be structured in a variety of configurations ranging from flat (one network with many nodes) to hierarchical (many interconnected networks with fewer nodes each). In Class A networks, the first 8-bit segment serves as the network prefix and may have a decimal value between 1 and 126. The three remaining segments function as the host, or computer, addresses on a particular network. Given that these three segments comprise 24 bits (i.e., 8 bits + 8 bits + 8 bits), Class A networks can accommodate a multitude of individual hosts (Semeria 1999). University networks are generally Class B. These networks have addresses that are divided into two 16-bit segments (i.e. the first two 8 bit octets, and the last two 8 bit octets of the IP address). The first 16-bit segments in this class of networks have decimal values between 128 and 191. Class C addressing is generally used for small networks and computers that are not part of any local area network. In these networks, the first three segments of the IP address structure specify the network address, and the fourth segment identifies the host address. The first octet for this type of network address has decimal values between 192 and 223 (Rony and Rony 1998).

The allocation of IP number space is coordinated on the basis of a hierarchical distribution model with the Internet Corporation for Assigned Names and Numbers (ICANN), the successor to the Internet Assigned Numbers Authority (IANA),[6] at the summit (see figure 2.1).

Figure 2.1: Administration of IP Address Space

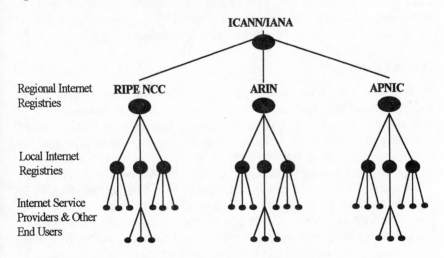

Although the IP address space is coordinated by the entity at the top of the hierarchy, responsibility for the assignment of specific blocks of numbers is delegated to three geographically dispersed nonprofit regional Internet registries:

- The American Registry for Internet Numbers (ARIN) services North America, South America, the Caribbean, and Sub-Saharan Africa;[7]
- Réseaux IP Européens (RIPE NCC) acts as the regional Internet registry for Europe, the Middle East, and some regions of Africa;[8] and
- The Asia Pacific Network Information Center (APNIC) is the regional Internet registry for the Asia-Pacific region.[9]

The regional Internet registries make specific numeric address allocations to network service providers and other sub-regional Internet registries located in the geographical regions they service (Internet Architecture Board and Internet Engineering Steering Group 1995). In turn, local network service providers and sub-regional Internet registries assign the portions of address space allocated to them to other Internet service providers (ISPs) and to end users in their respective regions.[10]

Although IP numbers underpin the Internet addressing system, they are primarily of interest to network administrators. For the average network user their utility as an identifier is limited, in part because they are difficult to remember. The problem created by numerically based identification is compounded further by the fact that the range of addresses used at various organizational and individual levels is relatively unstructured. Therefore, reliance on these numeric sequences makes the task of deducing which addresses apply to whom rather arduous. This dilemma is resolved by the mapping of alphanumeric character strings, or domain names, to IP addresses.

Domain Names

At their most basic level, domain names are little more than symbolic representations of a list of addresses on a particular network. The mapping of these alphanumeric character strings to IP addresses is made possible through the use of a hierarchically structured, distributed addressing architecture known as the domain name system (DNS). Whereas an IP address identifies a specific connection on a particular network, a domain name points toward a particular host or computer. Therefore, if this machine moves to a different network, the IP address must change, but the name used to identify the host may remain the same (Krol 1989). That said, it is possible for a host to have more than one identifying alphanumeric character string as well as more than one IP address if it is connected to different networks.

The hierarchical nature of the DNS is based on an inverted tree schemata with "branches" stemming from the root, or "." *(dot)*. At nodal points, or domains, these branches divide into more branches leading to alternative nodal points, or subdomains (see figure 2.2). Domains are labels assigned to the nodal points and define "a region of jurisdiction for name assignment and of responsibility for name-to-address translation" (Su and Postel 1982:1). The domain name of a node is the list of labels on the path between the node and the root of the tree. Therefore, sister nodes under the same parent node cannot share the same label. However, the same label may be used to identify nodes that do not share the same parent node (Mockapetris 1987a). Simply put, domain names must be unique because they define a specific location within the tree. The domains immediately below the root are known as top-level domains (TLDs) and may be divided into three groups: (i) generic top-level domains (gTLDs); (ii) national, or country-code top-level domains (ccTLDs); and (iii) top-level domains restricted to use within the United States.

At the time of writing there were five generic top-level domains in use: *.com, org, .net, .edu, .int*.[11] Of these, *.com* was, and remains, by far the most popular with approximately 22 million names registered in it at the start of May 2001.[12] In addition to the generic top-level domains, potential name registrants may also choose to register names in any of the more than 250 available country-code top-level domains. The vast majority of country-code top-level domains are based on the English language two-character codes detailed in ISO-3166, which is an international standards agreement establishing two and three character abbreviation country codes for sovereign nations (e.g., *.ca* for Canada, *.fr* for France, *.de* for Germany) (International Telecommunication Union 1999). There are two top-level domains whose use is restricted to agencies of the United States government: *.gov* and *.mil*. The former originally was intended for use by any kind of government office or agency, but was later set aside for exclusive use by agencies of the United States federal government (Federal Networking Council 1995; Postel 1994). Similarly, the latter is restricted to use by the United States military services and its agencies.

Figure 2.2: Structure of the DNS

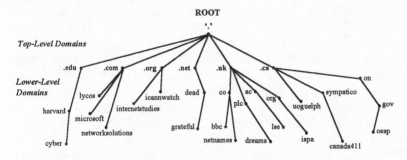

Below top-level domains there is an assortment of lower nodes, or subdomains. The names that registrants register within the generic top-level domains are usually at the second level. For example in figure 2.2, the *icannwatch* label represents a second-level domain within the *.org* top-level domain. One of the advantages of the hierarchical nature of the DNS is the relative ease with which domains may be divided into lower level subdomains. This feature makes Internet addressing highly scaleable. Referring again to figure 2.2, we see that

Harvard University has registered the name *harvard* at the second level of the
.edu top-level domain, and has elected to further subdivide this domain by creating a third level domain, *cyber*. The domain name *cyber.harvard.edu* identifies the host computer for Berkman Center for Internet and Society at the Harvard Law School.

The administrators of many country code top-level domains also have incorporated the scaleable nature of the DNS into their management strategies for
the national domains they oversee. Differences in the way in which country-
code top-level domains are administered are also reflected in figure 2.2. For
example, the registry organization for the United Kingdom domain,[13] *.uk*, has
elected to subdivide this top-level domain into a number of second-level categories (i.e. *.co.uk*, *.ac.uk*, *.plc.uk*, *.org.uk*) reflecting the intended use of registered
names.[14] In contrast, the registry organization for the Canadian domain,[15] *.ca*,
originally had chosen to subdivide this domain such that various aspects of Canadian political geography were incorporated into domain names. Prior to December 1, 2000, second-level domains under *.ca* were restricted to provincial
and territorial abbreviations and the names of national organizations. Similarly,
third-level subdomains were constrained to locality names, as well as provincial
and territorial organization names. Consequently, local organizations and individuals were able only to register fourth-level domain names. For example, the
domain name *osap.gov.on.ca* identifies the host computer for the Ontario Student Assistance Program (OSAP); a financial assistance program sponsored by
the provincial government of Ontario to provide loans to university students
who are Ontario residents.

Aside from its hierarchical structure, another distinguishing characteristic
of the DNS is that its successful functioning is not dependent upon the maintenance of a unique, centralized list of domain names. It is this particular feature
that allows the DNS to function as a distributed database. The diffuse nature of
this architecture is made possible by the system's reliance on name server and
resolver programs for the mapping of names to numeric addresses. Name servers contain comprehensive information about a specific subset of the domain
space, as well as indicators to other name servers that can be used to identify
the information available at any other part of the "tree." Despite the fact that
reference is often made to the "root" of the DNS in a manner that implies sin-
gularity, this "root" is, in fact, represented by thirteen root servers. They are
labeled "A" to "M." Each individual root server contains information about all
the domains below the root and the location of name servers containing additional data about the contents of specific domains. These thirteen root servers
are maintained by various corporate, education, and government organizations
in a number of countries. The A, B, C, D, E, F, G, H, J, and L root servers are
maintained in the United States. The K and I root servers are maintained the
United Kingdom and Sweden, respectively, while the M root server is maintained in Japan (Murai 1999).[16]

By convention, the data contained within the "A" root server is considered
generally to be the official, or authoritative, version of the root zone.[17] The data

it contains about domains are regularly downloaded by the other twelve root servers. Should something happen to the "A" root server, the diffuse structure of the DNS enables network administrators to easily circumvent the "A" server by configuring their respective name servers to point toward any of the other twelve root servers.

The role of resolver programs in the name-to-address mapping process is to extract the information contained within name servers so that they may (i) respond to requests for information from other name servers, and (ii) pursue queries by referring to other name servers. For example, when an individual network user at the London School of Economics and Political Science (LSE) enters an address such as *example.com* into his or her Web browser, the name server at the LSE undertakes a multiple address look up process to locate the host of this domain. Should the name server be unable to locate *example.com* within the list of addresses in its database, it then contacts other name servers connected to the network in order to identify whether such a location exists, and if so, where.[18]

Having demonstrated how the DNS works, we now move on to an examination of the underlying values that influenced the development of this hierarchical distributed architecture, and the administrative norms that evolved with it.

Evolution of the Internet Domain Name System[19]

Throughout the 1970s the number of computers connected to the ARPAnet,[20] the precursor to the modern Internet, was relatively limited. The host name-to-ARPA Internet address mappings for every computer connected to the network were maintained in a centralized database—HOSTS.TXT—at the Stanford Research Institute Network Information Center (SRI-NIC). Given the limited number of computers connected to the ARPAnet, it was relatively easy to update and regularly distribute this information to all the host computers. Since most of the computers connected to the network primarily were timeshared mainframes located in research institutes, the naming convention for network hosts was based on a *<user>@<host>* structure, with the host name generally being application dependent (Su and Postel 1982). By the early 1980s the character of the ARPAnet began to change, as timeshared hosts increasingly were replaced by local networks comprised of individual workstation computers.

The increase in the number of networks and individual hosts connected to the ARPAnet created three major problems for the existing addressing scheme (Albitz and Liu 1997; Mockapetris 1983a, 1987a). First, the rise in the number of hosts resulted in a dramatic increase in the amount of bandwidth[21] required to distribute updated versions of the HOSTS.TXT file. Second, the frequency of data updates impeded the manageability of this centralized data file. Third, although hosts were required to have unique names and the Network Information Center theoretically could assign addresses in a manner that assured the uniqueness of host names, local organizations tended to make their own decisions about names and addresses.

This situation led to a growing recognition among members of the networking community that, in the light of the growing sophistication of networking applications, a general purpose naming service would be required if the community's twin goals of network interoperability and interconnection were to be upheld. Various proposals for the development of a name space, and its management, were put forth in response to the need for identifying computers on different networks (Mills 1981; Postel 1979; Su 1982; Su and Postel 1982). The common themes that emerged from these proposals were: (i) the notion of a hierarchical name space where the hierarchy roughly corresponded to organizational structure; and (ii) boundaries between differing levels of the hierarchy should be denoted by names using "." *(dot)* (Mockapetris 1987a).

The most significant of these proposals, RFC 819,[22] was distributed to the networking community in August 1982. Following on the heels of an earlier decision to extend the *username@hostname* mailbox format for computer mail to *username@hostname.domain*, RFC 819 announced the decision to replace the name field *<host>* with a composite name field *<domain>* when identifying networked computers.[23] The intent of the new convention was to allow for the creation of a "tree-structured administrative dependent, rather than a strictly topology dependent, hierarchy" (Su and Postel 1982:1).

The following year RFC 882 and RFC 883 were published (Mockapetris 1983a, 1983b). These two documents expanded upon the generalized naming convention outlined in RFC 819, and formalized the technical specifications required for implementing the hierarchical and distributive database underpinning the evolving domain name system. The addressing structure outlined in these documents primarily was based on a series of technically orientated assumptions about the needs and usage patterns of the research-based network user community. These included:[24]

1. Network identifiers, addresses, routes, or similar information should not be required as part of a name.
2. Both the addressing database and the administration of names should be maintained in a distributed manner due to its size, the frequency of updates, and financial considerations.
3. Trade-offs between the cost of acquiring data, the speed of updates, and the accuracy of caches should be controlled by the data source.
4. Names should be capable of being used for multiple applications including retrieving host addresses, mailbox data, and other undetermined information.
5. The domain name space should not be constrained by different protocol families.
6. Name server transactions should be independent of the communications system that carried them.
7. The system should be useful across a wide spectrum of host capabilities, including personal computers and timeshared hosts.

The technical specifications that evolved from these assumptions influenced the manner in which the DNS was managed and administered. The norms regarding the assignment of responsibility for the management of top-level domains were outlined with the release of RFC 920 in October 1984. This was the first document to describe what would be, in effect, the system of domain naming as it existed prior to 1995. This document listed the six generic top-level domains that would be at the core of the new addressing system (see table 2.1), and acknowledged that the top-level domains for nation-states would be based on the English two-letter country codes established in ISO-3166. It also noted that although no domains had yet been established for multilateral organizations, such action would be undertaken at a future date.

Table 2.1: The Six Initial Top-Level Domains

Categories	Intended Use	Administrator
ARPA*	Current ARPA-Internet hosts	DARPA
GOV	Any government-related domains meeting the second-level requirements†	DARPA
EDU	Any education-related domains meeting the second-level requirements	DARPA
COM	Any commercial-related domains meeting the second-level requirements	DARPA
MIL	Any military-related domains meeting the second level requirements	DDN
ORG	Any organization-related domains meeting the second- level requirements	DARPA

* *The ARPA domain was identified as a temporary domain that would be phased out as the existing ARPA-Internet hosts made arrangements to join other domains.*
† *The requirements for second-level domains presented in RFC 920 were ambiguous. The general guideline offered for second-level domains was that they have 50 hosts. However, it was recognized that "it makes sense that any major organization, such as a university or a corporation, be allowed as a second level domain – even if it has just a few hosts" (Postel and Reynolds 1984:5).*

It was in RFC 920 that the association of domains with specific organizations, and the concept of domain registration entailing a hierarchy of delegation among organizations, initially were outlined. Within this document domains were defined as administrative entities whose purpose and expected use were to, "divide the name management required of a central administration and assign it to sub-administrations" (Postel and Reynolds 1984:1). This reflected an attempt to establish a decentralized approach to the administration of the domain name space paralleling the hierarchical distributed technical structure of the evolving addressing system.

The Defense Advanced Research Projects Agency (DARPA) was proposed as the initial administrator for the *.arpa, .gov, .edu, .com,* and *.org* domains, and the Defense Data Network (DDN) was to administer the *.mil* domain. Responsibility for the day-to-day administration of the domain name system fell to the SRI-NIC which was recognized as the agent for both DARPA and DDN.

On January 1, 1985, the domain name system was formally implemented as the addressing infrastructure for computer networks connected to the ARPAnet and/or the Defense Data Network. The United States Defense Communications Agency conferred responsibility for management of the DNS root, including the assignment of IP numbers, on the Information Sciences Institute (ISI) at the University of Southern California, while the SRI-NIC was awarded responsibility for managing domain name registrations.[25] Subsequent DNS-related developments in 1985 included:

1. Registration of the first DNS domains—*cmu.edu, purdue.edu, rice.edu,* and *ucla.edu*—in April;
2. In May, *think.com* was registered as the first *.com* domain;
3. *css.gov* was registered as the first *.gov* domain in June;
4. In July *mitre.org* was registered as the first *.org* domain; and
5. *.uk* was registered as the first two-letter country-code domain in July (Rutkowski 1997b).

At this point in the discussion an important caveat must be made. Although the United States Defense Communications Agency had awarded responsibility for managing the DNS root and assigning of IP numbers to the ISI, in practice, this "burden" essentially fell on one person: Jon Postel. Postel was a researcher at the University of Southern California's Information Sciences Institute who had been involved with computer networking since the beginnings of the ARPAnet. As a graduate student of the University of California at Los Angeles (UCLA), Postel had been present when the initial ARPAnet connection between UCLA and the Stanford Research Institute was made in the autumn of 1969. His personal influence over internetworking, and in particular the DNS, should not be underestimated. His actions regarding the assignment of network numbers, and the moral authority he commanded within the networking community, enabled him to exert a level of control over Internet addressing that was virtually unchallenged prior to the mid-1990s.

Aside from the recognition he had earned within the networking community for the substantial number of RFCs that he authored, the trusteeship role he acquired was predicated also on the key administrative tasks he conducted to facilitate the development of internetworking. The way in which he acquired responsibility for these tasks further reflects the informal manner in which technical problems associated with the development and construction of the ARPAnet, and subsequently the Internet, were addressed prior to the mid-1990s. While still a graduate student, Postel had volunteered to be the person responsible for keeping track of who wrote which RFC, as well as maintaining the distribution list to whom these documents should be sent.[26] Over time this task evolved into the position of RFC-editor responsible for publishing technical standards, records of best current practice, and information statements. In 1972, he appointed himself as the numbers czar. This entailed being responsible for assigning the numbers used in network protocol implementations, as well as organizing,   standardizing,   and   disseminating   these   numbers   to other network users (Postel 1972). Postel maintained both of these positions until his death in October 1998.

In November 1987, responsibility for the assignment of IP numbers was transferred from the ISI to the SRI-NIC (Romano and Stahl 1987). As a result, the SRI-NIC now acted on behalf of the ARPAnet and the Defense Data Network as both the registrar of top-level and second-level domains and as administrator of the root domain name servers (Stahl 1987). Despite this organizational transfer of responsibility, Postel maintained his authority for assigning all Internet protocol parameters other than Class A, Class B, and Class C 32-bit addresses, as well as the *.us* country-code top-level domain.

A year later, in December 1988, the first mention of the existence of an entity known as the Internet Assigned Numbers Authority (IANA) was made in RFC 1083.[27] However, no references to the founding, the persons responsible for such action, or the reasons underpinning the creation of this organization were ever offered, nor was such information ever posted on the IANA Web site. In essence, IANA was a term coined by Postel to describe his activities in ensuring that every Internet protocol had a unique identifier and to differentiate his ISI networking-related contract work from the Network Information Center that was established under contract to SRI to assign IP numbers (Postel 1996c). The function of IANA has been described as follows:

> A great many aspects of the Internet protocols are subject to extension, usually by assignment of new values for existing attributes. Services like Telnet and FTP depend on the assignment of "well-known" TCP and UDP ports for initiation of the service; and numerous options are defined with IP, TCP, and the other protocols. To coordinate the assignment of ports, values for options, and the like, the Internet has established the Internet Assigned Number *[sic]* Authority (IANA), which is operated by the University of Southern California's Information Sciences Institute (USC-ISI). Anytime *[sic]* a specification permits extensions, the task of registering those extensions and assigning an appropriate extension name or number is performed by IANA...Registration with IANA does not make an extension a "standard" but rather standardizes the mechanism for referring to it. This distinction is fundamental. IANA's task is to standardize the way systems refer to resources and mechanisms. (Crocker 1993b:53)

The subtle manner in which IANA first appeared and the significant role it played in terms of bearing the ultimate responsibility for the coordination of the IP address and domain name space clearly reflect the informal manner in which internetworking was administered while it remained in the education and research realms. This is further highlighted by the fact that IANA never existed as a formal organization and was never legally constituted. In essence, IANA defined a function rather than an entity. Elaborating on this state of affairs, Rony and Rony (1998:120) draw upon Winston Churchill's 1939 description of the USSR's war activities to characterize IANA as "a riddle wrapped in a mystery inside an enigma." A somewhat similar view was expressed in a dialogue between Jonathan Zittrain, a professor of law from Harvard University, and David Clark, a professor at the Massachusetts Institute of Technology and former chair of the Internet Architecture Board (IAB).[28] While speaking at a public presentation shortly before Postel's death, Clark summarized the peculiarities of IANA as follows:

> The person who has been making all of these judgmental administrative decisions for the Internet since its beginning is Jon Postel, who is the embodiment of something more formally called the Internet Assigned Numbers Authority, IANA. People are sometimes amused—"Oh, it must be this grand thing called IANA"—when they want to get a number, and in fact Jon is this guy with long hair and a beard and sandals who lives overlooking Marina del Rey, and you call him on the telephone and he says, "Well, you want some numbers, yeah." That's the Internet Associated Numbers Authority. It is as public a service and as non-profit as you can imagine, it's just this guy.... Technically speaking, the responsibility for carrying out the IANA is an institutional responsibility... we are tremendously dependent on what has been twenty years of incredibly good judgment from Jon, and yes, if he fell in a hole or decided he wanted to take up Zen or something, I don't know what we would do. If it was ten years ago, ... (inaudible) gotten the way we could. I mean, a hundred of us then caucused and selected a new person, but now with the world being so commercial, if we lost the personal stature he brings to this, I honestly don't know what we would do. I mean, we would have to do something that's much more either convoluted, Machiavellian, or public, and I don't know which one that would be. (Zittrain and Clark 1997)

There are three salient features in the above passage. First, it highlights the casual manner in which administrative decisions about Internet addressing were made prior to 1995. Second, it emphasizes the extent to which the coordination of this technical infrastructure was dependent upon the decision making prowess of just one individual. The key point to bear in mind here is that Postel's stewardship of Internet addressing was not based on legal contracts. Rather, his "authority" over this infrastructure was a product of the status he had established within the technical meritocracy that characterized the sociopolitical structures of the international networking community. Thirdly, Clark's comments also point toward one of the core predicaments underlying the controversies associated with attempts to reconfigure the Internet addressing regime during the latter half of the 1990s[29]—that is, *the conflict between the informal manner in which the basic Internet related administrative arrangements traditionally had been propagated, and demands by other parties, particularly commercial entities with an interest in Internet addressing, for the creation of a clearly defined administrative structure whose authority was legally constituted.*

Before proceeding with a discussion of how this conflict manifested itself, we briefly return to our examination of the informal structures and processes that characterized the administration of Internet addressing prior to 1995.

In 1991, the United States Defense Information System Agency (DISA) sought new tenders for the SRI-NIC management contract. The contract was awarded to a private entity called Government Systems Inc. in October of that year. This marked a shift away from the education/research-based management of one of the Internet's core functions, toward core service provision by a commercial entity. The tenure of Government Systems Inc., as the responsible entity for managing the Network Information Center, was short lived. In the spring of 1992, the United States National Science Foundation (NSF)[30] released a project solicitation seeking tenders for the provision and coordination of registration, database, and information services for the NSFnet[31] internetworking backbone.[32] This amounted to a call for the establishment of a new Network Information Center—the InterNIC Registration Services.

In January 1993, the NSF delegated the functions of domain name registration, domain name server registration, network number assignment, and autonomous system number assignment to another private entity, Network Solutions Incorporated (NSI).[33] In addition to the awardee party, two other entities, AT&T and General Atomics,[34] were awarded collaborative partnerships to assist in the provision of a "*seamless interface* for Internet users in accordance with the 'INTERNIC' concept" (National Science Foundation and Network Solutions Incorporated 1993: Article 2). AT&T was awarded responsibility for the provision of database services to extend and supplement the resources of the NSFnet. General Atomics, on the other hand, was awarded responsibility for the provision of information services including the development of a reference desk and a database of comprehensive networking materials. All three parties were awarded these responsibilities on the basis of a cooperative agreement, spanning a five year period from January 1, 1993, to September 30, 1998.[35] In essence, this agreement granted NSI a government-sanctioned monopoly over both the registration of second-level domain names in the generic top-level domain categories and the provision of registration services for the research networks funded by the NSF.

Given that the number of names being registered in 1993 was still relatively low and, more importantly, fees were not being levied for registering domain names, there was relatively little controversy associated with this newly formed monopoly. Moreover, despite the fact that the cooperative agreement granted NSI responsibility for operating the InterNIC, it placed an important stipulation on its activities. Specifically, the services rendered by NSI had to be provided in accordance with RFC 1174. The specific provisions of the RFC cited in the cooperative agreement recognized IANA as being responsible for "the allocation and assignment of various numeric identifiers needed for the operation of the Internet," and stipulated that it had the "discretionary authority to delegate portions of this responsibility" to other organizations (Cerf 1990b:1). Simply put, Article 3, sections C and D, of the cooperative agreement emphasized the continued role of IANA in overseeing the administration of the DNS and implied that NSI's activities in this realm were to be guided by IANA.

Two words in the last sentence of the above paragraph, *implied* and *guided*, highlight the informal administrative arrangements characteristic of how Internet addressing was coordinated prior to 1995. At issue here is the fact that no contractual relationship existed between NSI and IANA, nor was there any contractual relationship establishing the basis for, and/or scope of, IANA's authority in overseeing the administration of the DNS.

This administrative informality was further reinforced in March 1994 with the release of RFC 1591, *Domain Name System Structure and Delegation*. This document outlined the administrative procedures to be followed for adding new country-code top-level domains to the root, the standards to be upheld by the actors responsible for managing top-level domains, and the procedures to be followed by registries when accepting domain name registrations. Interestingly, it was noted within this document that, aside from country-code top-level domains, "it is extremely unlikely that any other TLDs will be created" (Postel 1994:1). Reflecting both the distributive nature of the DNS and the collectivistic ethos that had hitherto guided its evolution, the key principles set forth within this document were that: (i) the DNS be administered in a highly decentralized manner on the basis of delegated responsibilities; and, (ii) that, "concerns about *rights* and *ownership* of domains are inappropriate. It is appropriate to be concerned about *responsibilities* and *service* to the community" (Postel 1994:4).

Although these values had come to be seen by members of the networking community as an important dimension of internetworking, as this medium became increasingly commercialized, representatives of other entities that had not been associated closely with the development of this infrastructure perceived this administrative informality and ambiguity as problematic. Specifically, and as Mueller (1999a) has pointed out, for those entities seeking to appropriate value through the assertion of property rights in this realm, the ambiguous bases of decision making authority that characterized the medium of internetworking raised questions about the legal liability of the agents responsible for coordinating core internetworking functions. It was this clash of perspectives that set the stage for the start of the domain name wars.

The Domain Name Wars

Challenging NSI's Monopoly and IANA's Authority

Although the domain name wars clearly were sparked by a number of interrelated factors, one of the key variables underlying these controversies was the rapid growth of computer internetworking throughout the 1990s. Between January 1991 and January 1995 the number of computers connected to the Internet expanded by approximately 1,600 percent from 376,000 to 5,846,000.[36] By July 1999, the number of computers connected to the Internet surpassed 56 million and it was believed to have exceeded 100 million by early 2001.[37]

Not too surprisingly, the demand for domain names has grown, albeit more slowly, in proportion with the expansion in network connectivity. By mid-1995, NSI's market share of domain name registrations accounted for 75 percent of the total domain names registered throughout the world.[38] As of March 1996, it cumulatively had registered 306,347 names in the *.com,. edu, .org, .net,* and *.gov* top-level domains.[39] By the end of 1998, NSI's cumulative registration levels for these domains had reached 3,362,000 (Network Solutions Inc. 1998). As was noted earlier in this chapter, the most popular top-level domain is *.com*. In the period from January 1993 to March 1996, it accounted for approximately 89 percent of the total names registered by NSI. Highlighting the continued popularity of this domain, as of May 18, 2001, it accounted for approximately 60 percent of the total names registered world wide.[40] The growing demand for names in this domain created numerous scarcity related problems putting potential domain name registrants, NSI, and the institutions traditionally responsible for coordinating the domain name system at odds with one another.

Network Solutions Inc.-Related Controversies
By the end of 1995, two major controversies had engulfed NSI's registration activities. The first was centered around the way in which the registry was dealing with the fact that domain names must be unique. Prior to July 1995, NSI's approach toward domain name registration was based on a policy of *first come, first served* as outlined in RFC 1591.[41] As the potential value of establishing an online presence began increasingly to be recognized by commercial and noncommercial entities, this policy created problems both for the registry and potential registrants. The *first come, first served* approach was particularly contentious for those entities for whom the inability to register their preferred name(s), because of prior registrations by third parties, had corresponded with perceived infringements of their trademark and/or intellectual property rights. The result was a profusion of litigation pitting the rights of trademark holders against those of domain name holders who had registered names first.[42]

One of the significant features of the lawsuits that were launched against the registry and individual domain name holders was the direct challenge they posed to the way in which the DNS had been traditionally administered and coordinated. These challenges reflected a clash between the informal and diffuse administrative structures that had evolved while internetworking was predominantly in the education and research realms, with the desire of some newer Internet stakeholders to establish more formalistic regulatory structures. Up until this point in time, the two key principles guiding the way in which domain name registration requests were processed had been set out in RFC 1591. They were:

1. The designated manager must be equitable to all groups in the domain that request domain names. This means that the same rules are applied to all requests, all requests must be processed in a non-discriminatory fashion, and academic and commercial (and other) users are treated on an equal basis. . . .
2. In case of a dispute between domain name registrants as to the rights to a particular name, the registration authority shall have no role or responsibility

other than to provide the contact information to both parties. The registration of
a domain name does not have any Trademark status. It is up to the requestor to
be sure he is not violating anyone else's Trademark. (Postel 1994:4-5)

The legal challenges set in motion by entities seeking to redress perceived infringements of their intellectual property raised numerous questions about the
legal validity of these principles and the authority upon which they rested.

NSI's response to the legal disputes between trademark and domain name
holders further exacerbated the conflicts between itself and these two parties. On
July 28, 1995, it released the *NSI Domain Dispute Resolution Policy Statement.*
Although this policy statement affirmed NSI's continued adherence to the principle of *first come, first served,* domain name registrants now had to warrant that
their use and registration of a particular name did "not interfere with or infringe
the right of any third party in any jurisdiction with respect to trademark, service
mark, tradename *[sic]*, company name or any other intellectual property right"
(Network Solutions Inc. 1995: Article 1, section C). In addition, the holders of
domain names were required to "defend, indemnify and hold harmless" (Article
4) NSI, the NSF, and IANA, should legal actions be taken against the registry
because of the registration or use of a particular name. However, as Gould
(1999:10) notes, the policy's "real bite" was in the registry's assertion that it had
the "right to withdraw a Domain Name from use and registration on the Internet
upon thirty (30) days prior written notice (or earlier if ordered by the court)
should NSI receive an order by a United States court or arbitration panel of the
American Arbitration Association (hereinafter 'AAA') that the Domain Name in
dispute rightfully belongs to a third party" (Network Solutions Inc. 1995: Article
5).

This policy statement was the first of five widely criticized dispute resolution policies published by NSI between July 1995 and December 1999. The bulk
of the criticisms levied against these policies focused on specific objectionable
factors and the finer aspects of policy litigation (Maher 1996; Oppedahl 1997;
Rony and Rony 1998; Shaw 1996). In broad terms, NSI's approach to dispute
resolution was widely criticized on the grounds that, by seeking to focus on the
"rights" attached to second-level domain name registration, they were grafting
trademark law onto domain name registration in a manner that favored the rights
of trademark holders over those of the registrant who first registered a given
domain name.

The second major controversy pertaining to NSI centered around its status
as a monopoly provider of domain name registration services. This status had not
been particularly controversial when the number of domain name registrations
was relatively small and the registry operated under the original terms of its
cooperative agreement with the National Science Foundation. However, the
surge in demand for names in the *.com* domain in late 1994 and early 1995
had begun to overburden the registry's facilities. Citing increased operating
costs that exceeded the budgetary allocations received by the registry, and the
"inappropriateness" of the United States federal government's subsidization of

domain name registration services, NSI submitted a proposal to the NSF in which it sought to obtain permission to charge users for registering domain names.

On September 14, 1995, the National Science Foundation ignited a powder keg when it modified its cooperative agreement with NSI, authorizing it to begin charging domain name registrants a fee for the provision of registration services. This amendment marked the end of the free domain name registrations in the *.com, .org, .net, .edu,* and *.gov* top-level domains. Under the terms of the amendment NSI was authorized to impose an annual fee of US$50 per year per second-level domain name registered in these domains, of which it was entitled to retain 70 percent. The remaining 30 percent was to be allocated to an "interest-bearing account which will be used for the preservation and enhancement of the 'Intellectual Infrastructure' of the Internet" (National Science Foundation 1995: Amended Article 8). The National Science Foundation, however, undertook to pay the fees for registrations in the *.gov* and *.edu* top-level domains.

The introduction of service charges immediately was condemned by an array of network users. This controversy pitted NSI against domain name holders, as well as prospective providers of Internet services seeking access to the restricted market for registering domain names. On the one hand, existing domain name holders and new registrants now were faced with having to pay US$100 in order to register a domain name because initial name registrations were required to span a two year period. On the other hand, the potential lucrativeness of providing domain name registration services immediately was recognized by several entrepreneurial actors, enticing them to seek entry into this restricted market (Mueller 1999a). At the end of the 1994 financial year (December 31), NSI reported a net revenue of approximately US$5 million. By the end of 1996, its net revenues had increased to approximately US$19 million and were in the range of US$94 million by the end of the 1998 financial year (Network Solutions Inc. 1998).

Prior to the September 14 announcement, there had been ongoing discussions within the Internet engineering community about various aspects of domain name policy and other governance related issues. However, the intensity of the criticisms leveled against NSI in response to the introduction of registration fees catalyzed the focus of many of these technical and policy discussions toward expanding the number of available top-level domains.

IANA-Related Controversies
Throughout the year preceding the NSF's decision to authorize charging for domain names, there had been numerous discussions within the networking community about the ownership of the name and number space that IANA coordinated. The roots of these discussions stemmed from the attempts by Jon Postel to have IANA chartered by the Internet Society (ISOC). Having been formed by an assortment of individuals who had been involved, over the long term, with Internet-related standards making activities, the ISOC was incorpo-

rated as a not-for-profit corporation in 1992. The principal rationale for its creation had been to provide greater legal and financial security for the Internet standards making process (Cerf 1995b; Zittrain and Clark 1997). In July 1994, Jon Postel sent Vint Cerf,[43] the then president of the ISOC, a draft charter that sought to transfer IANA's function away from a government contract with the ISI at the University of Southern California to the ISOC.[44]

Despite the fact that the proposed charter had not yet been distributed to, or endorsed by, other members of the Internet standards making community, by October 1994 IANA was claiming that its role "as the clearinghouse to assign and coordinate the use of numerous Internet protocol parameters" was chartered by the Internet Society (Reynolds and Postel 1994:1). When the draft charter eventually was distributed to members of the Internet standards making community in February 1995, its contents raised numerous questions about the nature of the ownership of the domain name and IP address space. Responding to the request for comments about the chartering of IANA by the Internet Society, Robert Aiken, a former United States Department of Energy official, who at the time also was a member of the United States' Federal Networking Committee,[45] wrote:

> Is ISOC claiming that it has jurisdiction and overall responsibility for the top level address and name space—as some (see below) believe it does? If yes—how did ISOC obtain this "responsibility", —if NO then who does own it? I think these questions MUST be answered first before addressing the question of who addresses conflicts in domain bame *[sic]* registration and how. *Inquiring minds want to know!* (Aiken 1995)

Aiken's query intensified the growing debate about who, or what, could claim jurisdiction over the domain name and IP address space, and the basis upon which such claims rested. Some participants, Aiken among them, maintained that given its historical role as the primary financier for the development of the Internet, the government of the United States had the strongest claim to such authority. Others who had been more closely associated with the technical development of this networking infrastructure asserted that although IANA's authority regarding IP address and domain name space was directly, and historically, associated with its contract work for the United States government, the time had come to "settle the responsibility on the Internet Society as an nongovernmental agent serving the [global internetworking] community" (Cerf 1995a).

The issue of jurisdiction, or authority, over the domain name and IP address space, was further complicated by the fact that by this time the "authority" over the various segments of the DNS had become internationally dispersed. Although NSI had been granted responsibility for administering the "A" root server, the twelve other root servers were administered by an assortment of organizations, including IANA, both within and outside the jurisdiction of the United States government. In addition, since 1990 much of the responsibility for assigning specific portions of the IP address space had been delegated to geographically dispersed regional Internet registries whose activities also were not constrained either by the United States government or IANA. Ultimately, the diffuse and ambiguous manner in which authority was exercised over the DNS root suggested that there could be no justification for any attempt by the government of the United States to exert hegemonic control over this component of the addressing infrastructure. Moreover, it remained unclear whether, or if, any entity could legally claim such authority.

It was in the midst of these internal debates about jurisdictional rights that NSI had begun to charge network users for registering domain names. One of the initial consequences of the registry's action was the creation of a number of electronic discussion lists devoted to this issue. The immediate response of a significant number of interested parties, including Jon Postel, was a call for the creation of alternate top-level domains and registries to compete against NSI. In a message to members of the ISOC board of trustees, Postel noted that the introduction of charges for domain name registrations provided "sufficient cause to take steps to set up a small number of alternate top level domains managed by other registration centers" thereby facilitating "competition between registration services to encourage good service at low prices" (Postel 1995). However, support for this view was far from unanimous.

Actors representing those who sought to protect their trademark interests opposed the introduction of more top-level domains. They claimed that any increase in the number of available top-level domains would hamper their already strained efforts at protecting their intellectual property rights. Some members of this faction called for the imposition of waiting periods between applications for, and final authorization of, names. This, they claimed, would allow for concerned parties to conduct searches for trademark violations and/or allow for challenges to be made against proposed name registrations. An opposing faction argued that domain names were merely a reflection of free speech, and, therefore, aside from expanding the number of available domains, no new policies regarding name registrations were required. According to the proponents of this view, existing laws provided sufficient protection for trademark and intellectual property interests. Other actors argued for the creation of new categories of top-level domains, paralleling the business classifications recognized by the International Trademark Association (INTA). Commercial names could then be registered in these "new" domains. Yet another faction asserted that generic top-level domains should be withdrawn, and that domain names should be required to fit into national registration schemes of country-code top-level domains.[46]

Throughout the autumn of 1995, discussions about these issues carried on apace, leading to the release, in January 1996, of a draft proposal authored by Jon Postel and two of his associates. In line with the traditional manner by which both proposed solutions to technical problems and new ideas were articulated within the Internet community, this proposal was released as an Internet draft document, and called for: (i) opening competition in domain name registrations in generic top-level domains, (ii) allowing for multiple registries for *.com* and other generic top-level domains, and (iii) providing IANA with the international legal and financial umbrella of the Internet Society (Bush et al. 1996).

The release of this document spurred into action a number of entrepreneurial actors who wanted to reap some of the financial windfall associated with domain name registrations. Included among this group of entities were AlterNIC, Iperdrome, and pgmedia, all of which sought to create alternative top-level domains (i.e., *.per, .web, .arts,* and *.xxx*), and to sell domain name registrations for these new top-level domains. However, IANA failed to authorize the introduction of these alternative domains into the root, and NSI refused to undertake the technical steps required to make these domains visible throughout the Internet. This led to a situation wherein, despite the technical feasibility of configuring name servers to point at alternative roots, relatively few network administrators were prepared to recognize these alternative roots as authoritative. As a result, the root servers operated by NSI and IANA remained authoritative and the attempts at establishing an alternative root system foundered (Mueller 1999a).

In June 1996, Postel released a more detailed draft proposal regarding the creation of new registries and the delegation of top-level domains. As with the earlier draft, the revised proposal also sought to incorporate IANA into the legal and financial umbrella of ISOC on the grounds that "as the net becomes larger and more commercial, the IANA needs a formal body to accept responsibility for the legal issues which arise surrounding DNS policy and its implementation" (Postel 1996a:3). In addition, this draft proposed a framework for introducing 150 new top-level domains that would be allocated to fifty new registries with no more than two-thirds in any one country. Each new registry would be entitled to manage three of the new top-level domains on the basis of a five year contract with IANA. According to this framework, entities applying to become registries would pay IANA a US$1000 application fee. Once accepted, the new registries would be required to pay US$10,000 plus one percent of their gross income into a fund managed by the ISOC. In response to complaints that these fees amounted to an unfair tax, the revised August 1996 version of the proposal maintained the initial application fee, but the sum to be paid to the Internet Society was reduced to US$2000 plus two percent of a registry's gross income (Postel 1996b).

At the end of June 1996, the ISOC president, Donald Heath, announced that the Postel framework had been accepted, in principle, by ISOC's board of trustees. Throughout the summer, Robert Shaw, an International Telecommunication Union (ITU) advisor on the Global Information Infrastructure, outspokenly criticized the Postel plan. He, and others, argued that this approach would result in the establishment of multiple "mini-monopolies" that would merely replicate existing registration related problems and subject registrants to "lock-in" by predatory registries. Shaw also espoused the view that Postel's framework would make the implementation of any form of unified dispute resolution extremely difficult to establish. In September 1996, he was invited to be one of the speakers at the Coordination and Administration of the Internet Workshop, hosted by the Harvard Science and Technology Program's Information Infrastructure Project. In his presentation to the attendees he decried the lack, to date, of substantial participation in domain naming proceedings by any non-U.S. public policy officials and what he viewed as IANA's lack of authority to award highly lucrative contracts for registries. Shaw argued that

> the point being made here is not to question the important 'trusteeship' role that IANA has played—only that any expansion of that role outside of the traditional Internet technical community would be based on claims that wouldn't bear much scrutiny. . . . For ISOC (or any group) to claim responsibility for delegating international name space when there are such high stakes (e.g., financial) involved appears unsustainable. The Internet has become far too commercial and strategically important as a global communications tool to simply perpetuate the same informal arrangements that have kept it glued together until now. (Shaw 1996)

This critique of the manner in which domain naming policy was being promulgated appears to have persuaded Donald Heath to reconsider the legal, political, and economic complexities associated with any expansion in the number of available top-level domains. In October 1996, the ISOC announced that it was putting together an international "blue ribbon panel" to "undertake defining, investigating, and resolving issues resulting from current international debate over a proposal to establish global registries and additional international Top Level Domain names (iTLDs)" (Internet Society 1996). So began phase two of the wars.

The gTLD-MoU Initiative

In mid-November 1996, the ISOC announced that an 11 member panel, the Internet International Ad Hoc Committee (IAHC), had been formed to seek a resolution to the debates regarding the establishment of additional global registries and international, or generic, top-level domains.[47] The committee was chaired by Donald Heath and included one representative from the International Telecommunication Union (ITU), Robert Shaw; one representative from the World Intellectual Property Organization (WIPO), Albert Tramposch; and, one representative from the International Trademark Association (INTA), Sally Abel. Also included in the committee were five technical engineers appointed by IANA, the Internet Architecture Board, and the Internet Society, as well as one representative from the National Science Foundation. In addition, the Internet Society appointed David Maher, an intellectual property lawyer, to the committee.

Of the five technical engineers selected, three represented international interests. Jun Murai, an associate professor at Keio University in Tokyo, had played a fundamental role in the development of Japan's Unix-to-Unix Copy

Protocol (UUCP) and IP networks. Geoff Huston was the technical manager of Telstra, a telecommunication company and Australia's largest Internet service provider, and previously had been technical manager of the Australian Academic and Research Network. Hank Nussbacher was an Israel based networking consultant who had played a major role in fostering IBM's presence as an Internet service provider in Israel. The two remaining technical experts, David Crocker and Perry Metzger, were Americans who had been associated closely with the development of various aspects of internetworking in the United States and had played active roles in the Internet Engineering Task Force for a number of years.

Approximately one month after its formation, the IAHC released for public comment its *Draft Specifications for Administration and Management of gTLDs* on December 19, 1996.[48] The recommendations set forth in this document differed significantly from the administrative structures and management processes outlined by the Postel framework. First, whereas the Postel approach had envisaged the introduction of 150 new top-level domains, in the IAHC proposal this number was reduced to seven.

Second, the Postel proposals were premised on the notion that top-level domain registries were entities within which two discernible administrative operations were functionally integrated (i.e., the NSI model). The first of these, the registry function, consists of collecting, storing, and maintaining name data as well as operating the name servers that provide updated authoritative lists of domains throughout the Internet. The second, or registrar, function, focuses on the provision of retail services such as receiving applications for names and reserving them if they are not already taken. According to the Postel plan, private for-profit entities combining these two functions would compete against one another in the provision of domain name registration services. In contrast, the plan set forth by the IAHC entailed separation of the registry and registrar functions. Based on an assertion that the top-level domain name space was "a public resource and is subject to the public trust," the IAHC proposed creating a nonprofit monopoly registry, with approximately twenty to thirty globally dispersed for-profit registrars, chosen by lottery, sharing access to the same top-level domains (International Ad Hoc Committee 1996). An additional twenty to thirty registrars would be added annually, subject to annual reviews of the system's efficiency.

The third difference between the Postel and the IAHC proposals centered on the issue of dispute resolution. Postel had sought to distance the administration of the DNS from the protection of trademarks and intellectual property rights. He claimed that the DNS "should provide for the needs of the many rather than protecting the privileges of the few" (Postel 1996a:5) and emphasized the need for parties seeking to protect their intellectual property to recognize that domain names were "intended to be an addressing mechanism and are not intended to reflect trademarks, copyrights or any other intellectual property rights" (Postel 1996a:3). In contrast to this view, the IAHC sought to reduce the growing collisions between trademarks and second-level domain name allocations by linking trademark protection with the administration of the DNS. The new framework recommended that registries for generic and country-code top-level domains should publicize applications for second-level domain names for a period of sixty days prior to the assignment of requested names to applicants.

Despite allowing for a six-week period of public comment between the release of its draft and final reports, the IAHC and its proposals were heavily criticized for what many observers viewed as a failure to be sufficiently representative of the diverse interests of Internet stakeholders. A common theme running across these critiques was the perception that a core function of the Internet was being made subservient to the interests of trademark holders. In addition, during the period leading to the release of the IAHC documents, and for several months thereafter, this body was widely rebuked by the various factions associated with the domain name controversies for a perceived lack of procedural openness. Much of this criticism stemmed from the fact that, unlike the way in which Internet standards had been traditionally propagated, the IAHC's deliberations took place in closed sessions and no records or minutes of its meetings were kept (Simon 1998).

On February 4, 1997, the IAHC released the *Final Report of the International Ad Hoc Committee: Recommendations for Administration and Management of gTLDs.*[49] Included within this document were a number of substantive modifications to the committee's earlier draft. First, a framework was established for the introduction of seven new domains into the existing pool of generic top-level domains (see table 2.2). The final report also specified that eight new registrars, equally distributed among seven geographic regions, would be established to grant second-level domain name registrations under these new top-level domains.

Table 2.2: IAHC's Proposed New Top-Level Domains

Domain	Intended Users
.firm	Businesses or firms
.store	Businesses offering goods to purchase
.web	Entities emphasizing activities related to the World Wide Web
.arts	Entities emphasizing cultural and entertainment activities
.rec	Entities emphasizing recreation/entertainment activities
.info	Entities providing information services
.nom	Those wishing individual or personal nomenclature

Second, the final report included plans for the establishment of a governance framework in the form of a Memorandum of Understanding that both public and private entities were invited to sign. It would come into effect upon having been signed by the Internet Society and IANA. The principal document underpinning this framework was the *Memorandum of Understanding on the Generic Top Level Domain Name Space of the Internet Domain Name System (gTLD-MoU)*, for which the ITU was to act as the repository.[50] According to the tenets of the new framework, the administration and management of generic top-level domains, including the operation of a shared database repository for generic top-level domain registries, was to be coordinated by a consortium of new registrars operating as a Switzerland-based nonprofit association called the Council of Registrars (CORE). It was further stipulated that the stewardship of the top-level domain space would be assigned to a Policy Oversight Committee (POC) comprising members of the ISOC, IANA, the Internet Architecture Board, the ITU, the WIPO, the INTA, and CORE.

The third modification centered around the elimination of the sixty-day waiting period for publicizing requests for names. During the period of public consultation prior to the release of the final report, this idea, in particular, was vilified by an assortment of actors for granting trademark interests too much influence vis-à-vis the administration of the DNS.[51] In its place, the final report created a system of administrative domain name challenge panels to be administered under the aegis of the Geneva-based Arbitration and Mediation Center of the WIPO. This aspect of the report created an extremely complex procedure of mandatory arbitration allowing for intellectual property holders to petition a panel of international experts to determine if a registered name violated the committee's policy that domain names containing internationally known trademarks could only be held by the trademark owner.

Presented as a fait accompli, the gTLD-MoU was signed by Donald Heath and Jon Postel on March 1, 1997, at an official signing ceremony organized under the auspices of the ITU. In the light of the various economic, political, social, and technological interests at stake, the initiative immediately became mired in controversy. Nonetheless, over the next several months some 223 public and private organizations signed this document.[52] The individuals responsible for the creation of this framework claimed that this amounted to an international consensus in favor of the MoU. The plan's detractors, on the other hand, argued that in no way could such a limited number of signatories be considered representative of the internationally diverse internetworking interests.

Some critics declared that this initiative was attempting to establish a formal regulatory framework for Internet governance paralleling traditional telecommunication regulatory regimes. For example, Rutkowski (1998b, 1998c) decried it as an attempt by the ITU to assert illegitimate jurisdiction over the Internet. Those who supported the establishment of alternative registries, or who were sympathetic to this notion, argued that by limiting the expansion of top-level domains the gTLD-MoU failed to sufficiently open the market for domain name registrations. Perceiving this framework as a threat to its control over the *.com* domain, NSI launched an anti-MoU lobbying campaign claiming that the initiative placed the stability of internetworking at risk.[53] Highlighting the fact that with the exception of Albania no government representatives had signed the gTLD-MoU, other commentators, including government and industry representatives, questioned the authority of the ISOC, IANA, the ITU, and the WIPO to establish a quasi-governmental role for themselves.[54]

Despite the controversies surrounding the gTLD-MoU, throughout the remainder of 1997 its supporters proceeded apace with an attempted implementation of its operational framework.[55] However, in July 1997 the government of the United States dealt a serious blow to this initiative. In the light of the impending expiration of the cooperative agreement between the National Science Foundation and NSI,[56] on July 2, 1997, the United States National Telecommunications and Information Administration (NTIA), an agency of the Department of Commerce, issued a notice of inquiry to solicit public comments on "the current and future system(s) for the registration of domain names." Contained within the notice of inquiry was the following statement, "The government has not endorsed any plan at this stage but believes that it is important to reach consensus on these policy issues as soon as possible" (United States Department of Commerce 1997:35896). This declaration marked the start of phase three of the Domain Name Wars.

United States Government Green and White Papers

The United States Department of Commerce allowed for a seven week period during which public comments about the administration and management of the DNS were solicited. The deadline for comments regarding the notice of inquiry ended on August 18, 1997. In total, approximately 430 comments from individuals and organizations were submitted.[57] Under the direction of Ira Magaziner, a senior policy analyst on Internet issues for the President of the United States, the Department of Commerce analyzed the submissions throughout the autumn of 1997. Congressional hearings focusing on domain naming policy also were conducted during this period.

On January 30, 1998, the Department of Commerce released its proposals, in the form of a Green Paper, on how to transfer the stewardship of the DNS to a private sector-based administration (United States Department of Commerce 1998b). This document noted that the four principles guiding the evolution of the DNS should be stability, competition, private bottom-up coordination, and representation. In spite of these principles, the scheme presented by the authors of this document was widely perceived by non-U.S.-based actors as being overly U.S.-centric. The creation of a new private not-for-profit corporation, to be headquartered in the United States and incorporated under United States law, was proposed. The purpose of this new corporation was to coordinate the functions that hitherto IANA had been responsible for (i.e. allocation of IP address space to regional registries, overseeing operation of authoritative root server, determining circumstances under which new top-level domains are added to the root, and coordination of the technical parameters required to ensure universal Internet connectivity). Significantly, the proposal also recommended how the board of directors of this new corporation should be structured.[58]

The Green Paper also called for a separation of registry and registrar functions, and advocated experimentation by allowing each of these functions to operate on a competitive basis. To this end, the proposal called for a period of transition within which five new registries and five new top-level domains would be introduced into the DNS and monitored by the new corporation. The results of this experiment could then be used to guide future additions to the root. With regard to trademark considerations, the approach set forth in this document implied moving away from the quasi-centralized governance structure proposed by the gTLD-MoU toward a more decentralized governance model akin to the earlier Postel framework. The Green Paper stated that the United States government was opposed to the establishment of "a monolithic trademark dispute resolution process at this time" (United States Department of Commerce 1998b), favoring a framework wherein registries and registrars established their own minimum dispute resolution procedures.

Throughout February and March 1998 the Department of Commerce solicited public comments about the Green Paper. More than 650 responses were received.[59] These comments revealed that many Internet stakeholders, predominantly based outside the United States, viewed the Green Paper proposals as lacking international accountability and as raising the potential for the establishment of United States jurisdiction across the Internet as a whole. Likewise, the creators and supporters of the gTLD-MoU initiative were outraged that their efforts at international domain name reform had not even been mentioned in the Green Paper. A somewhat similar view was reflected by the numerous respondents who indicated that, despite not endorsing the gTLD-MoU, the initiative had elements that were worthy of further consideration. In particular, there was a perception that the gTLD-MoU framework allowed for far greater international participation in the development of domain naming policy than that which was proposed in the Green Paper. The European Union's response was especially adamant about this point, making several references to the need for greater consideration of the achievements of the gTLD-MoU initiative, concluding that "no decision should be taken as to the creation of new gTLDs before an international consensus is reached" (Council of the European Union 1998).

During April and May 1998, the public comments were reviewed by the United States Department of Commerce and used to develop a statement of policy regarding the management of the DNS, *Management of Internet Names and Addresses* (United States Department of Commerce 1998a). This document came to be known as the White Paper. If the Green Paper was indicative of an attempt by the United States government to become more directly involved in establishing domain naming policy, the release of the White Paper, on June 5, 1998, seemed to mark its retreat from this realm. This policy statement clearly shifted the responsibility for the creation of a governance structure onto the private sector. The policy set out in this document reiterated the view that the guiding principles of the evolution of the DNS should be stability, competition, private bottom-up coordination, and representation. It also adhered to the notion that a new private, not-for-profit corporation responsible for the coordination of specific domain name related functions should be created and both headquartered and incorporated within the United States. However, whereas the Green Paper had stipulated how the board of directors of this new corporation should be structured, the White Paper identified global representativeness as an important priority and stressed that the organizers of the new corporation would be responsible for deciding on the allocation of seats. The new policy also retained the distinction between the provision of registry and registrar services. However, it noted that it would be up to the new corporation, and not the United States government, to determine whether private for-profit registries should be incorporated into the DNS. The new corporation would also have to establish the minimum selection criteria for new registrars. In addition, the White Paper noted that the United States government would not seek to implement any new top-level domains. This responsibility also was divested to the new corporation.

The White Paper did not set out a specific dispute resolution policy. Rather, its recommendations regarding this matter mirrored the framework proposed earlier by the gTLD-MoU initiative. To this end, the WIPO was called upon to initiate a process, incorporating the participation of both trademark and non-trademark holders, leading to: (i) the development of recommendations for a uniform approach to trademark/domain name disputes involving cyberpiracy, but not conflicts between legitimate trademark holders with legitimate competing rights; (ii) the recommendation of processes for protecting famous trademarks in the generic top-level domains; and (iii) an evaluation of the effects of adding new generic top-level domains and related dispute resolution procedures on trademark and intellectual property holders (United States Department of Commerce 1998a).

According to the tenets of the White Paper the period of transition to the establishment of private sector administration of the DNS was anticipated to last for approximately two years, during which time the United States government would continue to participate in a policy oversight role until the new corporation was established and operationally stable. A target date for full transition to private sector administration was set for September 30, 2000. The release of this document initiated the fourth phase of the ongoing attempts to establish a regulatory framework for the administration and management of Internet addressing.

Internet Corporation for Assigned Names and Numbers (ICANN)

Shortly after the release of the White Paper, an organization calling itself the International Forum on the White Paper (IFWP) was formed by an ad hoc coalition of globally dispersed professional, trade, and educational associations representing a diversity of Internet stakeholder groups, including Internet service providers, content developers, trademark holders, networkers, intergovernmental groups, policy experts, and end users.[60] The purpose of this new organization was to convene a series of public meetings whose aim was to establish a consensus on the founding principles of the new corporation proposed in the White Paper. Bearing in mind that the cooperative agreement between the NSF and NSI was set to expire on September 30, 1998, IFWP-sponsored meetings were held throughout the summer of 1998 in Reston, Geneva, Singapore, and Buenos Aires. At these meetings Internet stakeholders with diverse interests convened without the involvement of a third-party judge. The meetings were structured as "workshops" wherein the participants divided themselves, on the basis of individual choice, into small working groups. The focus of these groups was devoted to structural and procedural issues relating to the new organization that was to be formed, and processes by which trademark and privacy issues, as they related to the future entity, could be resolved. Plenary sessions were held at the end of each meeting during which a representative from each group presented the "sense" of their respective group's discussion, including dissenting views. An electronic public discussion list by which interested parties could participate in discussions pertaining to this issue was also created.

Representatives of NSI joined the process from the start. IANA representatives, on the other hand, did not become involved until the Geneva meeting. At this session there was a clash of views between IANA and the other IFWP participants. During the earlier Reston meeting, all attendees had participated as equals in seeking to persuade others of the merits of their respective visions of how the new corporation should evolve. However, at the Geneva meeting, Jon Postel presented the attendees with draft bylaws, inviting them to use these as a basis for their discussions and debates regarding the new corporation. This invitation was rejected by the participants on the grounds that a consensus on the principles, or constitution, of the new corporation had to be established before any discussion of bylaws could proceed. Although IANA continued to participate in the IFWP process, it simultaneously proceeded apace with the development of revised proposals of draft bylaws for the new corporation. These were made publicly available for comment on its Web site.

By the beginning of September 1998, the IFWP meetings appeared to have succeeded in attaining an internationally based rough consensus regarding the principles of the new corporation.[61] The time had come to transform these ideas into a document. It was at this point that the IFWP process collapsed. The IFWP steering committee[62] had tried to arrange a final wrap-up meeting, to be attended by participants from the earlier meetings and representatives from IANA. The aim of the proposed meeting was to transform the international consensus into a framework document outlining the bylaws and articles of incorporation for the new corporation. However, representatives from IANA indicated to the conference organizer, Dr. Tamar Frankel, a legal scholar from Harvard University who had chaired the four IFWP meetings, that they would work to subvert the outcome of such a meeting.[63] Thus began a series of events that appear to have been mired in a degree of Machiavellian intrigue. Shortly before the meeting was set to start, IANA announced that it had privately negotiated an agreement with representatives of corporate Internet stakeholders, the Internet technical community, and some members of the IFWP steering committee, including representatives from the Commercial Internet Exchange (CIX)[64] and the Association for Interactive Media (AIM),[65] to resist the holding of a final meeting. This was followed, on September 17, 1998, with a release by

IANA and NSI of a jointly developed set of bylaws and articles of incorporation reflecting, to a limited extent, the results of the IFWP process.[65] This was the death knell for the IFWP process, and the proposed wrap-up meeting was canceled.

On September 28, IANA reissued a modified framework proposal within which two clauses from the joint draft that may have constrained the new corporation's authority over NSI were removed. This action, coupled with what had happened vis-à-vis the cancellation of the IFWP wrap-up meeting, served to further increase the intrigue and speculation surrounding these events. It was this fifth iteration of the proposed framework that IANA submitted to the NTIA on October 2, 1998. According to the documents submitted by IANA, the new corporation was to be incorporated in California and named the Internet Corporation for Assigned Names and Numbers (ICANN). A particularly contentious aspect of the IANA submission was the fact that it included a list of the interim members of the board of directors for the new corporation.[66] At issue here was the fact that, contrary to the White Paper's emphasis on the need for openness and consensus building, the selection process had been conducted behind closed doors without public knowledge of this undertaking. The interim board was presented as a fait accompli. The intrigue surrounding IANA's submission further increased when, one week later, the United States Department of Commerce announced that NSI's cooperative agreement was being extended through to September 30, 2000. In addition, the cooperative agreement was amended to authorize NSI's continued operation of the primary root server, as well as providing for the development, deployment, and licensing by NSI of a mechanism enabling multiple registrars to accept registrations for the generic top-level domains (United States Department of Commerce 1998c).[67]

The ICANN framework was not the only submission received by the United States government. Additional proposals were submitted by (i) the Open Root Server Confederation, a grouping of proprietary registries advocates,[68] and (ii) a hastily organized working group comprised of nine individuals who had been involved closely with the IFWP processes from the start, and who were appalled by its apparent usurpation by those with vested interests in perpetuating a regulatory agenda for administering and managing the DNS.[69] This group identified itself as the Boston Working Group and was highly critical of the ICANN framework. Its members asserted that ICANN failed to meet the standards established by the White Paper, both in terms of content and the means by which the proposal had been derived. Specifically, they claimed that, in addition to being susceptible to capture by self-interested factions and failing to guarantee an open membership structure, the ICANN framework reflected an organizational structure with vague lines of accountability that limited the means for individual participation.[70] Similar concerns were voiced by an assortment of Internet stakeholders, including the Open Root Server Confederation, the European Internet Service Providers Association (EuroISPA)[71] and the Electronic Freedom Foundation.[72]

On October 20, 1998, the NTIA advised ICANN of the United States government's intention to begin transferring responsibility for the technical management of the DNS to this newly formed organization. Citing the "significant concerns about substantive and operational aspects" of ICANN expressed by Internet stakeholders, the government requested that the new organization amend its bylaws to ensure that they were "consistent with the principles of stability, competition, bottom-up coordination and representation" (Burr 1998). Specifically, ICANN was advised that once concerns about its accountability (representational and financial), the transparency of its decision making processes, its means of avoiding conflicts of interest, and its role vis-à-vis country-code top-level domains had been addressed, work on a transition agreement between it and the United States government would commence.

On November 23, 1998, ICANN announced that its bylaws had been revised to address the concerns outlined above.[74] Despite this undertaking, in the eyes of many Internet stakeholders, the way in which ICANN came into being undermined, from the start, its legitimacy as a coordinating body and seriously hampered attempts by the interim board to garner the trust of Internet stakeholders (Clausing 1998a, 1998b; Lessig 1998b; Post 1998). Since that time, and despite attempts to assuage concerns about its activities, ICANN's attempts at legitimizing its role as the entity responsible for overseeing the technical administration of the Internet have remained precarious.[75]

Conclusion

The Internet is comprised of the hardware and software that make internet-working possible and of the formal and informal organizational structures that are evolving around this technological configuration. The structures responsible for coordinating and administering core functions, such as addressing, are important dimensions of the architecture. The focus of this chapter has been on the relationship between the domain name system and the administrative structures and processes that evolved in tandem with it. A number of key themes have been addressed to provide a backdrop for examining the issue of Internet governance in greater detail.

The way in which attempts to reconfigure the institutional parameters of this technological infrastructure have proceeded since 1995 have been at odds with the traditional technologically orientated values and norms that influenced the evolution of Internet addressing. Whereas the domain name system used to be coordinated on the basis of informal administrative arrangements, certain interests appear to have been able to influence the propagation of a clearly defined administrative structure whose authority is now legally constituted. The sociopolitical processes associated with these events, combined with the technical features of the DNS, have assisted in defining, and constraining, the options of actors seeking to redefine the institutional parameters of the Internet and its governance. This raises a number of questions about the way in which politics and power have influenced the development and implementation of coordination structures for managing and administering domain name registrations and allocations. The next chapter examines current perspectives on Internet governance as they relate to the issue of domain naming. Emphasis is given to developing a specific understanding of the processes by which change is occurring in this medium.

Notes

1. Norms are defined here as "a standard of appropriate behavior for actors with a given identity" (Finnemore and Sikkink 1998:891). Within the sociological context these behavioral rules are often referred to as "institutions" and defined as "a relatively stable collection of practices and rules defining appropriate behavior for specific groups of actors in specific situations" (March and Olsen 1998:948).

2. Some commentators have characterized these controversies as being akin to a kindergarten playground, "replete with a goody-goody, scores of screaming 4-year-olds, a big bully and a teacher who can't quite control the situation" (Barrett 1999).

3. Gould (1996b:199) defines these terms as referring broadly to "human and computer interactions across open networks and without reference to geographical location (and therefore legal jurisdiction) or real-world social understanding."

4. Until a few years ago, it had been assumed that the available store of 32-bit IP addresses (2^{32}, or 4,294,967,296) was more than would be required. As a result of the rapid growth of internetworking, by the mid-1990s concerns arose within the Internet engineering community about the potential exhaustion of the existing IP address space. These concerns were allayed in June 1999 when implementation of the IPv6 protocol and its 128-bit address space commenced. The first deployment of IPv6 addresses was announced by the Internet Assigned Numbers Authority on July 14, 1999 (www.iana.org/ipv6-announcement.txt [last accessed July 14, 1999]). See also Markoff (2001).

5. Classes D and E also exist to support IP multicasting and IP related experimentation, respectively. These two classes are not dealt with here as they are beyond the scope of this study.

6. A detailed discussion of these two organizations is provided in the subsequent sections of this book.

7. See rs.arin.net (last accessed May 14, 2001).

8. See www.ripe.net (last accessed May 14, 2001).

9. See www.apnic.net (last accessed May 14, 2001).

10. In most cases, the local Internet registries for IP addresses are also local Internet service providers.

11. On November 16, 2000, the Board of Directors of ICANN, the organizational body responsible for overseeing the administration of the DNS, approved the addition of seven new TLDs into the root. The domains selected were: *.aero, .biz, .coop, .info, .museum, .name, .pro*. They were expected to become operational at some point after May 2001 (www.icann.org/announcements/icann-pr16nov00.htm [last accessed May 14 2001]).

12. See www.netnames.com (last accessed May 5, 2001).

13. Initially, the *.uk* domain was controlled by one individual. This responsibility was later delegated to a committee of Internet industry representatives known as the UK Naming Committee. On August 1, 1996, the activities of the Naming Committee were divested to Nominet UK.

14. Only four of the ten second-level domains used in the *.uk* domain are presented in figure 2.2. The *.co.uk* domain is intended for use for commercial purposes, *.ac.uk* is used by institutions for higher education, *.org.uk* for non-commercial organizations, and both *.plc.uk* and *.ltd.uk* are used for limited companies. In addition, there are domains for Internet service providers, *.net.uk*; schools, *.sch.uk*; government bodies, *.gov.uk*; police forces, *.police.uk*; and the Ministry of Defence, *.mod.uk*. See www.nic.uk/rules.html (last accessed May 15, 2001).

15. The registry for the *.ca* domain previously was an entity known as CDNnet. It was based at the University of British Colombia and was managed on a voluntary basis by a committee of 19 individuals from Canadian education institutes, government, and Internet service providers. On December 1, 2000, there was an operational transfer of responsibility for overseeing this domain. The new registry organization for *.ca* is the Canadian Internet Registration Association (CIRA). See www.cira.ca (last accessed January 20, 2001).

16. Nine of the thirteen root servers contain information for both the root and the top-level domains. The four other root servers contain information for the root alone. These four "root only" servers were launched to test the feasibility of the maintaining the root information separately from additional information about the top-level domains (Murphy 1997).

17. There is a subtle distinction between a zone and a domain. A zone is a technical term used to define a portion of the domain name space that is served by a primary server and one or more secondary servers. Zone files may contain data about an entire domain, a domain and its subdomains, or a portion of a domain (Albitz and Liu 1997; Rony and Rony 1998).

18. A graphical representation of how DNS query works is available at: www.superuser.net/manual/dnsgraph.html (last accessed May 11, 2001).

19. Naughton (2000:275) makes an important observation about the perils one faces when writing about the history of the Internet. He writes, "The tale of how this remark-able system came to be built is an exceedingly complicated one, but to relate it one must hack a narrative path through the jungle and, in the process, do some injury to truth." Clearly, his comments are equally applicable within the context of this study.

20. Initially, the ARPAnet was a computer network-based communication link be-tween scientists and research contractors that was operated under the authority of the United States Department of Defense Advanced Research Projects Agency (ARPA). For a detailed historical account of the evolution of the ARPAnet, see Hafner and Lyon (1996); Naughton (2000); Abbate (1999); Leiner et al. (1998).

21. The amount of bandwidth required to distribute this information was equal to the square of the number of hosts on the network (Mockapetris 1987a).

22. The Request for Comments (RFC) document series is the official publication channel for Internet documents that provide information about Internet standards, speci-fications, protocols, organization notices and individual points of view, see Huitema et al. (1995).

23. The decision to extend the mailbox format for computer mail was reached at a meeting held on January 11, 1982, to discuss addressing issues in computer mail. The meeting was attended by twenty-two representatives from networking-based research institutes and computer companies associated with the ARPAnet (Postel 1982).

24. In addition to RFC 882 and RFC 883, see also Mockapetris (1987a, 1987b).

25. The Defense Advanced Research Projects Agency (DARPA) had divested its re-sponsibility for operating the ARPAnet to the United States Defense Communications

Agency in the summer of 1975.

26. During the early stages of the development of internetworking these documents were distributed to members of the networking community by post.

27. This particular document was one in a series of quarterly memos distributed to the Internet community of the time describing the state of standardization of protocols used in the Internet.

28. The Internet Architecture Board (IAB) originally was called the Internet Activities Board. It is a "coordinating committee for Internet design, engineering and management" that is comprised of an "independent committee of researchers and professionals with a technical interest in the health and evolution of the Internet system." Its primary role is to oversee the Internet standards making processes by offering direction, when needed, to the Internet Engineering Task Force (IETF). The latter is the principal body engaged in the development of new Internet standards specifications. For additional information about the IAB, see Cerf (1990a) and Carpenter (1996b). The definitive outline of the functioning of Internet Engineering Task Force is provided by Malkin (1994).

29. In the political science literature, regimes are defined as "a set of principles—explicit or implicit—norms, rules and decision making procedures around which expectations of actors (States) converge in order to coordinate actors' behavior with respect to a concern to them all" (Krasner 1983:2).

30. The United States National Science Foundation is an independent agency of the United States government. It is responsible for initiating and strengthening scientific and engineering research. See www.nsf.gov (last accessed May 15, 2001).

31. The NSFnet was created, in 1985, as a networking "backbone" to link five supercomputer centers located at various sites throughout the United States. At the same time, the NSF informed American-based academic institutions that if they created community networks, the agency would provide these networks with access to its backbone network. This led to a rapid increase in the number of universities connected to the NSFnet. By the time it ceased operations on April 30, 1995, NSFnet had become the major backbone of the Internet in the United States.

32. In hierarchical networks, the term "backbone" refers to the top-level transmission paths that other transit networks feed into. See whatis.techtarget.com/definition/0,289893,sid9_gci211629,00.html (last accessed May 15, 2001).

33. The history regarding the manner by which NSI became involved with registration activities is somewhat convoluted. In his account of the evolution of computer networking in the United States, Postel (1996c) makes the following claim: "USC files proposal with NSF for funding for ISI to operate the .US Domain registry for the period 1 Oct 92 through 30 Sep 97. Government Systems, Inc spunoff [sic] a new company, Network Solutions, Inc, and teaming with ISI, won a NSF contract to provide various IP number and domain registration services." Rony and Rony (1998) raised doubts about the accuracy of this portrayal of events, questioning how it was that NSI could be considered a "new" company when in fact it was incorporated in Washington, D.C., in 1979.

34. General Atomics is an American company specializing in diversified research and development in energy, defense, and other advanced technologies. It has a long history of being a government contractor and facilities operator for the United States government and other organizations, including the U.S. Department of Energy, U.S. Department of Defense and the U.S. National Science Foundation. See www.general atomics.com (last accessed May 15, 2001).

35. Although this agreement originally was made by the U.S. National Science Foundation, responsibility for its administration was transferred to the U.S. National Telecommunications and Information Administration (NTIA), in the U.S. Department of Commerce on September 9, 1998.

36. Source: Internet Software Consortium, www.isc.org (last accessed January 4, 2000).

37. Source: Internet Software Consortium, www.isc.org (last accessed January 4, 2000).

38. See www.netnames.com/template.cfm?page=statistics&advert=yes (last accessed January 4, 2000).

39. See www.networksolutions.com/en_us/legal/internic/coop-stats/mar96.html (last accessed May 15, 2001).

40. See www.netnames.com (last accessed May 18, 2001).

41. Historically speaking, this type of policy had proven to be equally contentious in the allocation of radio spectrum frequencies and the establishment of satellite orbital slots. See Neuman et al. (1998) for an account of the former and Smythe (1972) for an overview of the latter.

42. For detailed discussions of the relationship between trademarks and domain names see, Dueker (1996), Gigante (1996), Maher (1996), Nathenson (1997), Oppedahl (1997), Rony and Rony (1998), and Mueller (1998c).

43. Vint Cerf, along with Robert Kahn, was one of the co-developers of the Transfer Control Protocol/Internet Protocol (TCP/IP) suite of communication protocols.

44. See www.wia.org/pub/postel-iana-draft1.htm (last accessed May 15, 2001).

45. Established in 1993 as part the United States National Science and Technology Council's Committee on Computing, Information and Communications (CCIC), the Federal Networking Council (FNC) acted as a forum for networking collaborations among federal agencies to meet their research, education, and operational mission goals and to bridge the gap between the advanced networking technologies being developed by research. The Federal Networking Council's charter was revoked in October 1997. See www.fnc.gov (last accessed January 6, 2000).

46. For a detailed critique of this particular view see Mueller (1998a).

47. See *New International Committee Named To Resolve Domain Name System Issues* (November 12, 1996). www.iahc.org/press/iahcmembers.html (last accessed May 15, 2001).

48. See www.iahc.org/draft-iahc-gTLDspec-00.html (last accessed May 15, 2001).

49. See www.gTLD-MoU.org/draft-iahc-recommend-00.html (last accessed May 15, 2001).

50. See www.gTLD-MoU.org/gTLD-MoU.html (last accessed May 15, 2001).

51. The committee received in excess of 400 submissions from interested actors.

52. See www.itu.int/net-itu/gtld-mou/simple.htm (last accessed May 15, 2001).

53. Under the gTLD-MoU framework, NSI was to become a member of the Council of Registrars, and, as such, its activities would have been subject to the auspices of the Policy Oversight Committee.

54. A concise overview of comments from an array of interested parties is provided in Rony and Rony (1998:534-543).

55. By December 1997, there were approximately 80 globally dispersed organizations listed as CORE registrars. See corenic.org/language.htm#English (last accessed January 10, 2000).

56. Recall that the agreement was set to expire on September 30, 1998.

57. The submissions remain available at www.ntia.doc.gov (last accessed May 11, 2001).

58. Under the terms of this proposal, the board of directors would have been constituted by three members each representing one of the global regional Internet registries; two members were to be appointed by the Internet Architecture Board; two members appointed by a membership association (to be created) representing domain name registries and registrars; and seven members designated by another membership organization (to be created) representing Internet users.

59. All of the comments remain available at www.ntia.doc.gov/ntiahome /domainname/130dftmail (last accessed April 11, 2001).

60. See www.ifwp.org, (last accessed July 20, 1998).

61. A list of the points of consensus regarding the objectives/principles of the new entity as well as its powers, structure, and responsibilities is available at cyber.law. harvard.edu/ifwp/consensuslist.asp (last accessed January 12, 2000).

62. A list of the volunteer steering committee members is available at www.ifwp.org /steering.html, (last accessed January 13, 2000).

63. The specific reasons for the actions of the IANA representatives were never made public. Exchanges between some of the concerned actors involved in these events are available at lists.ifwp.org/archive (last accessed January 13, 2000).

64. The Commercial Internet Exchange is a United States-based association of Public Data Internetwork service providers.

65. The Association for Interactive Media is a lobbying organization that represents the interests of organizations that conduct business on the Internet.

66. The proposed bylaws and articles of incorporation for the new corporation are available at www.iana.org/bylaws-coop.html and www.iana.org/articles-coop.html (last accessed January 12, 2000).

67. A full listing of the initial board members, including biographies, is available at cyber.law.harvard.edu/ifwp/icannboard.html (last accessed January 12, 2000).

68. One, albeit somewhat biased, account of the possible relationship between IANA's actions and the government announcement to extend the cooperative agreement is offered by Cook (1998).

69. See www.open-rsc.org (last accessed January 13, 2000).

70. The members of this working group included Karl Auerbach, an Internet technologist and chairperson of an Internet Engineering Task Force Working Group; Mikki Barry, president of the Domain Name Rights Coalition; Peter Dengate Thrush, a patent lawyer who is counsel to the New Zealand branch of the Internet Society and the chairperson of the *.nz* registry, Domainz; Patrick O'Brien, CEO of Domainz; Milton Mueller, Associate Professor and Director, Graduate Program in Telecommunications and Network Management, Syracuse University School of Information Studies; Ellen and Peter Rony, co-authors of the *Domain Name Handbook: High Stakes and Strategies in Cyberspace*; Eric Weisberg, principal and general counsel for a rural Texas ISP, Internet Texoma; and David Schutt, an information systems manager for a manufacturer/end user, interested in access to resources and electronic commerce. See www.cavebear.com/bwg (last accessed January 12, 2000).

71. See www.ntia.doc.gov/ntiahome/domainname/proposals/bosgrp/submission-letter .html (last accessed January 12, 2000).

72. See www.euroispa.org/papers/icann.html (last accessed January 13, 2000).

73. See www.eff.org/pub/Infrastructure/DNS_control/ICANN_IANA_IAHC/1998092 3_eff_new_iana_bylaws.letter (last accessed January 13, 2000).

74. The revised bylaws are available at www.iana.org/icann/bylaws-pr23nov98.html (last accessed January 13, 2000).

75. A comprehensive collection of commentary and criticism, from an array of perspectives, about ICANN's activities is available at www.incannwatch.org (last accessed May 15, 2001).

Chapter 3

Don't Believe the Hype!

If we are to have some alternatives to the jurisprudence of digital libertarianism we will have to offer a richer picture of Internet politics than that of the coercive (but impotent) state and the neutral facilitative technology.
—Boyle (1997)

One of the key themes to emerge from the previous chapter is that the controversies associated with the restructuring of the Internet domain name system (DNS) have reflected different actors' perceptions of the goals of this technological configuration and how these goals might best be achieved. The parameters of these controversies, and the types of choices which they entail, suggest that the fundamental issue within this context is one of *managing* a process or situation. Moreover, the level of debate arising from these disputes appears to have been directly related to, if not indicative of, the economic significance of the technology involved. As a consequence, the controversies that have arisen within this realm have not been restricted solely to the technical features of the DNS. Rather, they have encompassed a reconfiguration of the institutional parameters of the Internet and its governance.

The outcomes of these collective exercises in decision making affect the flexibility and perceived efficacy of the domain name registry system, as well as other aspects of internetworking. Unfortunately, in having adopted prescriptive overtones, and by electing to focus primarily on end results, the bulk of Internet related "governance" literature does not sufficiently address the sociopolitical dimensions of the restructuring process. The perspective set forth in this chapter is premised on the assertion that since the collective and individual actions of industry players, Internet and non-Internet organizations, governmental authorities, and specific individuals have been integral in determining the suc-

cess and/or failure of proposed organizational and administrative innovations, the need for an examination of politics and power arises. By seeking a
specific understanding of the *processes* by which change has been managed
vis-à-vis the restructuring of the DNS, the sociopolitical perspective set out
here challenges the view that the outcomes of collective exercises in decision making within the Internet context are the result of organic bottom-up
decision making processes. Therefore, the aim of the discussion in this
chapter is to present a theoretical framework for examining how these decision making processes are influenced by the dynamic relationship between
technology and the political activities of interacting entities.

The chapter opens with an examination of prescriptive approaches to
Internet governance. Rather than contributing to an understanding of *how*
the governance of internetworking is evolving, these approaches appear to
primarily reflect bipolar perceptions of how it *should* evolve. In the second
section, process-orientated approaches to Internet governance are examined.
Although these perspectives offer greater insights into the dynamic relationship between technological change and emergent network characteristics,
they too appear to underestimate the significance of the social dynamics of
governance processes. In the third section a theoretical framework for understanding processes of organizational change within the context of cyberspace is presented. This framework offers a means for exploring the ways in
which the sociopolitical processes and ambiguities involved in the development and implementation of coordination structures for managing network-
based interactions, and transactions, influence the flexibility and perceived
efficacy of these structures.

Perspectives on Internet Governance

In recent years, there has been a dramatic and varied surge of literature focusing on "Internet governance." In fact, this term has become an imprecise
catch-phrase that often is used in connection with a multitude of regulatory
and coordinating standards.[1] In some contexts the regulatory aspects of governance have been emphasized by those actors who point to the necessity for
establishing rule sets, or regulations, vis-à-vis such issues as the protection
of intellectual property rights, freedom of speech, information flows, privacy, access, and content. In other contexts, the term "governance" has been
used to denote the informal and formal coordinating processes that make
network-based interactions, and transactions, possible on the Internet. In
addition to these two approaches, the scope of the "governance" concept
also includes politically charged questions pertaining to who, or what, in the
cyber-realm has the right to make authoritative decisions, and on what such
authority is based. The definition of governance adopted here refers to those
processes of coordination and regulation that culminate in the production of
a social order (Rhodes 1996; Rosenau 1990, 1992; Tang 1995).

In terms of Internet addressing, the semantic ambiguity characterizing the
use of governance reflects, in part, the fact that the controversies associated

with domain naming form only one aspect of a complex "governance" picture involving a multitude of different issues and actors. Despite the somewhat ambiguous application of this concept, it is possible to divide the literature on Internet governance into two schools of thought: *commons* approaches and *decentralized* approaches. Corresponding roughly to the interpretative differences between regulatory and coordinating standards, each school has offered conflicting visions about the means of, and necessity for, constraining various dimensions of cyberspace. Before proceeding any further it must be emphasized, however, that this division is somewhat artificial and is offered primarily for the purpose of achieving some analytical clarity. This conceptualization blurs the fact that various points of consensus have existed among the participants involved in the restructuring process. Bearing this in mind, the next two sections offer an historical overview of the arguments advanced by proponents of each school of thought.

The Commons School

Perspectives rooted in the commons school of thought have advocated the establishment of stable rules vis-à-vis property rights (intellectual and physical), means of exchange, and the enforcement of order on the basis of hierarchy. The key assumption underpinning the notion of governance associated with these perspectives is that there is such a thing as "the Internet." That is, "the Internet" is seen as encompassing numerous elements (technical and nontechnical), which when taken together, constitute a conceptual whole or "commons." Since each of these constituent elements is seen to be interdependent, subscribers to this interpretation have tended to advocate the implementation of various top-down regulatory frameworks to ensure the well-being of the conceptual whole.

In an early position paper illustrative of this approach, Foster (1996) focused on the conflicts that had arisen as a consequence of the global nature of domain names and the lack of global trademarks.[2] His aim was to make a case for incorporating the United Nations into any eventual Internet-centered governance framework. Foster argued that in the absence of global trademark law, the legitimacy of the DNS as a global system was dependent upon its recognition by the world's governments. Failure to achieve any formal recognition, he claimed, risked destabilizing both the DNS and its supporting organizations. He maintained that the Internet community needed to work cooperatively with business associations and national governments toward "the creation of an environment where the global domain name system can coexist with various national trademark laws" (Foster 1996:4). Rather than supporting the creation of new institutional bodies, he insisted that the legitimacy of the DNS as a global system was contingent upon registration with the United Nations and its specialized bodies, specifically, the International Telecommunication Union (ITU) and the World Intellectual Property Organization (WIPO).

In contrast to Foster's assertions about the need for the direct involvement of existing international multilateral organizations, Gould (1996a) suggested that contemporary Internet institutions could form the basis for a type of constitutional governance which "when enhanced, might stave off most calls for external regulation." His view was premised on the assumption that a form of governance derived from common Internet practice would be superior to that based on any externally imposed organization. He postulated that the core Internet functions should be treated as public resources and that once the core Internet institutions were privatized (i.e., no longer dependent upon the United States government for funding), the legitimacy of their authority over core functions (i.e., allocation of IP addresses, registration of domain names) would likely need to be embedded in some form of nonterritorially based Internet constitution. Using the example of the European Union's supranational constitution, Gould concluded that a constitution for the Internet might be based on the principle of teleocracy—that is, a form of governance based on a particular goal or objective. The strength of this principle, he averred, was that it would enable the objectives for which Internet institutions operated (i.e., ensuring efficient functioning and development of internetworking) to take precedence in cases where disputes arose. Conceding that the establishment of a fixed system of Internet governance seemed unlikely given the diffuse nature of Internet organizations, he suggested that responsibility for monitoring adherence to constitutional principles could rest with an "Internet regulator." Gould (1996a) opined that such a regulator could be "perhaps responsible to the Internet Society" and based on the regulatory model adopted in the United Kingdom to oversee the commercial operations of privatized public utilities. Under this model, the commercial operations of public utilities are conducted at "arms length" from the U.K. government on the basis of government consideration of consumer and commercial interests.

Mathiason and Kuhlman's contributions to the domain name-related governance debates also were rooted in the belief that elements of the Internet are of public interest and, consequently, that some form of regulation was inevitable. In their initial study, Mathiason and Kuhlman (1998b) analyzed the comments obtained by the United States Department of Commerce (DoC) in response to its *Notice of Inquiry on the Registration and Administration of Internet Domain Names* in July/August 1997.[3] Having recognized that there are multiple and differing interests associated with domain name-related issues, these authors advanced the view that the "international public sector" would be best suited to "maintain the coherence of the Internet in the context of technological and economic change" (Mathiason and Kuhlman 1998b:29). They concluded that divergent interests with a stake in the Internet and its governance should seek to organize themselves under the aegis of an international framework convention agreed upon by governments, but requiring the consent of all Internet constituencies.[4]

Mathiason and Kuhlman (1998a) continued with this line of argument and compared the comments submitted to the DoC in the response to the Green Paper in February/March 1998 to those the DoC had obtained from its initial notice of inquiry. Their analysis suggested that in the six months separating these two episodes, international interest in Internet governance had increased[5] and that a rough consensus on some general governance principles had begun to emerge.[6] Stressing that "the task of sorting out the roles and responsibilities of the numerous national, international and private entities cannot be left to Darwinian processes at this point in the development of a global enabling technology," Mathiason and Kuhlman (1998a:22) argued for the establishment of a comprehensive Internet regulatory regime founded on the creation of a framework convention paralleling the United Nations Framework Convention on Climate Change.

One of the striking features of the positions outlined above is an apparent failure to consider the potential role of internetworking technologies in shaping, or influencing, the formation of internetworking-related governance processes. As a result, these views tend to be characterized by an emphasis on the ways in which regulatory mechanisms in the physical realm might be transposed onto, or adopted into, the cyber-realm. In other words, these arguments appear to be premised on a conception of "governance" that entails a top-down imposition of constraints in order to meet regulatory ends. In addition, they do not give sufficient consideration to the fact that, in some instances, internetworking technologies may provide the means for sufficiently skilled users to bypass regulations that they find objectionable.

The Decentralized School

Outlooks grounded in the decentralized school of thought have also espoused the necessity of establishing a property rights regime for the cyber-realm. However, supporters of this perspective have tended to reject notions of "the Internet." They assert that the "the" is based on myth and conveys a flawed view of what are, in fact, merely processes of internetworking made possible by a series of interlinked computer networks, and a compendium of hardware and software. Advocates of this view place a strong emphasis on the "private" nature of internetworking, highlighting the extent to which name servers, leased lines, and even domain names are privately owned. The key assumption underpinning these perspectives is that the institutional norms that developed in tandem with the evolution of internetworking preclude the need for any external regulation or coordination of the modalities of cyberspace. In other words, since there is no "whole," the only policy required is one of laissez-faire.

In a paper written prior to the commencement of the Internet Ad-Hoc Committee's (IAHC) initiative, Gillett and Kapor (1996) suggested that the organizational model of internetworking was a type of decentralized self-governance that had emerged as a result of the interplay between technological design factors, and certain commonly shared *cultural* values within the Internet community.[7] The success of this model, they argued, was based on a shared belief throughout the internetworking community in the efficacy of protocol interoperability. In broaching the issue of domain naming, Gillett and Kapor asserted that, in the light of the historically rooted path dependence[8] of internetworking, and the fact that the stakeholder community for domain name assignments is global, the principle of decentralization should underpin any model for coordinating Internet addressing. In short, these authors were suggesting that the structures of contemporary, and future, Internet-related governance institutions would be recognizably similar to those internetworking structures that had come into existence at an earlier time to satisfy important technical and social purposes.

Gillet and Kapor's argument was premised on the assumption that the functionality and authority of diffused coordination mechanisms could be more easily legitimated in distributed network environments. In terms of functionality, they claimed that naming and addressing were different issues that were best dealt with by separate organizational and technical approaches. Using country-specific domain name registries as examples of distributed authority, they expressed the view that authority is more easily legitimated at the local level when it is administered by locally selected authorities, in accordance with local policies. In her response to the DoC's Green Paper, Gillett reaffirmed this position, arguing that the management of top-level domain databases should be shared by multiple entities, so as to avoid the possibility of registries "locking-in" their customers by restricting the portability of domain names (Gillett 1998).

Building upon the notion of decentralization, Milton Mueller has consistently argued against both the propagation of an Internet-centered "regulatory agenda" and the policing of trademark rights by domain name registries. Specifically, he has claimed that the Internet does not need governance, but rather that an institutional framework for establishing a system of property rights is required (Mueller 1997b). His position on this matter was clearly outlined in his submission to the DoC's *Notice of Inquiry on the Registration and Administration of Internet Domain Names* in which he wrote:

> Loose references to "self-governance" and "private sector initiative" are not helpful. They only obscure the legitimate and unavoidable role governments must play in the definition, enforcement, and adjudication of property rights. Without clearly defined property rights, there is no "private sector." Without stable rules governing the nature and use of resources, there can be no "self-governance." (Mueller 1997a)

In fact, Mueller has been critical of the application of the very term "governance" to internetworking, claiming that the notion of control embedded within this concept is anathema to the facilitation of internetworking. Accordingly, he has argued that

> The guiding principle of the governance debate is no longer the facilitation of internetworking. Instead, everyone seems to be focused on *restricting* the ability to internetwork in order to protect or advance the socio-economic interests of various stakeholders. The institutional problem of coordinating internetworking, which is difficult enough to solve, has become a pretext for address-

ing a variety of unrelated political agendas, from the regulation of free speech to the policing of trademark registrations. The simple but revolutionary idea of enabling internetworking has been all but buried by an avalanche of political dung. (Mueller 1998b)

Aside from his personal involvement in the processes associated with the formation of the Internet Corporation for Assigned Names and Numbers (ICANN) and its supporting organizations, Mueller's contributions to the avalanche have primarily focused on two aspects of the governance debates: (i) advocacy of increased competition in the top-level domain namespace by expanding the number of available generic top-level domains (Mueller 1997a, 1997b, 1997c, 1998a), and (ii) opposing attempts to forge strong links between the domain name registrations and the protection of trademarks (Mueller 1997a, 1997b, 1998c, 2000).

In terms of the first issue, Mueller maintained that expanding the number of available gTLDs would allow greater scope for price competition and service innovation. This, he averred, would foster a system better suited both to the nonterritorial basis of internetworking and a regime of free international trade in Internet-related services. With regard to the second issue, in Mueller (1998c), he provided the first publicly available empirical study of the interaction between domain names and trademarks. The study itself was based on a statistical analysis of 121 cases of conflict between domain name registrants and trademark owners.[9] Having presented evidence suggesting that "real" trademark infringements[10] through the use of domain names were rare occurrences he concluded that "trademark owners have been able to claim property rights in Internet domain names that go far beyond the rights they have under existing legislation and case law governing trademarks" (Mueller 1998c:13). In line with these assertions, Mueller continues to advocate the need to minimize opportunities for political and legal interference in the growth of cyberspace and has become an outspoken critic of both ICANN and its WIPO-based Uniform Dispute Resolution Policy for adjudicating conflicts between domain names and trademarks (Mueller 1999a, 1999b, 2000).[11]

Another key figure of the anti-regulation camp was Anthony Rutkowski, a former chief of International Telecommunication Regulations and Relations between Members at the ITU, and former executive director of the Internet Society.[12] He claimed that the rapid growth of the Internet[13] was a product of commercial and technical product developments that enhanced the value of internetworking and facilitated the use of these technologies by large numbers of people. According to Rutkowski, one of the consequences of these developments was the transfer of the control, or "governance," of the Internet's most significant facets to companies operating in a robust marketplace thus invoking traditional public governance and dispute resolution mechanisms (Rutkowski 1998a). He maintained therefore, that "from a public policy standpoint, it is not clear why such Internet related name system services and products should be treated any differently than any other enhanced, private networks and services"

(Rutkowski 1997a).

His opposition to the establishment of regulatory bodies in this realm clearly manifested itself in his hostility to the gTLD-MoU initiative which he described as "fraught with perilous scenarios, and fundamentally wrongheaded" (Rutkowski 1998b). Subsequently, he claimed that ICANN's temporary board members were deluding themselves that they constituted the world's Internet regulatory body:

> What someone hasn't told them—and their lack of understanding has engendered—is that they have no authority and no ability to implement anything, other than what they care to make available and hope that people use . . . attempting to regulate "the Internet" is like trying to walk around with a sand castle in your hands. (Rutkowski 1999:10)

This aversion to any governance model involving the United Nations or other intergovernmental bodies was premised on two interrelated factors. The first was an objection to any potential acquisition of jurisdiction over Internet resources by the ITU, which Rutkowski viewed as "perhaps the last major international home of adherents to the top-down managed cartel and public utility models of telecommunications" (Rutkowski 1998c). The second was his conviction that domain names should not be considered a public resource. This view was clearly outlined in his response to the DoC's *Notice of Inquiry on the Registration and Administration of Internet Domain Names* in which he wrote,

> Denominating domain names as a global public resource seems at best a perversion that is orthoginal [*sic*] to reality, and a poor public policy making choice that has significant permanent administrative implications. Thus, an additional principle should be adopted that asserts domain names are globally unique private expressions that describe an open network based information object. (Rutkowski 1997a)

Ultimately, Rutkowski's rejection of conceptualizing domain names as a global public resource led him to advocate framework proposals, and aspects of issue specific proposals, that sought the establishment of alternative self-organizing private contract solutions to domain name-related issues.

In comparing perspectives rooted in the commons and decentralized approaches to Internet governance, it becomes apparent that what we are dealing with is a debate, or more accurately a multitude of debates, about optimal governance strategies. In contrast to the approaches rooted in the commons perspective, the outlooks falling under the decentralized category appear to give greater credence to how the specific features of internetworking technologies might influence governance processes in the virtual realm. Simply put, they appear to be premised, in part, on a view of "governance" as a coordination standard, or options to permit interactions. However, neither of these prescriptive end-result orientations were intended to account for the emergent, or changing, structures of Internet centered coordination regimes. Consequently, they offer relatively little insight into the processes actually shaping the governance trajectory of the Internet and its domain naming system. In fact, the bulk of the Internet governance literature that is rooted in these two schools of thought risks transforming internetworking into a conceptual black box. Therefore, another approach is required if we are to understand the dynamic relationship that exists between institutional forms delivering technology and the network structures that emerge over time.

Process-Based Approaches to Internet Governance

An unfortunate consequence of approaching the issue of Internet governance from ideologically rooted interpretative frameworks (i.e., the need for some sort of formalistic regulation to ensure collective benefit of the "whole" versus collective benefit of the "whole" as a product of the workings of the invisible hand) is a tendency to focus on one dimension of social order at the expense of another. One of the weaknesses of such bifurcated conceptualizations of social order is their tendency to perpetuate analytical blind spots or distortions (Smythe 1977; Wendt and Duvall 1989). Moreover, the significance of the blind spots resulting from an emphasis on end results, and/or optimal governance strategies, cannot be underestimated unless one is prepared to overlook the importance of procedure as such:

> In most areas of human endeavor—from performing a symphony to orchestrating society—the processes and rules that constitute the enterprise and define the roles of its participants matter quite apart from any identifiable 'end state' that is ultimately produced. Indeed, in many cases it is the process itself that matters *most* to those who take part in it. (Tribe 1972:83)

Within the Internet context the difficulties of analyzing these constituent processes and rules are further exacerbated by the need also to consider the role that internetworking technologies might play in shaping and influencing emergent governance processes.

Although not centered specifically on domain naming controversies, process-orientated approaches to matters of Internet governance incorporate elements both of the commons and decentralized schools into their analyses. The distinguishing feature of these perspectives is a concern for the procedures whereby outcomes are produced, and for the history out of which outcomes within the cyber-realm evolve. Their collective emphasis lies in the processes by which rules are effectuated and how specific attributes of internetworking technologies influence rule making processes. When taken together, these perspectives parallel the notion of *technological politics* set forth in Hadjilambrinos (1998), Huigen (1993), and Winner (1977, 1986, 1993). At the root of this notion is a recognition of technology as something that is socially constructed, coupled with an acknowledgment that technologies influence the environments which they create. Concomitantly, design alterations to existing artifacts or systems are recognized as having the potential to bring about changes to the critical character of a social milieu. This suggests that technologies are not neutral but rather that they have political properties in so far as they may influence the authoritative allocation of values within a given context.[14]

In an early examination of the distinctive features of law making in cyberspace, Post (1995) argued that an asymmetric distribution of power existed between the various nodes from which rules might be issued in the electronic realm. Describing those entities that define network protocols[15] as "primary controllers,"[16] Post put forth two propositions about the construction of social orders in internetworking environments. The first was that those entities and institutions which defined network protocols possessed competitive advantages over other controllers in the electronic domain. One possible consequence of such asymmetric distributions of control advantages, he theorized, was the potential for these nodes, or controllers, to become the loci of substantive rule making in cyberspace.

His second, and more contentious, proposition suggested that despite the state's monopoly on the application of coercive sanctions, its ability to impose sanctions in the virtual realm was constrained by the ability of internetworking technologies to facilitate regulatory arbitrage.[17] Noting that control emanated at the level of individual networks, he asserted further that although forms of top-down control might be exerted over specific networks, the aggregate range of such rule sets was unlikely to lead to any form of centralized control of cyberspace. Reflecting the ethos of digital libertarianism,[18] Post concluded that the "law of cyberspace" would be largely determined by a free market of regulations in which network users would be able to chose those rule sets they found most congenial.

These ideas were developed further in Johnson and Post (1996a, 1996b) in which it was argued that the legitimacy of rule sets governing activities in online environments could not be traced to any geographically based polity because no geographically localized set of constituents possessed a stronger claim to regulate than any other group within this realm. They maintained that the various dimensions of internetworking, including Internet addressing, could be governed by "decentralized, emergent law" wherein customary and privately produced laws, or rules, would be produced by decentralized collective action leading to the emergence of common standards for mutual coordination. On the basis of this assertion, Johnson and Post (1996b) claimed that the "jurisdictional and substantive quandaries" created by transnational electronic communication networks could be resolved by "conceiving of cyberspace as a distinct 'place' for the purposes of legal analysis, by recognizing a legally significant border between cyberspace and the real world." In short, these authors were advocating the establishment of new legal institutions or a form of cyberspace sovereignty based on and reflecting the diffuse technical and social structures of the virtual realm.[19]

Dismissing claims that anarchy and/or chaos necessarily ensue without hierarchical controls, they suggested that "the technical protocols of the net have in effect created a complex adaptive system that produces a type of order that does not rely on lawyers, court decisions, statutes, or votes" (Johnson and Post 1996a). They proposed that internetworking technologies would lead to the emergence of a form of cyber-federalism in which individual networks and/or online communities would be governed by different locally defined rule sets. Maintaining that processes of decentralized emergent law could function as an efficacious governance system,[20] Post and Johnson (1997a, 1997b) postulated that that within online environments these processes might also lead to the redefining of notions of civic virtue. The ability of network users to enter or exit online spaces, they suggested, increased the probability that the traditional institutions of representative democracy (i.e., election of representatives of civic virtue to address problems of collective action) would not be replicated in online environments. Rather, individual network users were more likely to process and act directly upon information they perceived as affecting their personal utility in particular decision making arenas.

In other words, those most intensely affected by, or with a marked interest in, a given issue would be most likely to join and seek to influence relevant decision making forums. Post and Johnson (1997a, 1997b) concluded that within virtual environments, at least, the democratic tradition of rational debates among elected representatives would likely be replaced by more dispersed and complex interactions at localized levels. To this end, their arguments appear to have been based on the utilitarian assumption that social norms promulgated through the interactions of rational agents seeking to maximize their individual preferences produce outcomes, at the local level, that are in the common self-interest of those agents who participate in the decision making process.[21]

In contrast to Post's and Johnson's arguments about the futility of attempting to regulate cyberspace, others have stressed that this realm has always been a regulated environment—the regulations, or laws, being built into the hardware and software that constitute the Internet. Despite sympathizing with the view that internetworking is leading to the disintegration of territorial and substantive borders as key paradigms for regulatory governance, Reidenberg (1996) claimed that new models and sources of rules were being created in their place. He identified two distinct regulatory borders arising from complex rule making processes involving states, the private sector, technical interests, and citizen forces. Each of these borders is seen to establish and define behavioral rules within its respective realms of the networking infrastructure. The first type of border encompassed the contractual agreements among various Internet service providers. The second type of border Reidenberg identified was the network architecture. The key factor at this level, he argued, was the technical standards because they establish default boundary rules that impose order in network environments. Noting that in evolving internetworking environments technical standards could reflect, or affect, fundamental public concerns, Reidenberg pointed out that technical standards could be used as instruments of public policy.[22]

In Reidenberg (1998), the notion that networking technologies impose a set of default rules, or *Lex Informatica*,[23] on communication networks was more fully developed. *Lex Informatica* refers to the laws, or default rules, imposed on network users by technological capabilities and system design choices. Reidenberg asserted that whereas political governance processes usually establish the substantive laws of nation-states, in *Lex Informatica* the primary sources of default rule making are the technology developer(s) and the social processes through which customary uses of the technology evolve.[24] It is these laws, or default rules, he claimed, which define both possible behaviors in cyberspace and the values that are upheld within this realm. It follows, therefore, that changes to this architecture could alter the values embraced in cyberspace. To this end, he argued that since *Lex Informatica* could be seen as an important system of rules analogous to a legal regime, it was incumbent on policy makers to redirect their rule making strategies away from traditional regulatory approaches toward an understanding and recognition of the rule sets "embedded in network designs and standards as well as in system configurations" (Reidenberg 1998:554-555).

According to this view, current Internet-related conflicts and controversies—domain naming and others—reflect a state of flux in which *Lex Informatica* and established legal regimes are intersecting. In instances where technological rules are better suited to resolve policy issues (i.e. content filtering made possible by technology versus attempts at state censorship of online content), Reidenberg advocated substituting technical modalities for law. He postulated that technical arenas, and more specifically informal and formal standard setting forum coupled with market forces, would increasingly serve as the critical sources of information policy. Although *Lex Informatica* may constrain the law's ability to deal with certain problems, Reidenberg stressed that this trend would not necessary imply a reduction in government activity in the regulatory domain. He contended that in the light of *Lex Informatica's* dependence on design choices, the attributes of public oversight associated with regulatory regimes could be maintained by shifting the focus of government actions away from direct regulation of cyberspace toward influencing changes to its architecture.

Expanding upon the view that the values embraced by cyberspace could be altered by the implementation of changes to its architecture, Boyle (1997) also disputed claims about "the state's supposed inability to regulate the Internet." He argued that those exhorting this tenet underestimated the ways through which states may exert power on the regulatory process. Boyle maintained that by defining the problem of regulation primarily as a search for "neutral and facilitative" technological solutions, perspectives rooted in the assumptions of digital libertarianism failed to give adequate attention to the complicated social systems of private entities acting as agents of regulation. Specifically, he claimed that such approaches tended to insulate from closer scrutiny the state's attempt to "design its commands into the very technologies that, collectively are supposed to spell its demise" (Boyle 1997).

Reorienting the focus of analyses of the Internet and its governance in a Foucauldian light,[25] demonstrated how rather than circumventing state rules, certain information technologies might be interpreted as providing the state with "a different arsenal of methods to regulate content materially rather than juridically, by everyday softwired routing practices, rather than threats of eventual sanction" (Boyle 1997). He also illustrated how governments may be seen as obtaining advantages by privatizing the regulatory entities, or Panopticon,[26] of cyberspace. The advantages of privatized and technologically based rule enforcement, he argued, rested with the fact that in such cases policing would occur far from the scrutiny of public law. Consequently, this could be interpreted as offering states freedom from some of the constitutional and other constraints that would restrict their activities were they to regulate directly. Boyle drew attention also to another analytical blind spot perpetuated by the mantra of technical solutions being "intrinsically more desirable than the exercise of state power by a sovereign." Drawing on Foucault's assertions about the contradictory nature of the theory of sovereignty, he pointed out that this inclination toward the superiority of technical solutions may reflect the operation of relations of power in such a way as to conceal their actual procedures.[27] According to this interpretation, the attractiveness of technological solutions to problems presented by information and communication technologies may not be based solely on pragmatism, but rather on the fact that such solutions divert attention away from questions of private and public power.

Another key contributor to the development of process-orientated analyses of the Internet and its governance is the Stanford University law professor Lawrence Lessig. He, too, is dismissive of claims regarding the futility of regulation in cyberspace, asserting that the changing architecture of the Internet imposes the most troubling form of online regulation because "the shackles built by programmers may well constrain us most" (Lessig 1997). Lessig points out that rather than assuring freedom, there are no guarantees that changes to the architecture of cyberspace will not move in the direction of increasing control, or highly efficient regulation (Lessig 1999a). To this end, his concerns conform to the view that rather than offering liberation, the information revolution may represent a restructuring and reorganization of relations of power in a manner that reduces the freedom of society as a whole (Beniger 1986; Gandy 1993; Webster and Robins 1986; Robins and Webster 2001).

Lessig's approach to matters of Internet governance is rooted in the assumption that behavior in both the physical and virtual realm is regulated by four modalities of constraint (Lessig 1998d, 1999a, 1999b). In contrast to the looser usage of "regulation" in the preceding discussion, within this context regulation refers to a choice between the direct behavioral constraints that the four modalities might effect and the indirect constraints that they might give rise to. The first modality of constraint noted by Lessig is law. It regulates behavior by the imposition of sanctions *ex post*. The second modality consists of the social norms which regulate behavior by enforcing understandings and expectations within particular communities. A third modality of constraint on behavior is established by markets through price and availability. The fourth modality, architecture, refers to the constraints imposed upon behavior by the world as we find it. While observing that regulation is the sum of the interactions of these four modalities, Lessig contends that within physical and cyber domains, architecture is the most important because it establishes conditions of entry and existence, as well as reflecting different philosophies of social ordering.[28] He labels the architecture of cyberspace, "code." It refers to the "software and hardware that constitutes cyberspace as it is—the set of protocols, the set of rules, implemented, or codified, in cyberspace itself, that determine how people interact, or exist in this space. . . . It [*code*], like architecture, is not optional" (Lessig 1998d:4).

In contrast to the other perspectives examined in this section, Lessig's emphasis on the importance of focusing on the values underpinning code is not restricted to the potential for government encroachment into the virtual realm. He is equally apprehensive about the values that might be built into code by private interests. He asserts that the desire to remove government(s) from the virtual realm has blinded people to an important dimension of stakeholder governance; once the state is removed, actors representing private interests pursue their own ends, and there is no certainty that these interests will be any less controlling. To this end, he has consistently highlighted the need for finding ways to ensure that the types of checks and balances that get built into constitutional democracies are also incorporated into the code of cyberspace (Lessig 1998c, 1998d, 1999a, 1999b).

Lessig argues that since the mid-1990s the "invisible hand of commerce" has brought about control-oriented changes to the architecture of cyberspace. Prior to 1995 this architecture inhibited zoning,[29] in so far as users could more easily maintain their anonymity while online, and difficulties associated with personal verification meant that privacy was better protected than it is at present. Since that time, however, in accordance with the drive to facilitate electronic commerce the code of cyberspace has changed to accommodate a better zoning of this space (Lessig 1996a, 1996b, 1998d, 1999a, 1999b, 1999c). Lessig contends that this shift in zoning patterns has implications for how code is regulated and developed.

For example, he has expressed concern about the use, by some Internet service providers, of the Mail Abuse Prevention System (MAPS) to limit the distribution of unwanted and unsolicited e-mail, or spam.[30] Noting that "there's little agreement about what the spam rules should be, and even less agreement about how they might be enforced," Lessig claims that the "real problem is that vigilantes and network service providers are deciding fundamental policy questions about how the Net will work—each group from its own perspective," thereby perpetuating a system of "policy-making by the "invisible hand" (Lessig 1998e). The danger with this approach to altering the architecture of e-mail, he argues, is not that policy is being made per se, but rather that "those making the policy are unaccountable . . . [*and*] that policy is being made by people who threaten that if you complain or challenge their boycotts through the legal system, then you will suffer their boycott all the more forcibly" (Lessig 1998e).[31]

A key contribution of Lessig's work in this domain is the attention he draws to the need for questioning whether the architectures of cyberspace protect such values as liberty, free speech, protection of privacy, and access. Implicit within this and the other process-oriented approaches examined above is a recognition that "governance" in cyberspace entails a mixture of regulations imposed by the architecture, and the regulations of entities that regulate various domains of this realm. A key weakness with these approaches, however, is that they tend to be highly speculative, primarily focusing on the processes by which architecture *may* influence regulatory procedures and the types of social orders that *may* be promulgated. As a result, these normative perspectives make it difficult to assess how the institutional foundations of regulation are established. Moreover, they do not account for the fact that the outcomes of the conflicts between social actors mediating the processes of technological change are contingent, in part, on the relative power of the entities involved. These shortcomings highlight the need for an empirical analysis of what social actors actually do, in contrast to prescriptive and/or ideologically laden speculation about what they *should* do. By seeking a more specific understanding of the *processes* by which change is being managed, a more detailed picture of Internet politics extending beyond "that of the coercive (but impotent) state and the neutral facilitative technology" may be developed (Boyle 1997).

Politics and Power

When Internet usage was still predominantly restricted to the research and academic communities, the coordination and regulatory mechanisms that administered the allocation of domain names were capable of meeting the information processing and communication needs of cyberspace. The rise of commercial activity in this realm, including the introduction of commercial companies offering Internet access and services (i.e. Demon, PSInet, America Online, CompuServe) brought the Internet into people's homes and workplaces. Accompanying this growth was a recognition of the potential value of establishing an online presence by increasing numbers of commercial and noncommercial entities. Although the resultant increase in demand for domain names did not impact fundamentally upon the technical infrastructure underpinning the DNS, it did undermine some of the institutional norms[32] and character of the original network (King et al. 1997).

As the World Wide Web increasingly became the application for conducting commerce online, an assortment of actors with perceived stakes in the future of internetworking increasingly challenged the legitimacy of the principles and procedures that hitherto had been used to coordinate various elements of the cyber-realm, including domain name allocations. The fact that none of the entities involved in these processes had an uncontested, or clearly legitimate,

claim to the authority required to establish new principles and procedures resulted in the politicization of this aspect of internetworking. Drawing from
Ruggie (1975), politicization here refers to making things more controversial
in society, including the potential "pushing" of decisions to higher levels of
decision making within government structures. Within some internetworking
contexts these political processes fostered organizational innovations that took
on the form of new governance regimes for country-level name spaces. The
political processes associated with the changes to the global addressing regime
also led to the emergence of a new organization charged with the responsibility of overseeing the functioning of the DNS as a whole—ICANN.

The conflicts associated with the emergence of new naming regimes at the
national and international levels closely parallel the historical disputes regarding other forms of global communications (i.e. radio spectrum allocation,
orbital slots, television broadcasting), in so far as they have all been "characterized not by Nash equilibria that are sub-optimal but rather by disagreements
over which point along the Pareto frontier should be chosen, that is, by distributional conflicts rather than by market failure" (Krasner 1991:336). The
intensity of the conflicts associated with attempts to reconfigure the Internet
domain name system is directly related to the fact that, despite often agreeing
on mutually undesirable outcomes, the actors involved have tended to disagree
on their preferred outcomes. Variations in the outcomes of these disputes, and
the types of organizational innovations fostered, have been principally influenced by the relative bargaining power of the actors involved. Yet, with the
exception of a limited number of studies (e.g. Froomkin 2000a; Geist 2001;
Mueller 2000; Paré 2000, 2002) the focus of the bulk of the Internet-related
governance literature has implicitly, if not explicitly, given greater credence to
the importance of determining the ideal institutional structures than to the underlying distribution of power capabilities underpinning emergent administrative innovations. The strength of applying a power-oriented approach for examining Internet politics rests with its ability to provide a less polemical, more
empirical, and sociologically richer understanding of politicking and policy
making in the cyber-realm.

The term "innovation" can be used to refer to the creation or renewal of
material artifacts, practices, ideas, as well as the processes through which the
latter are created, developed, reinvented, and/or diffused (Slappendel 1996).
Some authors have defined innovation as entailing "the generation, acceptance, and implementation of new ideas, processes, products, or services"
(Kanter 1985:20). Others have highlighted the material (i.e., technology,
product) and subjective (i.e., administrative, social) arenas within which
change occurs (Daft 1978). Noting that behavior within organizations is heavily influenced by the performance of routines or repertoires (i.e., sets of routines), Nelson and Winter (1982) assert that administrative innovations involve some change in routine where the latter is viewed as being based on
individual skills. More recently, Levitt and March (1988) have emphasized
systems of shared values and beliefs in defining organizational routines.

The shared values and beliefs (i.e. open decision making structures and processes, diffuse administrative structures, informal volunteer-based coordination) that influenced, and were influenced by, the evolution of internetworking have attained near mythical status and continue to function as the prevailing administrative concept within this realm.[33] Meyer and Rowan (1977:340) argued that organizations that incorporate practices and procedures that are defined by "prevailing rationalized concepts of organizational work" increase both their legitimacy and survival prospects, independent of the immediate efficacy of the acquired practices and procedures. In applying this assertion to the reconfiguration of both country-level and the global Internet addressing regimes, it may be hypothesized that the perceived legitimacy of any newly created organizational entities responsible for managing and administering the core functions of internetworking will be subjected to historically based path dependencies that coincide with the values and norms associated with the earlier history of the Internet.

Bearing in mind the way in which internetworking evolved, the concept of *political* adopted here incorporates social events and group interactions beyond the sphere of the state and government. Therefore, the characterization of political phenomena as social interactions primarily orientated toward the authoritative allocation of values is particularly apt (Easton 1965b). Easton suggested that there are three possible ways in which values may be authoritatively allocated: (i) deprivation of a valued thing already possessed; (ii) obstructing the attainment of otherwise attainable values; and (iii) the allocation of values to some, while denying them to others. The notion of authoritative allocation of values implies a simultaneous focus upon power and authority arrangements in human interactions, on the one hand, and the interactions occurring within those associations, on the other. Although he noted that in some situations occupants of authority roles "may not perform in a specifically political role," (Easton 1965b:212) his conceptualization of authorities was rather narrow in that he defined these institutions primarily as roles and occupants of roles within the governmental sphere. He recognized that authoritative allocations are made in all types of groups and organizations, but considered these other contexts to be "analogous to, rather than isomorphic with, the political system of a society" (Easton 1965a:51). The interpretation of authorities adopted in this study is broader in that it considers authorities to include those agents or groups of agents with the capacity to influence the final allocation of values within a specific setting. This is in line with other work that recognizes the importance of distinctive social actors and the politics of their interaction (Barley and Tolbert 1997; Finnemore and Sikkink 1998; Giddens 1995; Wendt 1987, 1998; Wendt and Duvall 1989).

Given that specific design features, or the arrangement of a device or system, may establish patterns of interaction, the choices made and the decisions that are ultimately implemented by social actors may be seen as representing a form of authoritative allocation of values. One of the assumptions underlying this view is that these processes occur within a *competitive* social milieu. Weber defined competition as "a formally peaceful attempt to attain control over opportunities and advantages which are also desired by others" (Weber 1978:38). This process, he wrote, "is directed against competitors who share some positive or negative characteristics; its purpose is always the closure of social and economic opportunities to *outsiders*" (Weber 1978:342). The extent to which social relations permit entry to any outsider defines their relative degree of openness, whereas relationships are seen as closed in so far as the subjective meaning and binding rules of the group exclude, limit, or subject the participation of certain agents to the meeting of certain criteria.

However, exclusion is only one dimension of closure. Attention must also be directed at the forms of recourse adopted by outsiders in response to being excluded: i.e. usurpation. Whereas exclusionary closure represents the downward use of power to create a defined group of inferiors, usurpation signifies the use of power in an upward direction by the excluded, in an attempt to win a greater share of the resources denied to them (Parkin 1979). Hence, usurpation may be seen as both a consequence of, and a collective response to, exclusion.[34] This discussion provides the foundation for the specification of a framework for an analysis emphasizing the role of politics and power in influencing both the shape of administrative innovations and the likelihood of their survival within the cyber-realm.

An examination of these interactive processes entails a recognition of the multifaceted nature of power relations. On the one hand, these relations may reflect the instrumental use of resources to attain specific goals by seeking to get an entity, or group of entities, to do something that they would not otherwise do (Dahl 1957; Lasswell and Kaplan 1950). On the other hand, the observation of power relations cannot focus solely upon overt conflict because power may be exercised in a manner that limits the scope of, or even restricts, decision making activities (Bachrach and Baratz 1962, 1963). There is also a third, less action-orientated view which suggests that power also operates in a more subliminal manner in the form of institutional norms and procedures that bind and constrain the arenas and directions of conflict and its resolution (Lukes 1974). Building on this multidimensional view of power, Frost (1989) and Frost and Egri (1990a, 1990b, 1991) presented a framework for examining the manner in which organizational politics influence the innovation process. More recently, their framework has been used in the industrial networks literature to interpret decision making processes within asymmetrical exchange networks of interdependent firms (Elg and Johansson 1997).

Noting that organizational politics consists of power in action as well as power of conception, Frost and Egri posited the notion of a dynamic relationship between two tiers of organizational or interest group politics. According to their model, the first or surface tier is represented in the day-to-day contests and struggles for collaboration. Politics at this level is seen as dealing with "attempts by one or more parties to exploit (bend, resist, implement) the rules of the situation they are in to their own advantage" (Frost and Egri 1991:236). This level of politics is seen as being played out in three domains: the level of individuals, the level of intra-organizational groups, and between or among organizations. The strategies and tactics employed at this level are interpreted through a games metaphor involving the attempted manipulation and influencing of outcomes with actors intending to benefit themselves or others involved in the game. For our purposes, surface-level politics may be articulated as the issue-specific conflicts regarding the various aspects of establishing new addressing regimes. For example, debates between interested agents about the necessity of expanding the number of available top-level domains or of the efficacy of the WIPO Uniform Dispute Resolution Policy may be seen as reflecting surface level politicking.

The second tier of this framework, deep structure, is less easily observable and refers to the power that influences "usually in hard to detect ways, not only the way the rules of a situation are played but the very way the rules are framed in the first place" (Frost and Egri 1991:236). More specifically, deep-structure power is believed to be coded in the cultural values, beliefs, and practices in and around organizations, as well as in the collective unconscious of social agents (Frost 1989). The power relationships at this level are seen to inform collective interpretative frames and the cognitive maps of the participants. Although the deep structure is embedded and implicit, some actors are able to recognize and harness this power to their advantage. Frost and Egri identify four deep-structure games that may overtly or covertly influence the authoritative allocation of values. The first, naturalization, refers to participants treating existing structures as inviolate. In this game, discussion of existing relations is restricted by presenting them as the "natural order" of things. Consequently, naturalization functions as a means of preserving prevailing power relationships. Second is neutralization, or the presentation of positions and activities as unbiased, or the only reasonable ones that exist. This involves the universalization of a singular position as being a position that is shared by all actors. Consequently, the position is presented as being a fact rather than a choice (Frost 1989). Third, legitimation strategies may be adopted by invoking higher order values to justify, sustain, or promote the self interests of an elite. These strategies prevent explanation of the direction and level of activities of actors with less power through the use of such higher order explanatory devices as the Protestant work ethic, sacrifice, honor, and loyalty. The fourth game, socialization, encompasses the manner in which existing arrangements and processes shape the values of some participants in a manner which benefits others.

An important facet of this framework is the emphasis that is placed upon recognizing the dynamic nature of the relationship between the surface and deep-structure tiers. Power in the deep structure is seen as shaping and influencing, but not determining, actions at the surface level. Surface actions, on the other hand, are believed to impact on the direction and nature of power in the deep structure, thereby influencing the future's surface-level politics. According to Frost and Egri (1991:242),

deep-structure power relationships are not static and can be used in a proactive

way to facilitate change. In that current deep-structure power is a deriva-
tion of past political activity, the outcomes of current political activity
form the future foundation of future deep-structure power relations.

In reviewing seven previously documented cases of social, product, and
administrative innovation, Frost and Egri (1991:259) proposed that the likelihood of acceptance for innovations that threatened power relations at the
deep-structure level was significantly reduced because they evoked the "full
breadth and depth of opposing political forces, strategies, and tactics." Allud-
ing to the metaphor of "corporate immune systems,"[35] this proposition implies
that the conflict over a proposed innovation consists of a conflict between
maintenance of the status quo and the attempted implementation of an innovation, or change. Within the context of restructuring the management and administration of Internet domain names, organizational transformations generally have been precipitated by a recognition on the part of the concerned
parties that a change in the allocation processes was required. Any conflicts,
and their resolution by social actors, manifested themselves in attempts to define the parameters of these changes. This suggests that, despite its usefulness,
there is a need for modifying Frost and Egri's framework in order to better
address the dynamics of administrative innovation within the context of cyberspace.

Analyzing Domain Name Governance

The modification to Frost and Egri's framework that is being proposed entails
drawing attention to a third tier. According to this tripartite view, the third tier,
or meta-structure, is seen as the internetworking architecture itself. The meta-
structure is expected to impose a set of default rules which inform the collective interpretative frames and the cognitive maps of the network users. However, the architecture is not regarded as being deterministic. Rather, it is seen
as having the potential to influence both the actors' deep-structure perceptions
of internetworking and the nature of power relations within the electronic realm.
Therefore, the actors' perception of the default rules created by the architecture
may or may not be influenced by the history of internetworking and the value
structures coinciding with its evolution. In the light of this interpretative diversity, within the modified framework it is expected that the cognitive maps of
actors participating in restructuring processes manifest themselves at the deep-
structure level, in accordance with how they perceive the architecture (i.e., public resource versus private resource). In the process of negotiating new administrative and coordinating mechanisms to oversee the management of the Internet
domain name system, this modified framework suggests that attempts at establishing the sociopolitical and cognitive legitimacy of new regulatory entities will
manifest themselves as conflicts between the advocacy of governance regimes
premised on open bottom-up decision making processes and more exclusionary,
or top-down, approaches to decision making. Focusing on the articulation of
meta-level   politics   and   power   relations   provides   a   means   by   which

to develop a richer understanding of the sociopolitical processes through which social actors have been seeking to identify and establish a popular consensus regarding the values that should underpin the Internet and its governance.

In this revised framework the notion of surface-level politics is used to reflect the conflicts associated with negotiating new management structures that accord with the deep structure and meta-level power relations. For example, in seeking to promote the merits of their respective positions, it is expected that social actors will participate in day-to-day contests and struggles for collaboration in accordance with their respective views of contemporary power relations in the electronic realm. That is, actors whose perceptions of the domain naming architecture are primarily influenced by the historical norms of values of internetworking would be expected to advocate governance regimes whose focus is restricted largely to functions of technical coordination. In contrast, actors whose perceptions are not heavily influenced by such norms and values are expected to advocate the establishment of governance regimes whose role extends beyond technical coordination, encompassing more intricately structured policy making and enforcement mechanisms.

The conceptual framework presented here provides a means for examining what the social actors involved in the reconfiguration of the Internet addressing regime actually do rather than becoming mired in normative assertions about what should be done. Viewing the process of change as a form of organizational innovation entails a recognition that the process of innovation is about ambiguity and encompasses disputes between social actors that are based on the differences in their respective perspectives about the outcomes of change. In addition, the politics of the change process are believed to be influenced by the ambiguity associated with the perspectives of social actors and the saliency attributed to particular issues. When applied to the issue of Internet governance the strength of this approach rests on its ability to incorporate both subjective and objective aspects of the processes and outcomes of change within the cyber-realm.

Conclusions

The discussion in this chapter has presented a critical juxtaposition of current perspectives on Internet governance as they relate to the issue of domain naming. It has been argued that by adopting prescriptive overtones, and by choosing to focus primarily on end results, the bulk of the Internet-related governance literature does not sufficiently address the political dimension of the restructuring process. As a result, the analytical strength of much of this work is weakened by its failure to seek a specific understanding of the processes by which change is occurring in this medium. In order to interpret the dynamics of Internet politics there is a need to understand how specific characteristics of the internetworking architecture influence and shape the organizations and actors responsible for managing and administering this technological infrastructure.

Having noted the limitations of the current literature on this topic, the assessment presented in this chapter emphasized the need to view the outcomes of negotiations associated with the establishment of Internet addressing regimes as a process of organizational innovation. It was argued that since the collective and individual actions of industry players, Internet and non-Internet organizations, governmental authorities, and specific individuals have been integral in determining the success or failure of proposed organizational and administrative innovations, the need for examining the role of politics and power arises.

The power-oriented approach is likely to provide a richer picture of Internet politics, in part, because it does not fall prey to ideologically motivated positions with respect to the appropriate roles of the private sector or governments in the evolution of governance regimes for the Internet. In addition, it offers a means of coupling investigations of the determinants of the technical architecture of the Internet and the way the social and political interests of its designers and users become embedded in that architecture. By giving power the pride of place, we may address such questions as: How are power relations and politicking influencing the emergent governance trajectory of internetworking? How have the historically rooted path dependent norms, or institutions, associated with internetworking been altered? What factors underpin the organizational legitimacy attained by the administrative innovations emerging from processes of institutional reconfiguration within the cyber-realm? Answering these questions will contribute to a better understanding of the Internet and its governance by providing a basis for formulating theoretical insights into the nature of an important aspect of governance in the cyber-realm.

Notes

1. Regulatory standards are generally imposed from the top down to advance the regulatory end of restricting behaviors associated with a given activity. Coordinating standards, on the other hand, may be imposed from the top down or emerge from the bottom up and limit an actor's liberty in order to make a given activity possible (Lessig 1999c). Within the literature about standards the former often are referred to as *de jure* standards and the latter as *de facto* standards (David and Greenstein 1990; David 1995).

2. For an overview of the conflicts that have arisen about the relationship between trademarks and domain names see Dueker (1996), Maher (1996), Oppedahl (1997), Rony and Rony (1998: chapter 7), and Helfer (2001).

3. Their analysis did not examine the content of the responses per se. Rather, it distinguished between the comments submitted by *eminents* (defined as those individuals who replied to the DoC request and were known specialists on the Internet, or persons who had been concerned with the domain name controversy) and *hoi polloi* (used to refer to individuals who replied, but who did not meet the criteria of the eminent category) on the basis of whether certain key issues or phrases were mentioned in individual responses.

4. The authors did not elaborate on how, or on what basis, constituencies might be defined.

5. Measured in terms of the total number of non-U.S.-based responses obtained by the United States Department of Commerce.

6. Both the increase in interest levels and the emergence of a rough consensus may be accounted for, in part, by the fact that the second Request for Comments called for responses on a specific regulatory framework proposal—the Green Paper—which was widely seen outside of the United States as being overly U.S.-centric.

7. These authors failed to mention, however, that the community to which they referred was dominated primarily by like-minded academics, predominantly based at American universities, who found it relatively easy to agree on how internetworking should be coordinated because of the homogenous nature of this grouping of individuals.

8. The notion of path dependence refers to a sequence of economic changes in which "important influences upon the eventual outcome can be exerted by temporally remote events, including happenings dominated by chance elements rather than systemic forces. . . . The dynamic process itself takes on an *essentially historical* character" (David 1985:332). See also David (1997) and Arthur (1994). An attempt to introduce and apply this concept within the field of political science is offered by Pierson (2000a, 2000b).

9. The cases selected for the study were limited to those for which published reports in printed or online media or records of court proceedings were available at the time of its undertaking. In the report, Mueller pointed out that although several registries were contacted, most were either too busy to provide information about such conflicts or lacked the accounting resources to do so. He also noted that Network Solutions Inc. refused to provide him with information about specific domain names or companies involved in conflicts on the grounds that releasing information about disputes to third parties was inappropriate.

10. Mueller defined "infringement" as conflicts in which the original registrant intentionally sought to trade off the resemblance between a domain name and another company's trademark.

11. In addition to Mueller's work in this area, the results of Michael Geist's recent study of the UDRP adjudication process also raises questions about the fairness of its decision making processes and outcomes. See Geist (2001).

12. On February 18, 2000, Rutkowski joined Network Solutions Inc. as vice president of Internet strategies.

13. Rutkowski also is cautious about notions of "the Internet," emphasizing that he uses it merely as a shorthand term encompassing "intranets (a/k/a enterprise internets), extranets, on line services, Email, World Wide Web, and countless hundreds of other networks, applications and services that woven [*sic*] through the backbone networks constituting the Internet" (Rutkowski 1998a).

14. For a critique of the approaches rooted in such assumptions, see Woolgar (1991), who argues that the presentation of technologies as political artifacts is overly dependent upon interpretative flexibility.

15. Within this context "protocols" refers to both digitally and nondigitally embodied network specifications.

16. Drawing from the Ellickson (1991) study of the extent and manner of the influence of legal rules on individual behavior, Post defines controllers as entities that provide substantive rules governing an individual's behavior.

17. Regulatory arbitrage refers to the ability, in certain circumstances, of individuals connected to the Internet to arrange their affairs in a manner that enables them to evade domestic regulations, by structuring their transactions or communications such that they may benefit from foreign regulatory regimes. See Froomkin (1996).

18. The ethos of digital libertarianism is perhaps most clearly articulated in John Parry Barlow's *Declaration of Independence of Cyberspace* (1996).

19. The concept of cyberspace as a sovereign place has been widely criticized on a number of grounds. Lessig (1996b) critiqued Johnson and Post's assertions for failing to address why it would be good or even right to recognize cyberspace as a sovereign place. Wu (1997) argued that assertions about the futility or impossibility of state regulation of internetworking were simply wrong. He claimed that despite being very difficult, Internet regulation was possible and stood to become increasingly so. Similarly Wilske and Schiller (1997) pointed out that international law permits more states to exercise jurisdiction than netizens might be aware. Noting that states have found means to regulate the moon and other celestial bodies, the deep seabed, and Antarctica, the authors argued that states were unlikely to respect the independence of cyberspace. Leaffer (1998) also rejected the notion of cyberspace sovereignty on the grounds that it is simply "not rooted in practical reality." He argued that governments already impose various forms of regulatory authority over the Internet and that remaining "pockets of decentralized autonomy" exist because of the benevolence of governments.

20. Post and Johnson (1997b) define a "governance system" as a set of institutions and mechanisms that enable inhabitants of an environment to solve the ever present problem(s) of collective action.

21. A critique of perspectives rooted in this utilitarian assumption is offered by Kornhauser (1992). He argues that the latter fails to address the fact that individual responses to social norms often differ from the types of behavior that economic rationality predicts.

22. Reidenberg was not the first to express this particular view of technical standards. An in-depth analysis of the political nature of technical standards may be found in Hawkins et al. (1995) and Mansell and Silverstone (1996).

23. The concept of *Lex Informatica* draws from the principle of *Lex Mercatoria*. The latter refers to the common ground rules that developed among traveling merchants during the Middle Ages to create trust and confidence in international trade. These practices developed into an international law of business that was independent of national laws (Berman and Kaufman 1978; Carbonneau 1990; Dezalay and Garth 1995).

24. See also Quintas (1996) on the role of software designers in default rule making.

25. According to Foucault, analyses of the operation of political power based on the triangle of sovereign, citizen, and right were misguided. What was required was a focus on more subtle, informal and material forms of coercion organized around the concepts of surveillance and discipline. See Foucault (1977, 1978, 1980, 1982).

26. The Panopticon defines a form of power relations. It refers to a surveillance paradigm based on Jeremy Bentham's wheel-and-hub prison construction plans, in which individual behavior is modified due to constant uncertainty about whether one's actions were being monitored (Foucault 1977; Gandy 1993; Samarajiva and Shields 1990, 1992).

27. On the peculiarity of the coexistence of disciplinary power and "grand juridical edifice" created by the theory of sovereignty Foucault wrote:

On the one hand, it has been . . . a permanent instrument of criticism of the monarchy and all the obstacles that can thwart the development of disciplinary society. But at the same time, the theory of sovereignty, and the organization of a legal code centered upon it, have allowed a system of right to be superimposed upon the mechanism of discipline in such a way as to conceal its actual procedures, the element of domination inherent in its techniques, and to guarantee to everyone, by virtue of the sovereignty of the State, the exercise of his proper sovereign rights. The juridical systems—and this applies both to their codification and to their theorisation—have enabled sovereignty to be democratised through the constitution of a public right articulated upon collective sovereignty, while at the same time this democratisation of sovereignty was fundamentally determined by and grounded in mechanisms of disciplinary coercion. (Foucault 1980:105)

28. This perspective on the political properties of technologies draws on two interrelated varieties of interpretations. The first is concerned with the manner in which specific design features or arrangements of artifacts and systems may influence the establishment of various power relations and patterns of authority within a given setting. The second variety of interpretation draws heavily from Engels' (1978) assertion that certain kinds of technology require specific structuring of their operational environments. It is primarily concerned with the linking of particular technological properties with specific institutionalized relations of power and authority. Winner (1986:3-58) offers a comparative analysis of these interpretative traditions.

29. Lessig defines zoning as "any technique used to facilitate discrimination in access to or distribution of some good or service . . . the techniques refer to law, as well as social norms; the architectures include both physical features of the world and cultural histories that make regulation salient, or possible" (Lessig 1996a).

30. MAPS is a program that deals with the problem of spam by coordinating a type of group boycott by Internet service providers. Post (2000) describes the program's operations as follows. The developer and manager of this institution has created a list of ISPs who are in his opinion, and in the opinion of those electing to participate in this program, fostering the distribution of spam. This list is called the Realtime Blackhole List (RBL). Those associated with MAPS define "fostering the distribution of spam" as providing "spam support services." The latter entails hosting Web pages that are listed as destination addresses in bulk e-mails, providing e-mail forwarders or auto-responders that can be used by bulk e-mailers, or allowing "open-mail relay" (i.e., allowing mail handling servers to be used by nonsubscribers, which allows bulk e-mailers to "launder" e-mail by launching it from a site to which they cannot be traced). The individuals involved with MAPS provide its RBL list to other Internet service providers on the basis of a free subscription. Once subscribed, these Internet service providers have the option of setting their mail handlers to delete all e-mail originating from or going to addresses appearing on the list. As a result, the selected addresses essentially disappear from the Internet as far as the subscribing service provider and its customers are concerned. See *Maps Realtime Blackhole List* maps.vix.com/rbl/; *Mail Abuse Prevention System* mail-abuse.org/; *MAPS RBL Candidacy* maps.vix.com/rbl/candidacy.html; and *MAPS RBL Participants* maps.vix.com/rbl/participants.html (last accessed February 3, 2000).

31. David Post is critical of Lessig's position regarding the use of MAPS. He claims that instead of being negatively labeled as vigilantes, actors participating in the MAPS program can be just as easily characterized positively as activists. He asserts that "the kind of bottom-up, uncoordinated, decentralized process of which the RBL is a part strikes me as a perfectly reasonable way to make network policy and to answer fundamental policy questions about how the Net will work" (Post 2000).

32. Norms are defined here as "a standard of appropriate behavior for actors with a given identity" (Finnemore and Sikkink 1998:891). Within the sociological context these behavioral rules are often referred to as institutions and defined as "a relatively stable collection of practices and rules defining appropriate behavior for specific groups of actors in specific situations" (March and Olsen 1998:948).

33. In recent years the Open Source Movement has come to be seen by many as the primary upholders of this tradition (Castells 2001; Moody 2001).

34. Murphy (1988) is critical of the conception of exclusion and usurpation as polar opposites, arguing that it obscures the fact that exclusion is involved in usurpation. He suggests that usurpation is a special subtype of closure which results from processes of monopolization and which has as its consequence the acquisition of some of the resources of the dominant group.

35. "When you start something new, the system naturally resists. Its is almost as if the corporation had an immune system which detects anything that is not part of the status quo and surrounds it. If you are to survive, you will have to lull this immune system into ignoring you. You will have to appear to be part of the corporate self, rather than identified as a foreign body" (Pinchot 1985:189, quoted in Frost and Egri 1991).

Chapter 4

Transformation of the *.uk* Domain Naming Regime

We can build, or architect, or code cyberspace to protect values that we be-
lieve are fundamental, or we can build, or architect, or code cyberspace to
allow those values to disappear. There is no middle ground. There is no
choice that does not include some kind of building. Code is never found; it is
only ever made, and only ever made by us.

—Lessig (1999a)

The *.uk* domain is the third largest top-level domain in the world, preceded in
ascending order by the German domain *.de* and the generic top-level domain
.com. During the mid-1990s the addressing regime for the *.uk* name space un-
derwent a period of institutional transformation, the outcome of which was the
creation of a registry organization called Nominet UK. Formally established in
August 1996, Nominet UK has since grown from a membership base consisting
of a grouping of approximately 100 providers of Internet services into an organization composed of in excess of 1000 members.[1] The controversies associated with its formation entailed an overhaul of the structures responsible for
managing and administering the *.uk* domain. The discussion in this chapter
focuses specifically on the sociopolitical processes through which domain
naming policy evolved in the United Kingdom. A detailed analysis of these
proceedings is important because it illustrates the extent to which relationships
between social actors influenced the establishment, and institutionalization, of a
specific registry architecture. As such, the narrative that is presented is basically a story about the mediation of the contending interests of various organizations and individual actors.

The chapter opens with an overview of the historical background to the evolution of the principles and procedures for managing the .*uk* domain. This is followed by an analysis of the factors underpinning the de-institutionalization[2] of the organizational entity responsible for managing this domain prior to August 1996. In the third section, the sociopolitical interactions between actors involved in the creation of Nominet UK are explored. The discussion concludes with an examination of the ways in which the underlying distribution of power capabilities among the actors involved in this reconfiguration process influenced the structure of the administrative innovation that emerged and the legitimacy it has attained within the U.K. Internet sector.

Evolution of the U.K. Naming Committee[3]

Early Management of the .*uk* Domain

In the late 1980s the National Science Foundation (NSF), established NSFnet to provide an internetworking backbone for the United States. A parallel backbone system, the Joint Academic NETwork (JAnet), was developed in the United Kingdom throughout the 1980s under the auspices of the Joint Network Team (JNT), an entity that operated as part of the United Kingdom Higher Education Network Programme. The JNT was primarily composed of a small group of U.K. academics involved in computer networking related research. The gateway between the NSFnet and JAnet networks was maintained at the University of Kent at Canterbury. Although the internetworking facilities that were available in the U.K. throughout the late 1980s and early 1990s primarily were used and maintained by the academic and research communities, the U.K. Ministry of Defence (MoD) was also associated with JAnet in so far as it was investigating military applications of computer networking.

University College London (UCL) was the first organization in the U.K. to run the Internet Protocol (IP) suite for all its network services, and it operated the first "foreign" network connected to the ARPAnet. Prior to 1985, the UCL network was identified on ARPAnet through the use of the .*uk* domain. This particular name was chosen, in part, for reasons of convenience, and because the IP suite was not being used elsewhere in the U.K. In July 1985, .*uk* became the first two-letter domain to register with the Network Information Center (NIC) at the University of Southern California Information Sciences Institute (ISI), the precursor to the Internet Assigned Numbers Authority (IANA). Peter Kirstein, a computer researcher from UCL who had been directly involved in pioneering work on computer networking in the U.K., was assigned as the "responsible person" for the .*uk* top-level domain.[4] This decision involved the combined support of: (i) the Joint Network Team; (ii) the U.K. Department of Trade and Industry (through the Alvey Programme);[5] (iii) the U.K. Ministry of Defence; and (iv) Jon Postel at ISI.

In the period spanning 1985 to 1988 there were ongoing discussions between Jon Postel and Peter Kirstein regarding the appropriateness of using .*uk* as a two-letter top-level domain for the United Kingdom. RFC 920, and later RFC 1591, stipulated that two-letter codes for identifying countries should correspond with ISO-3166 two-letter country-codes. Postel had wanted the British networking community to switch to *.gb*, the official ISO-3166 two-letter country-code for the United Kingdom, as the top-level domain used to identify British computer networks. However, the failure of the U.K.-based computer networking community to reach any form of consensus on such a change resulted in a maintenance of the status quo.

As increasing numbers of commercial and noncommercial entities began going online during the early 1990s, the Joint Network Team was transformed into the Joint Network Team Association. This new entity was formed by the Higher Education Funding Councils for England, Scotland and Wales and the Office of Science and Technology on December 10, 1993. It currently trades as United Kingdom Education and Research Networking Association (UKERNA). This organization's mandate focuses on the management of the U.K.'s Higher Education and Research Community Network Programme. It is also responsible for managing the *.ac.uk* name space, and in conjunction with the U.K. Central Computer Technology Agency, the *.gov.uk* name space.

In April 1994, the Joint Network Team staff, who previously had been responsible for managing the Higher Education Network Programme, were formally transferred to UKERNA. At that time, the former leader of the Joint Network Team, Dr. William Black, was appointed director of the new organization. One of the indirect consequences of the formation of UKERNA was the transfer of official responsibility for the *.uk* top-level domain from Peter Kirstein to Dr. Black in the autumn of 1993. Although the Ministry of Defence had expressed support for Peter Kirstein retaining his authority for the *.uk* domain, for most of the actors involved in this process, the issue of who was authorized to be the official responsible person was not considered to be a particularly serious matter.[6] Simply put, the British internetworking community of the time saw this event as consisting of little more than the passing of a baton through an old boys' network.

Formation of the U.K. Naming Committee

Before 1993, all *.uk* domain registrations were handled by the Joint Network Team in accordance with its Name Registration Scheme (NRS). This was a centralized naming system for British universities which operated as an equivalent to the Internet domain name system. The primary difference between these two addressing systems was that under the NRS all entries into the registration database were made in *uk* domain order (i.e., *uk.ac.sussex*). At that time, a gateway between the U.K.-based Network Registration Scheme and the DNS was maintained at UCL, which translated names between the two addressing systems nightly. This service allowed American-based network users to see only normal DNS names for British hosts, while U.K.-based network users were able to read DNS names as NRS addresses.

Corresponding with the establishment and growth of the commercial Internet in the United Kingdom, an increasing number of organizations sought to register names in the *.co.uk* name space. As a result of this increasing demand, the Joint Network Team shifted away from the NRS toward utilization of DNS as the authoritative source of data for the *.co.uk* subdomain. Coinciding with this shift, EUnet GB Ltd,[7] a private commercial Internet service provider (ISP) founded by a group of U.K. academics and owned by the University of Kent at Canterbury, assumed responsibility for running and maintaining the *.uk* root name server on a voluntary basis.

Questions regarding the commercial legitimacy of EUnet GB's control of the registry database sparked the first controversy to significantly influence the manner in which the *.uk* name space was managed. Some of the emerging Internet access providers claimed that EUnet GB might be able to use its control of the registry database to gain an unfair commercial advantage over its competitors in the developing Internet sector. In early 1993 UnipalmPIPEX,[8] at the time the only U.K.-based ISP with its own international capacity, approached the Joint Network Team claiming that it was unfair to have one of its competitors, EUnet GB Ltd, controlling the domestic domain name registry. Shortly thereafter, Demon Internet,[9] the first commercial ISP offering low cost full Internet dial-up access in the U.K., also approached the Joint Network Team to express similar concerns about the manner in which the *.uk* domain was being managed. Through a series of informal discussions, representatives of these four organizations—Joint Network Team, EUnet GB Ltd, UnipalmPIPEX, and Demon Internet—agreed to adopt a more "democratic" approach toward the coordination of domain name registrations.

Under the new arrangement the Joint Network Team delegated authority for coordinating and administering the *.co.uk* subdomain to a Naming Committee composed of three commercial and two noncommercial Internet access providers. However, UKERNA maintained a right of veto over decisions reached by this committee.

The five founding Naming Committee members were:

1. The Joint Network Team (Network Registration Scheme) Administrator;[10]
2. JAnet;
3. EUnet GB Ltd;
4. Demon Internet Ltd; and
5. UnipalmPIPEX Ltd.

Through the voluntary activities of representatives from the member organizations, the Naming Committee operated as a self-governing body with no formal structure or chairperson. In essence, the term "Naming Committee" referred to a group of closed electronic discussion lists where domain name registration requests were processed, and naming-related issues discussed. In late 1993, BT Internet Services[11] became the sixth organization to join this body.

The means by which it did so highlight the degree of informality characteristic of the early administrative structures of the Naming Committee. Nigel Titely, who at the time was BT Internet Services technical services manager, was well known throughout the U.K. Internet community. He sent an e-mail message to a member representative of the Naming Committee requesting information about how to register a *.co.uk* domain name for a client. The individual that Titely had contacted responded by informing him that he would simply add BT Internet Services to the Naming Committee discussion lists because it was a known ISP.[12]

At this stage in the discussion, there are two aspects of the Naming Committee's operations that need to be singled out given their significance vis-à-vis the information provided thus far and that which is provided in the subsequent sections of this chapter. The first relates to the extent to which the actions of particular individuals, rather than organizations, played a crucial role in the development of the administrative mechanisms for coordinating the *.uk* domain. To this end, all of the former representatives of the Naming Committee's member organizations interviewed pointed out that their activities in this realm were subject to very little scrutiny by the upper management of their respective organizations. One of the common themes to emerge from interviews with former Naming Committee member representatives was a sense that, in the light of the *newness* of the Internet at the time, the respective organizations they represented tended to accord their individual activities in this realm a high level of autonomy.

Second, in its early days, the U.K. domain name registration system was relatively flexible, relying both on interactions and mutual cooperation between member Internet access providers. The interviewees generally emphasized that in its early days the registry system benefited from an ethos that stressed the importance of maintaining technical continuity and upholding its technical integrity. As a result, many interviewees felt that prior to 1995, the cumulative impact of this evolutionary process was the forging of "good" relations between competing organizations in the British Internet industry. These views about the cooperative nature of their interactions during the early to mid-1990s corresponded with an institutional ethos of consensual adoption of ethics and the propagation of voluntary technical standards, or rough consensus and running code.[13]

In October 1994 the London Internet Exchange (LINX) was established to provide a point of physical interconnection for ISPs to exchange Internet traffic through cooperative peering agreements.[14] This interconnection arrangement enabled members to substitute the need for a whole network of links to individual service providers to a single line into LINX. Simply put, this new entity established a hub within which the routers of individual service providers were linked via an Ethernet segment. In order to ensure that member organizations were serious backbone providers, membership of this association was made contingent upon meeting two criteria. First, applicants were required to own a permanent, independent, international connection to the Internet. Specifically, they had to demonstrate that they had paths from an IP address within the autonomous system[15] to at least four of the thirteen Internet root name servers, excluding the "K" server. Second, members also had to sell Internet services, including at least one public service allowing customers to connect to the Internet.[16]

The LINX subsequently was incorporated as a nonprofit association limited by guarantee,[17] in December 1995. Its five founding members were the five organizations that comprised the Naming Committee in October 1994: JAnet/UKERNA, UnipalmPIPEX, EUnet GB Ltd, Demon Internet Ltd, and BT Internet Services. Given that at this time the people acting as organizational representatives to the Naming Committee were primarily technical engineers, most were also directly involved, in varying degrees, with the establishment of LINX. Although the Naming Committee and LINX were completely separate organizational entities, the individual representatives to the Naming Committee arbitrarily agreed that LINX membership requirements should also be used as the criteria for establishing full membership of the Naming Committee. Consequently, every new company joining LINX simultaneously became a full, or voting, member of the Naming Committee. Those organizations that did not meet LINX criteria, on the other hand, were permitted to join the Naming Committee but had no voting rights. According to some of the founding member representatives, this decision was made primarily on the grounds that adopting the LINX membership rules was the easiest and most efficient way of establishing the criteria for joining the Naming Committee. However, this arbitrary action was to have negative long-term implications for the survival of the Naming Committee.

The U.K. Naming Committee Years

By late 1994 the technical, social, and political relationships that had evolved around the management and administration of the *.co.uk* name space appear to have attained a degree of closure. At the technical level, closure was reflected in the stabilization of the technology facilitating the registration of names in the *.uk* domain. Socially, the domain was managed by a relatively small homogenous group of technical engineers with shared perceptions of about how to structure and administer addressing needs within the *.uk* name space. At the political level, power relationships within the Naming Committee had been structured in a manner that allowed representatives from a relatively small number of ISPs to determine the acceptability of name requests. Simply put, the closure attained reflected the fact that by late 1994 internetworking in the United Kingdom was characterized both by the presence of relatively few actors with a limited variety of needs, and a relatively limited set of ideas about how best to meet these needs.

When the Naming Committee began processing requests for domain names in 1993, it was receiving on, average, two or three requests per week. By mid-1995, it was receiving in excess of 100 requests per day. This increase in demand for domain names began to accentuate procedural and structural weaknesses in the Naming Committee's registration practices. At the structural level, there was a growing division between a new and rapidly evolving commercially diverse internetworking-based industry and a technical infrastructure that was operated and maintained on a volunteer basis. Procedurally, the Naming Committee's administrative processes were highly contentious, fueling several disputes between full/voting and guest member representatives, as well as between individual representatives within the voting constituency. At the root of these controversies was a questioning of both the registry's decision making authority and its legitimacy. The next two subsections examine some of the issues underpinning these disputes. The first focuses on the Naming Committee voting structure, while the second examines the subjective manner in which the rules of registration were implemented. Taken together, these discussions highlight the power struggles between social actors that resulted from the techniques used to allocate domain names.

Voting Structure

In terms of the functioning of the Naming Committee, the state of closure described above manifested itself at two levels. First, the ability to submit requests for domain names was restricted to members of the Naming Committee. Individual network users, and providers of Internet services who were not members, were not permitted to apply directly to the committee for domain names. From the perspective of nonmembers, this was problematic because, despite the fact that EUnet GB was not charging committee members a fee for entering registered names into the registry database, member registrars were levying fees on their customers for providing domain name registration services.[18]

A second, and more obvious, manifestation of closure consisted of the Naming Committee's bifurcated voting structure. In order to offer domain name registration services in the *.co.uk* subdomain, prospective domain name registrars who were unable to meet the LINX/Naming Committee membership criteria (i.e. a permanent, independent, international connection to the Internet and the sale of Internet connection services) had to be introduced, electronically, to the other committee members by a full/voting member representative. In most cases, the introduction to the Naming Committee discussion list was done by the full/voting member from whom the applicant organization leased its network access. The new member organization was then granted guest status, and permitted to apply for domain names on their organization's behalf and that of their customers. However, they were not permitted to vote on domain name requests or policy-related matters.

Under this arrangement the domain name registration process was based on a system of peer review in which only full/voting member representatives were entitled to vote on the suitability of requested names. If no full/voting member representative raised an objection, a requested name usually was registered within two working days. If an objection was raised, formal registration of the desired name could be delayed for up to five working days. The presence of two or more objections resulted in the rejection of the requested name. Once a request for registration had been accepted it was passed on, electronically, to EUnet GB Ltd, where the information associated with the domain name application was entered into the registry database.

According to some of the founding Naming Committee member representatives interviewed, there was no preconceived rationale for denying voting rights to guest members.[19] When questioned about this issue, one founding member representative expressed the viewed that the "amateurish" nature of the Naming Committee's operations during this period was simply based on the fact that the speed with which things were happening prevented members from really thinking things through. Likewise, another member representative suggested that the rationale underpinning this decision was related to a desire to keep the vote counting process as simple as possible. That is, to minimize the level of administration associated with the voting process. It appears that in having underestimated the diverse range of organizations that might wish to offer domain name registration services, representatives of the full/voting member organizations assumed that entities not providing Internet access services did not require input into how the registry system was managed.

One of the consequences of restricting voting rights to only certain members of the Naming Committee was that this entity soon came to be seen by most guest member representatives, and some individual full/voting member representatives, as being not only closed, but elitist. When interviewed, one former full/voting member representative sympathetic to this view argued that the lack of congruence between LINX membership criteria and eligibility for full/voting membership meant that guest members were prevented from exercising the same powers as their respective access providers despite being dependent upon the committee's approval process.[20] This view was indicative of a popular consensus among critics of the Naming Committee that its exclusionary voting structure subjected smaller service providers to the tyranny of larger ISPs.

Although all full/voting member representatives were entitled to vote on domain name requests, there were large variations in the voting patterns of individual representatives. This was due, in part, to the fact that it was not incumbent upon members to exercise their voting rights. A number of individual full/voting member representatives who were opposed to the registration process, but who nevertheless had the authority to vote on requests for names, adopted a deliberate policy of not objecting to any requests for domain names. Contained within the box on page 77 is a series of exchanges which took place between two voting member representatives in response to a complaint received about differentials in voting behavior. The exchange illustrates some of the factors underpinning the variations in the voting behavior of individual representatives.

What is significant about the dialogue presented in the box on page 77 is the recognition by voting member representatives that the arbitrary and subjective nature of the Naming Committee's decision making processes was failing to protect Internet users from the negative consequences of the subjective implementation of an informal rule set. It also highlights a further problem with the Naming Committee's operational procedures.

Exchange Between Full/Voting Member Representatives

Member One: As far as I can see, the problem lies in several places. Firstly, not every voting member is fulfilling their obligations and objecting to everything they should.

Member Two: Perhaps I'm missing something here, but where is it written that full members are "obliged" to object to submissions to the Naming Committee? Especially since the rules are very much open to subjective judgement [*sic*], and other members' interpretations of the rules may not parallel your own?

Member One: This is resulting in (as *[name of individual]* said) a farcical situation where, if one keeps one's head down and keeps quiet after getting a couple of objections, the requested name will go through anyway, albeit delayed by a few days.

Member Two: Oh, I *do* agree that the situation is farcical. At this moment certain full members have decided to flex their muscles and arbitrarily post objections to almost every submission. They can; so they do. Many of these objections are quite unjustified and result in a good deal of unnecessary extra work on the part of the company putting the name(s) forward.

Member One: There wouldn't be a problem if every member was 100% honest in making submissions, and complying with all the rules every time, and every voting member was actually voting.

Member Two: So you're saying that because (in *your* opinion) not every member is 100% honest, the assumption must be that every member is *dishonest* until s/he can prove otherwise? Have you any idea just how insulting that is to the vast majority of members? You're right *[Member One's name]*, the present system is extremely flawed, but I think it needs resolving asap rather than waiting until August.

Member One: I think the situation with members objecting to the vast majority of names that are submitted has arisen because the submitters aren't formatting their requests properly, ie leaving out the trading: or regdno: field where appropriate. I agree, it's frustrating for the submitters, but it's frustrating for the voters, too.

Member Two: This would be fine and I have no problem with that, but at the moment lots of objections are being made where the requests are properly formatted and all the required information is present.

Member One: No *[Member Two's name]*, I think you misunderstand me. I am certain that every member is perfectly honest for the *vast* majority of the time, but it's my experience that rules tend to be bent in places. I'm happy to treat everyone as innocent until proven guilty, as long as their requests conform to the correct format I don't have a problem.

Member Two: But as I said above, lots of objections are being made, by various individuals, to requests that do conform to the correct format and comply with the present rules exactly. Sure, there have been submissions that look a bit suspect and I understand (without necessarily agreeing) why people have objected to those. It's the blanket objections to just about every name put forward that are the problem here.

Source: Excerpts from postings to the <naming-co@mhs-relay.ac.uk> discussion listJune 25-28, 1996.

If nonvoting members did not rock the boat and basically followed the guidelines, their requests generally were approved. The fact that acceptance of requests was contingent upon less than two members' disapproval meant that certain applications risked being subjected to more (or less) scrutiny than others.[21]

The subjective nature of this decision making process was particularly problematic for both registrars and domain name applicants alike. From the registrar perspective, the rejection of name applications meant that if a requested name was rejected for any reason other than prior registration by another party, they were faced with the task of having to explain the committee's arbitrary decision to their client(s). Moreover, the subjective outcomes of the application process also meant that registrars were unable to provide their clients with clear rules regarding the types of names that would be acceptable to the Naming Committee. From the applicant's perspective, the Naming Committee's lack of a precedent-based decision making apparatus had two consequences. First, it made the task of applying for names needlessly obscure. Second, this subjectivity meant that an individual registrant might not be able to establish an online presence based on the name they desired, even if the name they sought had not yet been registered.

The fact that all domain name requests submitted to the naming discussion list were made in a quasi-public forum further reinforced concerns among some members about the arbitrary and subjective nature of the Naming Committee's decision making processes. All committee members were able to identify who was registering domain names for whom simply by looking at the request-for-names messages posted to the discussion list.

Therefore, from a registrar perspective submitting requests for names entailed exposing one's clients to one's competitors. If a representative from company A saw that company B was submitting name requests for a particular customer, representatives of company A subsequently might attempt to poach, or entice away, company B's client(s). To this end, some committee member representatives likened the naming discussion list to "a source of free intelligence" that allowed members to keep tabs on their rivals. The fact that full/voting members also registered domain names on behalf of their clients in this quasi-public forum served to further bolster elitist perceptions of the Naming Committee because these same organizations had the authority to object to their competitor's requests for names.[22]

Subjective Implementation of Arbitrary Rules

The lack of a comprehensive, unambiguous rule set detailing the criteria and policies to be upheld for name registrations in this domain also perpetuated numerous disputes between individual representatives of the Naming Committee. In essence, there existed no formal rules for registering domain names. Rather, committee members, and their clients, were provided with guidelines outlining suggestions for *good* and *bad* names. The full/voting member representatives were supposed to base their decisions about the merit, or acceptability, of requested names on the basis of common sense interpretations of these informal rule sets. The guidelines offered to members stipulated that the *.co.uk* domain was a commercial domain that was intended for trading entities that traded for profit rather than for individuals. Some of the other suggestions regarding the choice of names emphasized that (i) the full name of the organization should be selected if it was not too long; (ii) two-letter domain names would not be accepted because they potentially could clash with the ISO-3166 two-letter country-codes; (iii) three-letter names would only be accepted if they corresponded exactly to the company name, or were a very well known acronym for the company; (iv) potentially offensive names would be rejected; (v) names that might confuse would be rejected on "common sense" grounds; and (vi) requests for multiple similar names by the same organization would be rejected because these would be better served by using subdomains of a common domain.[23]

Initially, the Naming Committee only approved registration requests in the *.co.uk* domain for limited companies on the grounds that this implied commercial legitimacy. This policy prevented entities not registered with Company's House (i.e. trading companies, partnerships, and sole traders) from registering domain names matching the character string under which they had established a commercial reputation. It also meant that companies trading under names differing from their officially registered name were prevented from registering the names by which they were publicly identified. In addition, attempts to enforce this subjective rule set perpetuated situations wherein requested names often were objected to, and/or rejected, on stylistic grounds. In numerous instances individual full/voting member representatives objected to requests for names while simultaneously suggesting alternatives more in line with their personal interpretation of the guidelines, and/or their individual preferences.

In order to overcome problems of this sort, a decision eventually was made by the full/voting member representatives to accept name registrations for entities not registered with Company's House provided that "proof of existence" was submitted on demand. However, the meaning of "proof" was never clearly defined. As a result, the verifiable information solicited upon submission of requests for names tended to be arbitrary and contingent upon the whims of individual representatives from full/voting member organizations. The evidence demanded ranged from requests to see company letterhead to demands for evidence of the existence of bank accounts in a respective company's name.

Objections to requested names were particularly contentious because they implied that some member representatives were subjectively policing registration requests. "My first impression was *shock* at the arbitrary rule set, and the arbitrary way in which it was imposed" is how one former guest member described his organization's first encounter with the Naming Committee.[24] Concern at this level focused on the authority, or lack thereof, of the Naming Committee's full member representatives to vote on the suitability of the domain name requests. Given the difficulties in enforcing this ambiguous rule set, some representatives argued that the process of voting on domain name requests was an impediment to the commercial provision of registration services. In a message posted to the Naming Committee discussion list highlighting their organization's frustration with this state of affairs, one guest member wrote,

> Look, lets be honest here—the objection procedures are a farce . . . full members are not living up to their obligations. [*Company name*] has tried to take the time and effort to stick to the rules and ensure the names we put forward are within the rules. But whats [*sic*] the point? Even if they aren't we'll get one or two obejctions [*sic*] and the names will be delegated within 6 days instead of 3. We do NOT want to abuse this system and have demonstrated that amply in the recent past, but we are waking up and the coffee is definately [*sic*] no longer even lukewarm. FULL MEMBERS—please live up to your obligations. We cannot continue to dissuade customers from selecting names only to find that others get those names on even an [*sic*] flimsier basis.
> PS: I am not inviting the full members to single [*company name*] out once again. We will abide by rules that are applied universally and justly. This is not a free for all. It is a service with guidelines. (Message posted to <naming-co@mhs-relay.ac.uk> June 25, 1996)

Between 1995 and 1996, the problem of subjective rule/guideline implementation was further aggravated by the rapid growth in the number of full/voting and guest members comprising the Naming Committee.

Table 4.1: Members of the Naming Committee (July 1995)

Voting Members	Nonvoting Members	
NRS	Advantage Communications	Bates Dorland Interactive
EUnet GB	ALMAC	Global Internet
BTnet	Aladdin	Compass Computer Group
Demon Internet	Athene Internet	North-West Net
JAnet/UKERNA	Cerbernet	Maxis Peripherals
UnipalmPIPEX	Cityscape	Netbenefit
Cable Online	Colloquium	Nethead
Internet Network	Easynet	Pavilion Internet
Services Ltd	Electric Mail	Pinnacle Internet
Netkonect	ExNet	PIPEX Dial
Technocom	Frontier Internet	Rednet
VBCnet GB	Ftech	Research Machines
	Hypereality Systems	SERVELAN
	Information Providers Ltd	The Direct Connection
	IBMPC User Group	The Internet in Nottingham (Innotts)
	Internet TV & Video Corp.	
	Internet Discovery Ltd	Total Connectivity Providers Ltd
	Matrix Publishing Network	
	Soft Options	Webmedia
		Winweb International

By July 1995 the number of full/voting members had expanded from five to eleven, with the number of guest members increasing to thirty-seven (see table 4.1). By August 1996 the number of full/voting members had more than doubled from the previous year, encompassing twenty-four organizations. Exact figures regarding the growth of guest members are not available. However, in accordance with the rapid growth of internetworking during this period their ranks also grew dramatically, expanding to approximately 100 organizations.

As the proportion of voting member representatives with a specific interest in the registration process decreased, the initial sense of goodwill and camaraderie that had previously characterized intermember relationships began to wane and an *us versus them* scenario began to develop between individuals seeking to exercise an ill-defined form of control over the registry process and advocates of a more open registry system. Proponents of a more closed process tended to be technical engineers acting as organizational representatives of full/voting members. Their primary concerns tended to focus on the technical and moral[25] dimensions of the registry system. Advocates of a more open registry system, on the other hand, argued that the existing domain name registration process was having a negative impact on the development of Internet-related commercial service provision within the United Kingdom. This group of actors maintained that existing registry practices prevented providers of Internet-related services from effectively providing the services their customers were requesting and limited the ability of interested parties to establish a presence on the World Wide Web. This view was reinforced by a sense that those full/voting member representatives who most frequently exercised their decision making authority by often objecting to requested names lacked an understanding of the commercial realities facing service providers, concerning themselves instead with how the Internet as a whole should evolve. Proponents of a more open registry architecture tended to favor the establishment of a neutral body that processed domain name registrations on the basis of a nonrestrictive formal rule set and gave primacy to the principle of *first come, first served*.

The Emergence of Nominet UK

In September 1995, a meeting aimed at redressing problems associated with the Naming Committee's operations was held in Cambridge. It was the product of a posting to the Naming Committee discussion list during the previous month, soliciting representatives' interest in arranging an informal social gathering. This meeting introduced a face-to-face element into the registry process, marking the first opportunity the majority of actors had to meet in person. In the light of several representatives' concerns about the registry's state of affairs, it was agreed that the meeting should allow for discussion of, and voting on, procedural issues of the *.uk* domain and its future management. The meeting was attended by thirty-five people including representatives from seven full/voting member organizations and eighteen guest member organizations (see table 4.2).

In terms of tangible outcomes, very little was achieved at this meeting. The attendees agreed that the registry system needed to be changed, but *how* remained elusive. General agreement was attained on the need to formalize rules regarding registration procedures and committee membership. However, no immediate action was taken. It was decided that henceforth any new full/voting members would be accorded "guest" status during their first three months in the committee. Also, the full/voting membership would from this point on include two full/voting members co-opted from, and elected by, the guest members as representatives of their interests. In addition, due to growing dissatisfaction with the operation and maintenance of the registry database, EUnet GB was required to commit to a service level agreement.[26]

Table 4.2: First Naming Committee Meeting—September 30, 1995

Voting Member Attendees	Number of Representatives	Nonvoting Member Attendees	Number of Representatives
BTnet	3	Alladin Internet	1
Demon Internet	3	Cityscape Internet	
EUnet GB	3	Services	2
UnipalmPIPEX	3	County Internet	1
Technocom	1	Electric Mail	1
VBCnet	1	Exnet Systems	1
UKERNA	2	Frontier Internet	
		Services	1
		Gill Jennings & Every	1
		Hypereality Systems	1
		The Internet in	
		Nottingham (Innotts)	1
		Intermedia	1
		Nethead	1
		Planet Online	1
		Rednet	1
		Soft Options	1
		Total Connectivity	
		Providers	1
		The Planet	1
		Web Media	1
Total	**16**	**Total**	**19**

In the light of the problems facing the Naming Committee, individual representatives from UnipalmPIPEX and BTnet each submitted proposals, reflecting their personal views, about the establishment of alternative registry procedures to UKERNA in November and December 1995, respectively.[27] The contents of these documents closely paralleled one another. Both called for the abolition of the existing Naming Committee structure and a shifting of the registration process away from its dependence upon the voluntary activities of U.K.-based providers of Internet services toward the establishment of a legal body that would ensure the provision of stable and efficient domain name registration services. A move toward a more centralized registry structure incorporating other neutral subdomains (i.e. *.ltd.uk*, *.org.uk*) was also recommended. In addition, both documents called upon UKERNA to play a greater role in overseeing the registry in order to reduce the likelihood of committee members exploiting the registration processes to their advantage. The proposal from the BTnet representative went further in this regard than its counterpart. It suggested that if UKERNA was not prepared to perform registration services, the rights of administration and operation of the commercial name space— *.co.uk*—should be sold off to an organization willing to run the U.K. Internet Naming Service in a manner that guaranteed high quality service levels.

In January 1996, a second meeting to assist in remedying the problems facing naming administrators was held. It was attended by twenty representatives of full/voting and guest members of the Naming Committee (see table 4.3).

Table 4.3: Second Naming Committee Meeting—January 8, 1996

Voting Member Attendees	Number of Representatives	Nonvoting Member Attendees	Number of Representatives
BTnet	2	Alladin Internet	1
Demon Internet	1	Cityscape Internet	
EUnet GB	2	Services	1
UnipalmPIPEX	2	Electric Mail	1
Cable Online	2	Webmedia	1
VBCnet	1		
UKERNA	4		
Internet Network			
Services Ltd.	1		
Xara Networks	1		
Total	**16**	**Total**	**4**

The meeting was chaired by Dr. William Black, the then director of UKERNA and the "responsible person" for the *.uk* domain. Building on the ideas contained in the proposals submitted by the BTnet and UnipalmPIPEX representatives, Black called for the creation of a neutral legal body to manage the name spaces under the *.uk* domain. Similar approaches to the management of top-level domains had already been adopted in the Netherlands, Germany, and Japan, as well as for the management of generic top-level domains (i.e. *.com*, *.net*, *.org*). Although being the responsible person appears to have given Black *de jure* power, his *de facto* power was dependent upon the support of the interested parties forming the British Internet industry. Consequently, input about this initiative was sought from a broad array of participants involved with this evolving sector.

Three working groups charged with developing proposals regarding specific aspects of this notion were created. Dr. Black took responsibility for developing a business plan for the proposed registry entity; Jag Minhas, a representative from BTnet, volunteered to establish a financial working group to create a funding model; and Anthony Barber, a representative from UnipalmPIPEX, volunteered to establish a working group to develop an operational model dealing with the technical requirements of the naming functions of the new entity.[28] The three working groups were composed of several representatives from a range of U.K.-based providers of Internet services who volunteered their time and services.

Drawing from the recommendations of the working groups, a formal proposal for the development of a new registry organization was presented to the U.K. Internet service provider community at a public meeting in April 1996. The proposal consisted of three components:

1. The establishment of a not-for-profit management company providing legal protection, limited liability, and a professional full-time organization to carry out the tasks, which at that time were being done on a voluntary basis.
2. The creation of a Steering Committee open to all who were prepared to pay the membership fees; and
3. The establishment of a charging regime for subdomains registered under the neutral domains.

This became the proposal for the establishment of Nominet UK.

The uncertainties associated with this initiative created further opportunities for disputes between individual actors, and groups of actors, with a perceived stake in the U.K.-based domain name registry process. Underpinning many of these controversies were concerns about the extent to which the proposed organization would successfully ameliorate the structural and administrative weaknesses of the Naming Committee. According to the Nominet business plan, the new organization would operate on the basis of a shared registry system wherein all the members would manage the registry in common. The organization would be composed of two executive and two nonexecutive directors, as well as a Steering Committee composed of all the member organizations. The committee was open to all interested parties willing to pay nominal annual subscription fees, and the function of members was to decide on policy pertaining to naming in the *.uk* domain and the appointment of nonexecutive directors. Given the problems associated with the voting structure of the Naming Committee, one particularly contentious aspect of this initiative was the proposed voting structure of this new organization. Many of the actors representing smaller service providers were critical of this aspect of the proposal, suggesting that it allowed for the grafting of what they perceived as the elitist structure of the Naming Committee onto the new registry.

Originally subscription fees were to be based on the annual turnover of individual members and, in turn, voting entitlements would be proportional to the fees paid—up to a maximum of £5000 (see table 4.4). However, at the first Annual General Meeting (AGM) the number of votes allocated to members was made contingent upon respective rates of name registration. In addition, provisions were made allowing all members to purchase votes, up to a defined limit (see table 4.5). Members with lower registration volumes were permitted to purchase additional voting entitlements for a set fee of £500 per vote, with the upper limit on the number of votes allowed per any member fixed at ten. The establishment of a voting structure wherein voting entitlements were proportional to registration volumes was seen as a means of ensuring that the Steering Committee would be representative of the relative commercial strengths of its members, thereby minimizing the risk of unrepresentative groups exerting undue influence on the registry's activities.

Table 4.4: Proposed Steering Committee Subscription Fees

Member Turnover (£)	Subscription Fee (£)	Number of Votes
more than 1,000,000	5,000	10
250,000–1,000,000	3,500	7
100,000–250,000	2,500	5
50,000–100,000	1,000	2
less than 50,000	500	1

Source: Adapted from Black (1996).

Table 4.5: Revised Structure of Nominet Subscription Fees

Number of Domain Names Registered	Subscription Fee (£)	Number of Votes
more than 400	5,000	10
300–399	4,000	8
200–299	3,000	6
100–199	2,000	4
50–99	1,000	2
less than 50	500	1

Source: Adapted from Gould (1997).

The business plan for Nominet had also indicated that it would introduce a charge for each name registered in neutral subdomains of the *.uk* name space. Prior to the commencement of its operations in August 1996, the registration of domain names had been provided by the Naming Committee as a free service. When Nominet began administering the *.uk* domain on August 1, 1996, the registration of a name in the subdomains it oversaw became subject to a £100 fee for the first two years of registration, followed by a renewal fee of £50 for each of the subsequent years for which the registration was maintained.[29] Member organizations were entitled to a forty percent discount on the cost of registering domain names. Despite this discounted rate, initially, there was some concern that these charges would be levied prior to names actually being entered in to the registry database, and that the prices charged might be out of the reach of smaller entities offering registration services. Such an approach potentially could have benefited larger providers of Internet services who could afford higher levels of capital expenditure up front. These fears were allayed by the levying of name registration charges to individual registrar organizations on a monthly per registration basis for registrations they submitted to the registry during the preceding month.

Another key area of controversy focused around Dr. Black and how best to limit the personal authority he could exert over the registry process. He offered to leave UKERNA to become the managing director of Nominet, and some segments of the U.K. Internet community feared that he might seek to take advantage of his position for personal gain. The Nominet proposal circumvented concerns about the potentially narrow commercial motives of Dr. Black by recommending the creation of a not-for-profit company limited by guarantee. In addition, there was some uncertainty regarding Dr. Black's suitability as managing director of Nominet. These concerns focused on his academic background. Some individuals asserted that the new registry should be managed by a person with a commercial background. Dr. Black acted as the managing director, on a voluntary basis, in the period between Nominet's incorporation in May 1996 and the commencement of its operations in August 1996. At the first AGM, the Steering Committee, or Nominet members, formally elected him to the position.

Figure 4.1: Registrar Perceptions of Nominet

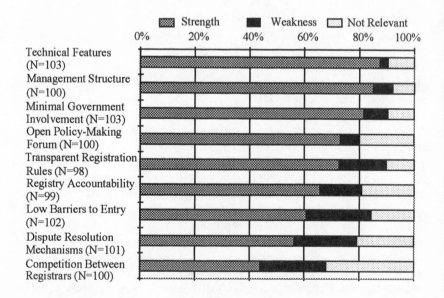

The data obtained from a survey of U.K.-based providers of Internet services, conducted in November 1998, provide evidence to support the view that at that time Nominet was generally held in high regard by a large majority of respondents and was perceived as having successfully remedied the structural and administrative weaknesses that characterized the Naming Committee.[30] This finding corresponded with the views expressed by a number of interviewees regarding the broad base of support for Nominet within the U.K.-based Internet industry. According to the survey results, the technical features of the registry were the most highly rated aspect of Nominet, followed by its not-for-profit management structure, and the minimal degree of government involvement in its registration activities.[31]

Nominet appears to have acquired sociopolitical legitimacy among U.K.-based domain name registrars, in part, because of the openness and transparency of the processes associated with its establishment and the type of organizational structure that was implemented. Each of these factors reflected the incorporation of practices and procedures that echoed the prevailing rationalized institutional rules, or "myths," associated with internetworking at the time of its formation. By establishing formal registration rules and practices Nominet removed ambiguities previously associated with the registration of domain names in the *.uk* name space. Moreover, it was able to enhance its sociopolitical legitimacy within the Internet sector by successfully incorporating the interests of a multitude of actors in its functioning in a manner that prevented any particular group of interests from exerting undue influence in this realm.

Politics and Power in the Nominet Formation Process

Before commencing with our analysis of the role that politics and power relations have played in influencing the governance trajectory of the *.uk* domain, it would be beneficial to reexamine, briefly, the value structures and norms that traditionally have underpinned the evolution of internetworking architectures. These value structures may be seen as functioning on three interrelated planes of reference. The first set of value constructs has a technocentric orientation and is rooted in the concept of end-to-end system design (Blumenthal and Clark 2000; Carpenter 1996a; David 2001; Lemley and Lessig 2000). This ethos entails placing intelligence at the periphery of the network in order to enhance opportunities for technological innovation and to empower network users. The second set of norms has a sociopolitical orientation, manifesting itself in an approach to the development of technical standards that is premised on the consensual adoption of ethics and the propagation of voluntary technical standards (Bradner 1996; Crocker 1993a; Hanseth et al. 1996; Malkin 1994). The third set of value constructs is grounded in a socioeconomic orientation reflecting a collectivistic ethos that emphasizes the importance of "service to the community" rather than rights and ownership (Postel 1994:4). Taken as a whole, this compendium of value orientations underpinned an approach to coordinating the architectures of internetworking that has become known as the Internet paradigm.

The empirical evidence derived from the narrative in the previous sections of this chapter appears to support the assertion that the transformation of the addressing regime for the *.uk* name space was marked by a period of closure and usurpation that encompassed a shift in the constellation of power relations among social actors. Moreover, the relatively low degree of politicization associated with the formation of Nominet reflected the fact that those actors that participated in these events tended to view the creation of this entity as being primarily a matter of technical coordination. The following are some of the key summary points that represent the evidence in support of this view:

1. The reconfiguration of power relations resulting from the transformation process was limited to U.K.-based suppliers of domain name registration services.
2. Virtually none of the political activity associated with the Nominet initiative was related to differences in the deep-structure interests of the actors that participated in the registry formation process.
3. The actors who participated in the registry formation process were able to define for themselves the constraints that would be placed on their domain name registration activities.
4. There was virtually no government involvement in the registry formation process.
5. There was virtually no involvement in the registry formation process of representatives of trademark and intellectual property interests.

In the period preceding the reconfiguration of the *.uk* addressing regime, a rough consensus had been attained by a relatively small number of technical engineers about how this domain should be coordinated. This consensus reflected the establishment of a form of closure based on a shared understanding of what the domain name system was and what it could do. As both the demand for names in the *.uk* name space and the number of actors with a perceived stake in the registration process increased, this state of closure was increasingly challenged. The demand for modifying the techniques used to facilitate discrimination in access to, and distribution of, domain name registrations and allocations reflected a desire to alter the way in which the *.uk* name space was zoned.[32] The contesting of the existing state of affairs manifested itself in the form of a loose collection of ideas arising from a variety of ill-defined and inconsistent individual preferences. The common theme emerging from these views was dissatisfaction with the operations of the Naming Committee. Hence, the transformation of the registry architecture was precipitated by a recognition among participants in the U.K. Naming Committee of its inability to effectively meet the needs of both U.K.-based suppliers of Internet services and Internet users.

The activities of the Naming Committee, coupled with its two-tiered voting structure, suggests that it was characterized by a series of power relations that favored larger U.K.-based providers of Internet services. This dichotomy implies a view of power relations that is based on overt conflict between member organizations and on the use of power in a manner that may have limited the scope of decision making activities within the Naming Committee. Those organizations that met the full/voting membership criteria (i.e. own permanent, independent, international connection to the Internet) possessed a level of decision making authority that was not shared by guest member organizations (i.e. those entities that could request names but had no direct input into the voting and policy making processes). This led many guest member representatives, and some full/voting member representatives, to argue that the Naming Committee structure subjected guest member organizations to the tyranny of the larger U.K.-based providers of Internet services who were full/voting members.

However, analyzing the overhaul of the *.uk* addressing regime on the basis of a distinction between large and small service providers offers an overly simplified view of the controversies that underpinned the reconfiguration of the *.uk* addressing regime. Two factors reinforce this assertion. First, every person interviewed about the functioning of the Naming Committee emphasized both the extent to which their respective organizations appeared to have been relatively uninterested in Naming Committee related activities per se, and the relatively high degree of autonomy accorded to their individual activities in this realm. Nonetheless, it should be noted that the extent of representative autonomy was somewhat different for the organizations that comprised the Naming Committee's guest membership. These organizations tended to be smaller companies (two to five employees), and it was often the personal views of senior managers and/or proprietors, and hence the organization, that were being articulated on the Naming Committee discussion lists. Therefore, in the light of the varying degrees of autonomy exercised by individual member representatives to the Naming Committee, an assessment of power relations premised on a distinction between large and small service providers falters unless the actions of some individuals can be directly equated with organizational agency.

Second, no policy making meetings of the Naming Committee were held until September 1995, by which time there was unanimous agreement among all member representatives of the need to address the problems associated with the administration of the *.uk* domain. Moreover, 80 percent of the attendees at the second meeting of the Naming Committee, in January 1996, which focused on the establishment of a new registry organization, were representatives from large service providers. These factors are particularly significant because they illustrate that despite being perceived by representatives of the smaller service providers as "oppressors," many representatives of larger service providers also did not support a maintenance of the status quo. Taken together, these findings suggest that within the context of the Naming Committee, power relations manifested themselves in the interactions between individual member representatives whose ability to make authoritative decisions reflecting their perceptions both of the goals of this architecture and how those goals might best be achieved differed.[33]

A significant number of the full/voting member representatives who chose to exercise their decision making authority tended to be technical engineers. Many of these individuals were inclined to view the Naming Committee architecture as a necessary extension of the technical hardware and software comprising the Internet and its domain naming system. This group of actors stressed the importance of maintaining the technical continuity and moral integrity of the Internet. Those member representatives who perceived the Naming Committee as being an impediment to the commercial success of internet-working within the United Kingdom either did not have the authority to participate in the committee's decision making processes (i.e. guest member representatives) or often chose not to exercise the decision making authority of the organizations they represented (full/voting members) when assessing name applications. These divergent views about the Naming Committee implied the presence of differences in the cultural values and beliefs of individual representatives regarding both the nature and necessity of restructuring the committee-based registry structure.

By applying the three-tiered conceptual framework presented in the previous chapter, it is possible to illustrate the multifaceted way in which the closure associated with the existing architecture was undone and a new consensus regarding the organizational innovation that emerged from this process— Nominet—was attained. It appears that those individual member representatives who exerted their decision making authority within the Naming Committee both overtly and covertly employed deep-structure tactics orientated toward the preservation of the prevailing power relationships. The most common tactics seem to have been strategies based on naturalization, legitimization, and neutralization. For example, naturalization strategies, or regarding the existing architecture as the natural order of things, manifested themselves in the actions of some full/voting member representatives who objected to multiple requests for names by a single registrant despite the lack of any technical justifications for the implementation of such a rule. Similarly, legitimization strategies often manifested themselves by justifying objections to requests for names through the invocation of higher values. For instance, applications for names were often objected to on the grounds that they were not sufficiently informative or adequately representative of the company names of the applicants. Finally, neutralization strategies, or the presentation of positions and activities as unbiased, manifested themselves in the claims that objections to names were based simply on the Naming Committee's registration guidelines. Taken together, these strategies influenced the authoritative allocation of values in a way that appears to be an attempt to justify, or maintain, elements of the status quo despite unanimous recognition of the need for changing the way in which the *.uk* domain was managed and administered.

In contrast, the individual member representatives who opposed the Naming Committee's registration practices, some of whom had decision making authority and many of whom did not, appear to have engaged primarily in surface-level politicking in order to manipulate and influence the outcomes of its decision making activities. For example, in deliberately challenging the boundaries of the domain name allocation process, opponents of the Naming Committee succeeded in altering its policy regarding the need for registered names to reflect either the trading or company name of the registrant. In addition, opponents of the Naming Committee further undermined its decision making authority by consistently pointing out discrepancies and contradictions in its decision outcomes. Overall, the actions of these individuals seem to have been oriented toward benefiting their respective organizations and other domain name registrars who also were opposed to the Naming Committee.

Given the hypothesized dynamic relationship between deep-structure and surface-level power relations, the struggles between social actors, combined with the rapid increase in both the volume of registration requests, and the number of full/voting and guest Committee members resulted in the undermining of the direction of power relations in the deep structure. Specifically, the surface-level actions of those representatives who opposed the Naming Committee succeeded in demonstrating the lack of congruence between the needs of U.K.-based Internet suppliers and users and the views of those representatives whose primary concern appeared to be focused on how the Internet developed as a whole within the United Kingdom. In so doing, the Naming Committee opponents managed to alter the direction of deep-structure power relations away from technical engineering interests toward more commercially oriented interests. Simply put, the outcomes of these collective interactions between social agents, combined with the technical shortcomings of the registry, undermined the Naming Committee's authority and legitimacy thereby fostering a shift in the way the *.uk* name space was zoned.

A significant dimension of these sociopolitical processes was the interactions between two specific individuals who were perceived by the other Naming Committee member representatives as advocating diametrically opposed value constructs. One individual was a strong proponent of the need for a more closed registry structure wherein applications were vetted by a committee prior to being added to the registry database. The other person argued for the establishment of open registration practices, where the suitability of names was not assessed. This individual maintained that the sole criterion for accepting names should be *first come, first served*. The personal exchanges between these two individuals were among the most acrimonious debates about the Naming Committee's procedures and structure to have taken place on its electronic discussion lists. The outcomes of their debates served as a catalyst for transforming the way in which the *.uk* domain was coordinated and administered. More specifically, the notion of establishing a legal neutral body to manage the name spaces under this domain emerged as a product of their exchanges in the form of the proposals for establishing alternative registry procedures. Given that these two actors were generally perceived by other Naming Committee representatives as antagonists, it is somewhat ironic that the proposals they put forth closely paralleled one another. Ultimately, these two proposals provided the impetus for Dr. William Black to become directly involved in, and subsequently to lead, the restructuring process.

The unanimous dissatisfaction with the Naming Committee registry system makes it unlikely that the proposal to establish a registry architecture in line with the principles of neutral service provision represented a threat to any deep-structure power interests. Consequently, the institutional formation process was able to proceed on the basis of addressing a problem of technical coordination rather than entailing broader debates about how the *.uk* name space should be governed. The relative lack of deep-structure politicking between the social actors involved in the transformation process appears also to have been linked to two other important factors. At the time when these events began to unfold, holders of intellectual property and trademark interests were not yet widely recognized, nor did they generally recognize themselves, as being potential stakeholders in the Internet addressing realm. To this end, representatives of these interests do not appear to have sought to become involved heavily in the events associated with the formation of Nominet. Based on the opinions expressed by representatives of such interests throughout the period of the domain name wars, it seems plausible that had such actors played a more active role in the administrative overhaul of the *.uk* name space, they may have sought to expand the debate to encompass broader policy issues. More specifically, representatives of trademark and intellectual property interests may have perceived the adoption of *first come, first served* registration practices and Nominet's approach to dispute resolution as a threat to their deep-structure interests. We may conclude, therefore, that the lack of participation by such actors appears to have limited the scope of the debates associated with the Nominet initiative.

The second factor that may have limited the extent to which this enterprise became bogged down in controversies about broader regulatory issues was the fact that the interpretative frames of the majority of participants in this process seemed to be grounded in a commons view of the Internet. That is, the necessity of maintaining a single entity responsible for overseeing the management and administration of the *.uk* name space was not fundamentally challenged, and the provision of domain name registry services was widely perceived as being a public service that should not be managed on a for-profit basis. Consequently, the key issue underpinning the transformation process was not about the necessity of establishing and formalizing a coordination mechanism. Instead, the primary questions centered around distributional capabilities, that is, the issue of how such a coordinating mechanism could be created such that both the regime formation process and its outcome were not subjected to undue influence by any individuals representing a particular set of interests. Consequently, most of the negotiations associated with this initiative occurred largely at the surface level and focused primarily on finding optimal strategies for ensuring the impartiality of the new organization.

An array of supportive political tactics focusing on the establishment of a rough consensus among interested parties was used in attempting to ensure the success of the Nominet proposal. On the whole, these tactics appear to have been premised on the behavioral norms and values associated with the Internet standards-making paradigm.[34] A major component of this paradigm continues to be the creation of working groups, as required, within the Internet Engineering Task Force (IETF) to address specific problems or to create particular standards. A key feature of these working groups is that they are open to participation by any interested party. However, due to the respect they have acquired over time for their contributions to the development of internetworking, the contributions of some individuals often carry more weight than others. As a result, this approach to standards making is largely meritocratic in its orientation.

Another key aspect of the Internet standards-making process is the means by which conclusions are reached and standards are settled. The first stage in the evolution of an Internet standard is the promulgation of a document known as an Internet draft, which is discussed by the relevant IETF working group which then recommends it for action to the Internet Engineering Steering Group (IESG).[35] If it is approved, the specification is proposed as a Proposed Standard RFC and discussions about the standard continue apace on the relevant electronic discussion lists and at IETF meetings for a period of six months. At this stage in the standards process, the proposed standard may be promoted to the status of draft standard once it has been reconsidered by the IESG. After an additional four-month period of review, the draft standard may be promoted to a standard. At each stage in this process participants are provided with opportunities to critique the actions of the IESG. The means by which the specification is accepted as a standard is best summarized in the credo, "We reject kings, presidents, and voting. We believe in rough consensus and running code" (Zittrain and Clark 1997). Reflecting the informal nature of IETF discussions, this phrase highlights the fact that discussions or debates about a standard are not resolved through voting. Rather, disputes are resolved through the negotiation of a consensus because particular working groups have no specified members and there is no means of dictating who those members should be.

When examining the Nominet formation process, elements of the IETF standards making process may be observed. For example, the openness component of the Internet standards making paradigm manifested itself in the creation of three working groups to develop a coherent proposal for change, from which no interested parties were restricted from participating. It was through processes involving cooperation and competition between social actors that participants in these working groups were able to define the parameters of the specific features of the proposed architecture (i.e. structure, technical base, funding model).

Drawing from the recommendations of these working groups, a formal proposal for the development of a new registry organization was presented to the United Kingdom Internet service provider community at a public meeting in April 1996. Reflecting the meritocratic nature of the Internet standards-making process, the legitimacy of Dr. Black's historically rooted authority over the *.uk* domain was broadly accepted by the British Internet community. However, this did not hold for the concept of Nominet before it was established. Given the widely held perception of Nominet's predecessor as a closed structure, the social, political, and cognitive legitimacy of the new registry architecture hinged upon its continued openness to participation by all interested actors as well as on its technical merit. Once the Nominet proposal had been released, additional comments about its contents were sought from all interested parties. Some of the comments led to modifications being made to the original proposal. For instance, when concerns were raised that the proposed voting arrangements might graft the perceived elitist voting structure of the previous registry onto the new architecture, the manner in which votes were to be allocated was altered.[36]

Once the new registry was established, membership in this new organization remained open to any interested parties, thus empowering all members to contribute to the making of domain naming policy for the *.uk* name space. According to those directly involved in these events, the initiative acquired legitimacy, in part, because its detractors were also incorporated into the planning processes and, later, into the company itself. For example, at Nominet's first AGM the membership elected one of the most vehement opponents of this organization as a nonexecutive director. According to this individual, getting "on board" offered a means of improving the system from within.[37] By the time that Nominet commenced its operations in August 1996 virtually all opposition had been diffused.

The fact that this initiative was entirely industry based with virtually no government involvement was another factor that accorded it socio-political legitimacy among interested parties. This sense of legitimacy was not restricted to industry perceptions of Nominet. It also affected the U.K. government's perception of the registry. Government interest in this undertaking had focused on concerns about the extent to which user interests (business and individual) were adequately represented in the restructuring process. According to the former head of Infrastructure and Convergence Policy at the DTI, the key issue from the U.K. government's point of view was that the registry system be open, transparent, and objective, which it perceived Nominet as being.[38] Therefore, Nominet's monopoly status was never really perceived by the U.K. government as problematic. Essentially, the DTI saw the Nominet approach as a good model reflecting a pragmatic industry-based decision.

Although the U.K. government was not directly involved in the registry formation process, it did have an indirect influence over these proceedings. This limited degree of influence manifested itself in the threat of sanction the government maintained over the activities of this new entity. More specifically, since Nominet exerted monopolistic control over the *.uk* domain, had it been incorporated as a for-profit entity, or if it was believed to be exploiting its monopoly status for its own advantage, the government could have initiated proceedings against the registry through the U.K. Office of Fair Trading. The fact that the government never questioned the necessity or desirability of Nominet's monopoly control over the *.uk* domain may be seen as reflecting, in part, the extent to which the proposed registry architecture was seen by the DTI as coinciding with U.K. public policy.

Taken together, the events associated with the formation of Nominet succeeded in constraining the extent to which these proceedings became politicized by fostering a perception among concerned parties that the initiative was: (i) inclusive; (ii) prevented the interests, or groups of interests, of any one organization from dominating the processes by which it was established; and (iii) independent, and not in competition with other industry players. The extent to which the success of this initiative was contingent upon these three factors suggests that the perceived degree of openness and transparency of this process of organizational change was the primary deep-structure consideration of the social actors involved. Consistent with the historically rooted values of internetworking, the openness of the interactive processes associated with the establishment of a new administrative regime provided the means of allowing interested parties to define the types of checks and balances that were incorporated into the architecture. In short, the relatively high degree of openness and transparency of the sociopolitical processes from which the Nominet proposal emerged, and later the way in which Nominet operated, facilitated: (i) the building of trust between the new registry and actors with a perceived stake in the outcome of the formation process; and (ii) the framing of the uncertainties connected to this initiative in such a way that the proposed innovation was viewed as credible by actors with a perceived stake in the outcome of these events.

As such, the initiative acquired legitimacy among the concerned actors because it incorporated practices and procedures that corresponded with the prevailing concepts of organizational work in both the physical and electronic realms. Specifically, it was perceived as a bottom-up endeavor which permitted actors to define for themselves the constraints that would be placed on their behavior. The fact that these constraints were congruent with British public policy served to minimize the degree of politicization associated with this endeavor as well as enhancing its legitimacy from the perspective of the U.K. government. Once established, the continued legitimacy of Nominet was related to its technical efficacy and to the maintenance of its neutrality.

Conclusion

This chapter has explored the flux between the relatively stable period of coordinated administration that characterized the management of the *.uk* domain prior to the mid-1990s, and the relatively unstable period of transition that fostered the emergence of Nominet UK. The changing directions of power relations initiated a process of institutional reconfiguration, while the processes by which new power constellations were established influenced the legitimacy of the administrative innovation that emerged from this process of change. The evidence also suggests that the process of reconfiguring the *.uk* addressing regime did not proceed in accordance with any specific plan. Rather, the outcome of this period of institutional transition was shaped over time both by the characteristics of the naming architecture and the dynamic processes of cooperation and competition between social actors.

Although the responsible person for the *.uk* domain possessed an historically rooted authority over this segment of the Internet, the continued legitimacy of this authority was contingent on it being perceived by interested parties
as neutral. The success of the Nominet initiative can be traced to the inclusive
strategies adopted to develop a coherent proposal for change that prevented any
particular interest, or groups of interests, from being perceived as exerting undue influence on the registry's activities. The bottom-up manner in which these
collective exercises in decision making was conducted was congruent with the
historically rooted values of internetworking. The outcomes of these processes
appear to have influenced the sociopolitical legitimacy bestowed on this inter-
mediary organization by all interested parties.

In the next chapter, attention is given to how U.K.-based providers of Internet services responded to the uncertainty fostered by controversies about the
technical management and administration of the domain name system as a
whole.

Notes

1. A complete listing of Nominet's current membership is available at:
www.nic.uk/members.html (last accessed January 12, 2000).

2. Oliver (1992:564) defines "de-institutionalization" as, "the process by which the
legitimacy of an established or institutionalized organizational practice erodes or dis-
continues."

3. The narrative presented in this chapter draws primarily from qualitative and
quantitative data obtained by the author from (i) personal interviews and e-mail exchanges with members of the U.K. Internet industry, government policy makers, and
other individuals who are known specialists on the Internet; and (ii) a review and analysis of primary archival documents, including the U.K. Naming Committee discussion
list archives spanning the period from August 1995 to August 1996. The interviews
were conducted by the author during the period spanning from April 1998 to March
1999. Interviewees were selected on the basis of their personal involvement in the U.K.
Naming Committee and/or direct involvement in ongoing attempts to restructure the
global Internet addressing regime. Some interviewees were active in both processes.
Access to many of the U.K.-related archival materials was a direct result of the benevolence of a number of interviewees. The majority of documents associated with the restructuring of the *.uk* domain are no longer in the public domain. Instead, they tend to
make up part of the personal electronic archives of individuals who, at the time, were
involved in this process.

4. The norms regarding assignment of "responsibility" for two-letter top-level domains initially were outlined in RFC 920.

5. This was an advanced information technology program consisting of a central di-
rectorate that allocated government funds to approved projects. The program focused on
four enabling technologies that were regarded as the "keys" to the new generation of
computers: software engineering, Very Large Scale Integration (VLSI) chip architecture,
intelligent knowledge-based systems and intelligent user interfaces.

6. Interviews with Dr William Black, Peter Kerstein, and one other individual associated with this process who requested to remain anonymous. Conducted by the author on April 8, 1998, September 3, 1998, and March 30, 1998 respectively.

7. Prior to April 1993, EUnet GB had been trading under the name UKnet, providing e-mail, news and full Internet access to more than 800 U.K. sites. It was also a founding member of the independently run EUnet Europe, serving as the British backbone portion of the latter organization's network. In July 1995, EUnet GB was acquired by the U.S.-based company, Performance Systems International Inc. (PSI). See www.psi.com (last accessed April 1, 1999).

8. PIPEX was founded in January 1992 by Unipalm, a U.K.-based company that produced computer networking products based on the IP protocol suite. When PIPEX commenced operation it consisted of fifty-six employees. In March 1994 the company was floated on the London Stock Exchange. In late 1995 it merged with UUNET, which subsequently merged with the U.S.-owned MCI Worldcom in December 1996. See www.uk.uu.net (last accessed April 1, 1999).

9. Demon Internet Ltd was founded in June 1992 by the staff of Demon Systems Ltd, a firm which specialized in software production. It originally sought to expand the market for telnet, e-mail, Gopher and FTP services to the British public. Up to that time, these services had remained largely restricted to those working in academic and research environments. Demon Internet grew from a subscriber base of 100 people at the time of its founding to in excess of 180,000 dial-up subscribers in May 1998, at which time it was purchased by Scottish Telecom, the telecommunication division of Scottish Power, for £66 million. See www.demon.net, (last accessed April 1, 1999).

10. The role of the NRS representative consisted of providing continuity between the segment of DNS under commercial control and those segments that remained under the direct control of the Joint Network Team.

11. This was a generic name that included all British Telecom Internet products prior to BTnet becoming a trademark name in January 1995. Prior to the formal launch of BTnet, BT Internet Services consisted of a team of six individuals responsible for virtually all aspects of the provision of corporate Internet services.

12. Interview with Nigel Titely conducted by the author on September 9, 1998.

13. For an overview of how this approach differs from more centralized approaches to the development and implementation of technical standards see Crocker (1993a), Malkin (1994), Hanseth et al. (1996), and Bradner (1996).

14. See www.linx.org (last accessed April 1, 1999).

15. An autonomous system is a unit of routing policy. It can be either a single network or a group of networks that is controlled by a common network administrator, or group of administrators, on behalf of a single administrative entity such as a university, business enterprise, or business division.

16. For a detailed listing of LINX membership requirements see the LINX *Memorandum of Understanding*, available online at: www.linx.org/mou.html (last accessed April 1, 1999). See also the LINX *Articles of Association*, at: www.linx.org/manda.html (last accessed April 1, 1999).

17. In the U.K., companies limited by guarantee have no shares or shareholders, and those who control the company have no financial interest in the company's assets.

18. Most interviewees claimed that the registration process was nevertheless very competitive because, in providing this service, registrars competed on the basis of price.

19. The companies comprising the guest membership primarily consisted of smaller organizations specializing in the provision of specific Internet services (i.e. Web design,

content providers, Web hosting), and other service resellers.

20. Interview with author conducted on June 5, 1998.

21. The number of objections required to reject a request was increased as the number of voting members increased. By July 1996 the number of member disapproval's needed to dismiss a request had increased to five.

22. In the light of these circumstances, some member companies began recommending to their clients wishing to register domain names that they do so under the generic *.com* top-level domain on the grounds that, *.com* registrations were not 'public' knowledge, and the acceptance of name applications was, at the time, contingent only upon whether or not the name itself had been previously registered by another party. Interview with the author conducted April 29, 1998.

23. This information was adapted from, *Application for a Domain Name within .co.uk Domain (8/12/94)*. This was a general information sheet, whose authorship was not attributed to any person(s) or organizations, that was made available to those seeking to register names in the *.co.uk* domains. A copy of this form was obtained from the personal Web page of an individual who was a representative of one of the founding members of the Naming Committee. See www.kfs.org/~jhma/naming-co/naming-co-tips.html (last accessed January 19, 1999).

24. Interview conducted by the author on May 1, 1998.

25. In this context "moral" refers to concerns about possible misuses of the DNS that might cast a negative light on internetworking. For example, allowing the registration of domain names which might be seen as offensive by some (i.e. *rudeword.co.uk*).

26. Representatives from UnipalmPIPEX had proposed that their organization should assume control of the registry database because they were better equipped than EUnet GB to meet any service-level agreements decided upon at this particular meeting. However, this motion was not passed.

27. See Barber and Davies (1995) and Minhas (1995).

28. These two individuals were the authors of the proposals for changing the *.uk* registry structure that were submitted to UKERNA at the end of 1995.

29. At the time of writing, Nominet charged £80 plus VAT per direct domain name registration, which was required to be paid in full in advance. However, it offered its members a substantial discount on the registration fees, charging them £5 plus VAT per domain name registration. See www.nic.uk/howto/fees.html (last accessed July 10, 2001).

30. A questionnaire was sent to 408 U.K.-based providers of Internet services — approximately one-half of the organizations offering domain name registration services in the United Kingdom at the time of its distribution. A 27 percent response rate was obtained (Paré 2000).

31. A more detailed analysis of the data obtained regarding Nominet revealed that the respondents' perceptions of each of the nine factors was independent of their respective organizational size, core business, and target clients.

32. Recall that Lessig (1996a) defines zoning as "any technique used to facilitate discrimination in access to or distribution of some good or service."

33. The intensity of participation in the Naming Committee's activities and interactions was fluid and occurred on a voluntary basis. Variations in participation levels may have influenced the constellations of power relations that emerged and some of the value allocation decisions that were made (Denis et al. 1996; Wallis and Dollery 1997).

34. See Bradner (1996) for a discussion of the Internet standards process. An examination of how this approach to standards-making evolved is offered by Gould (1999).

Much of the content of this and the next paragraph is derived from these documents.

35. The IESG is composed of the IETF chair and technical area directors.

36. It is worth noting that both the Naming Committee and Nominet architectures did deviate from the traditional consensus-based approach to the development of Internet standards in so far as a voting-based approach to resolving policy disputes was incorporated into each organization.

37. Interview with the author conducted on May 1, 1998.

38. Interview with the author conducted on May 13, 1998.

Chapter 5

Internet Addressing: The U.K. Perspective

At this level, there is a need to check one's political beliefs at the door.[1]

Having examined the sociopolitical processes associated with the reconfiguration of the *.uk* addressing regime, the discussion now turns attention to the ways in which U.K.-based providers of Internet services responded to the uncertainties arising from the events leading up to the formation of ICANN. The narrative presented in this chapter draws primarily upon the results of a statistical analysis of quantitative data collected from a postal questionnaire that was distributed to domestic domain name registrars during the autumn of 1998.[2] Emphasis is placed on the commercial characteristics of the organizational respondents, their opinions about a number of issues that were central to the debates preceding the creation of ICANN, as well as the extent of, and rationales for, their participation in the reconfiguration process. Domain name registrars are only one of the entities with a potential interest in the restructuring of the domain name system. Other entities with stakes in this process include, but are not limited to, holders of trademark and other intellectual property interests, commercial and noncommercial domain name holders, connectivity providers, international regulatory bodies, and national governments. Unfortunately, resources were insufficient to distribute the questionnaire to representatives from all of these groups.

The analysis presented is structured in accordance with the power-oriented framework outlined in chapter 3 and is divided into four sections. The first offers a brief overview of the methodology used to conduct the survey, as well as the motivations for collecting the various categories of information. The second focuses on the respondents' opinions about a number of specific issues whose resolution would be expected to fundamentally influence the future coordination of internetworking. In the third section, the extent of and rationales for participation in the reconfiguration process by U.K.-based domain name registrars is examined. The discussion in the final section focuses on the nature of the dynamic relationship between deep-structure and surface-level power relations. Whereas the empirical evidence derived from the narrative presented in chapter 4 appears to support the claim that the Nominet formation process was largely perceived by interested parties as being primarily a problem of technical coordination, the same cannot be said about the ICANN formation process. In this instance, the process of regime formation was transformed into a matter concerned primarily with issues that have broad implications for public policy.

Methodology

The boundaries for the survey were delimited by the Internet domain naming system. The management and administration of this technological configuration entails "governance" in so far as the policies promulgated and enforced at this level of internetworking influence specific network segments and may transcend cyberspace as a whole. The implications of policy making at this level are not restricted to the technical dimensions of addressing. Rather, they incorporate public policy issues relating to intellectual property rights, freedom of speech, content, and dispute resolution (Froomkin 2000b; Liu 1999). Collectively, addressing-related policies entail governance in so far as they may be seen to establish the parameters of a social order within the electronic realm.

The quantitative data presented in the proceeding pages was obtained from a postal questionnaire distributed to U.K.-based providers of Internet services in November 1998. At the time, attempts at creating a new entity to oversee the DNS in accordance with the tenets of the U.S. Department of Commerce White Paper were coming to an end. The purpose of the questionnaire was to identify how U.K.-based organizations offering domain name registration services in the United Kingdom were responding to uncertainties about the technical management and administration of the Internet.[3] The questionnaire was sent to 408 potential respondents—approximately one-half of the total number of organizations offering domain name registration services in the United Kingdom at the time. A 27 percent response rate was obtained, with a total of 106 completed questionnaires returned.[4]

The individuals queried were randomly selected on the basis of whether their respective organizations offered domain name registration services.[5] Overall, 81 percent of the participants were in senior management positions. Therefore, it is reasonable to conclude that the respondents were well-placed to provide information about the views and practices of their respective organizations.

The questionnaire comprised four sections, the first of which consisted of four descriptive questions pertaining to the organizational characteristics of the companies the respondents represented. In the second section, the respondents were asked a series of questions focusing on the domain name-related registration activities of their respective organizations.

The third part of the questionnaire focused on a number of issues associated with the ongoing international attempts to restructure the DNS. Some of the questions posed in this section were designed to assess the extent to which the respondents' respective organizations had been monitoring and/or participating in the events associated with the formation ICANN. This approach was used as a means of gaining insights into the respondents' participation in surface-level politicking. The respondents' deep-structure values were assessed by focusing upon their views regarding a number of fundamental domain name-related issues including: (i) the necessity of expanding the number of available generic top-level domains (gTLDs); (ii) the appropriateness of marketing country-code top-level domains (ccTLDs) as substitutes for gTLDs; (iii) whether trademark rights should be protected within the context of the domain name system; (iv) whether domain name registries and/or registrars should play a role in resolving domain name-related disputes; and (v) whether the WIPO should be directly involved in helping to resolve domain name disputes.

In order to directly address our concern with the role of power relations and politicking, the participants were also asked to rate the amount of influence they felt various entities associated with the restructuring of the Internet addressing regime had exerted on shaping domain naming policy. This particular aspect of the survey was designed to assess the reputational power of various parties with a stake in the restructuring process. One of the weaknesses of using a reputational approach to assessing power is a tendency for this methodology to produce pyramidal descriptions of power relations (Walton 1966a, 1966b). However, within the context of this study, this concern is alleviated by treating reputation itself as a resource and presenting "reputational leaders" as an aggregate of individual actors with resources that may or may not influence the outcome of decision making processes (Crenson 1971; Gamson 1966).

Organizational Characteristics of Service Provider Respondents

In terms of size, the data obtained from questionnaires returned completed reflected the views of a relatively balanced distribution of registrar organizations:[6]

- 34 percent of the sample represented organizations employing between one and five employees;
- 34 percent of the sample represented organizations employing between six and fourteen employees; and,
- 27 percent of the sample represented organizations employing more than fifteen employees.

From here on in, the respondent organizations are categorized as micro, small, and composite on the basis of the above differences in employee numbers.[7] The "composite" category incorporates medium- and large-sized service providers, that is, organizations employing more than fifteen people.

Figure 5.1: Respondents' Target Clients (N=104)

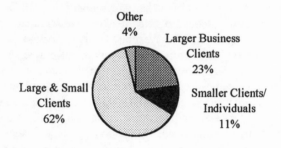

Figure 5.2: Respondents' Core Businesses

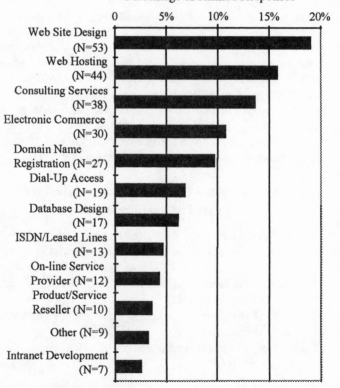

A majority of respondents indicated that their respective organization targeted its products and/or services to both large business clients and smaller clients/individuals (see figure 5.1).

A summary of the respondents' grouped rankings of their core businesses is provided in figure 5.2. Within the sample population, the five most common core businesses, in descending order, were: Web site design (19%), Web hosting (16%), consulting services (14%), electronic commerce (11%), and domain name registrations (10%). These rankings reflect, in part, a deliberate bias in the sample selection process. At the time of the questionnaire's distribution, there were only four organizations in the U.K. for whom the registration of domain names served as the primary core business—Netnames, NetBenefit, Virtual Internet, and Nomination.[8]

Although only twenty-seven participants rated the registration of domain names as one of their organization's top three core businesses, 79 percent of the 106 respondents indicated that provision of this service was considered to be an important dimension of their respective organization's overall competitiveness. A more detailed analysis of these data suggested that the level of importance attached to the provision of this service was related to a number of commercial factors. First, these perceptions correlated inversely with organization size ($r(s)$ = -0.241, $p<.05$),[9] suggesting that the larger organizations within the sample tended to view the provision of registration services as a less critical dimension of their overall competitive strategies than their smaller counterparts. Second, and as one might expect, a positive correlation was identified between attaching importance to the provision of registration services and the respondent organizations' average monthly registration volumes ($r(s)$ = 0.382, $p<.05$).[10] Finally, attaching importance to the provision of this service also seemed to be related to the respondents' target clients ($\chi^2=7.115$, df=2, $p<.05$). More precisely, a greater number of organizations specifically targeting larger clients than statistically expected indicated that provision of this service was not perceived as an important dimension of their organization's overall competitiveness.

Overall, the key characteristics of the participant organizations may be summarized as follows:

1. The respondents reflected the diversity of U.K.-based companies that potential registrants could approach to register domain names in the autumn of 1998.
2. The sample comprised an array of service providers of various sizes, specializing in the provision of a variety internetworking-based services, targeted to an assortment of potential clients.
3. The majority of companies who participated in the survey viewed the provision of domain name registration services as an important aspect of their competitive strategies.

On the basis of these characteristics it was concluded that the sample population reflected the diversity of U.K.-based providers of Internet services with a potential stake in how the domain name system was managed and administered at the end of 1998.

Deep-Structure Perspectives of Restructuring Process

Before proceeding with an analysis of the perceptions of U.K.-based domain name registrars vis-à-vis attempts to restructure the Internet addressing regime, it is useful to reiterate the key elements of the tripartite framework presented in chapter 3. The first, or surface-level, tier of the model is represented in the day-to-day contests and struggles for collaboration among social actors. The second tier, or deep structure, is described as consisting of the power relationships that inform the collective interpretive frames and cognitive maps of the participants to these exchanges. The third, or architectural, tier represents the technical hardware and software that comprises the networking architecture. The perceptions of social agents vis-à-vis the networking architecture may or may not be influenced by the history of internetworking and the sociopolitical structures that coincided with its evolution. Finally, the relationship between these three tiers is considered to be dynamic, with events at one level influencing, and being influenced by, what transpires in the other levels.

The discussion in this section is concerned primarily with the deep-structure perspectives of the respondents. As such, it draws upon observations of the respondents' opinions about five subject specific issues that, at the time, were at the core of discussions about the technical management of domain names. The five issues for which the participants' opinions were solicited included:

1. The necessity of expanding the number of generic top-level domains (gTLDs).
2. The appropriateness of marketing country-code top-level domains (ccTLDs) as substitutes for gTLDs.
3. Whether trademark rights should be protected within the context of the domain name system.
4. Whether registries and/or registrars should play a direct role in resolving domain name disputes.
5. Whether the World Intellectual Property Organization (WIPO) should be directly involved in helping to resolve domain name disputes.

Opinions about the issues listed above, combined with the amount of influence the respondents believed different actors were able to successfully exert in shaping the evolution of domain naming policy were expected to be indicative of the their interpretative frames and cognitive maps regarding the restructuring process.

Expanding the Number of gTLDs

When queried about the necessity of expanding the number of available gTLDs, approximately 55 percent of respondents viewed it as necessary, 34 percent indicated that it was unnecessary, and 11 percent claimed to have no opinion on the matter. A more detailed analysis of the data regarding this matter suggested that perceptions of this issue were independent of organization size (Goodman-Kruskal Gamma = 0.080, p>.05; Kendall's tau-b =0.046, p>.05; Stuart's tau-c = 0.051, p>.05), core businesses (χ^2=8.607, df=10, p>.05), and target clients (χ^2=2.281, df=2, p>.05). Views on this issue also failed to correlate in a statistically significant manner with average monthly registration volumes (r(s)=0.001, p>.05).

These findings suggest that, in November 1998, perceptions about the necessity of expanding the number of available top-level domains were not related to the commercial characteristics of the organizations the respondents represented. Instead, opinions about this issue appear to have been based upon individual convictions about how the Internet should evolve. To this end, some interviewees from the private and public sectors, as well as some of the open comments added to the returned questionnaires, emphasized that rather than increasing the number of available top-level domains better use of the .*us* ccTLD was a more appropriate method of alleviating many of the problems associated with the growing scarcity of desirable names in the .*com* domain.

The question of whether new gTLDs should be introduced into the domain name system and, if so, who should be authorized to undertake such an endeavor remains at the core of the controversies associated with the reconfiguration of Internet addressing. Those actors supporting a more rapid expansion of the number of gTLDs have argued that (i) they are easily created; (ii) such an undertaking would remedy perceived scarcities in existing name spaces; and (iii) such action would be consistent with increasing both consumer choice and innovation in the cyber-realm. Opponents of expansion, on the other hand, have consistently claimed that such action would lead to increased confusion among network users, as well as increasing the risk of trademark infringement, cybersquatting, and cyberpiracy.[11]

Up until the latter part of 1999 the approach taken by the ICANN to expanding the number of top-level domains was largely one of "wait and see". Drawing from the efforts of a series of working groups within the Domain Name Support Organization, in April 2000 the Names Council recommended to the ICANN board that it establish a policy for the introduction of a limited number of new gTLDs.[12] At the conclusion of its meeting in Yokohama, Japan, in July, ICANN announced that it would issue a formal call for proposals from entities seeking to sponsor or operate new top-level domains. The deadline for the receipt of proposals was set for October 1.[13] Forty-four applications for operating new top-level domains were received. In November, ICANN announced its selections for the registry operators for seven new top-level domains. They were:[14] .*aero*—Société Internationale de Telecommunications Aeronautiques

SC (SITA); *.biz*—JVTeam LLC; *.coop*—National Cooperative Business Association (NCBA); *.info*—Afilias LLC; *.museum*—Museum Domain Management Association (MDMA); *.name*—Global Name Registry Ltd; and *.pro*—RegistryPro Ltd

Substitution of ccTLDs for gTLDs

In the light of what some actors perceived as the insufficient number of generic top-level domains, and the increasing difficulties associated with obtaining a desired name within the coveted *.com* domain, some national registries have marketed their respective country-code top-level domains as substitutes for generic top-level domains. The use of national domains in this manner represents an attempt to increase the utilization of specific domains by attributing various types of meaning to them. Some observers have argued, however, that using national domains in this way blurs the distinction between commercial top-level domains and country-code top-level domains, thus increasing the likelihood of further trademark and intellectual property rights-based conflicts between registrants (Broersma 1998).

Some examples of country-code top-level domains that have been marketed as substitutes for generic top-level domains include: *.nu*, for Niue, a Polynesian island nation; *.tv*, for Tuvala, another Polynesian nation; and *.tm*, for Turkmenistan

The appeal of *.nu* for potential registrants lies in the fact that within the English language the term implies "newness," while in many Scandinavian languages it means "now," and in Yiddish the term is a casual greeting. The *.tv* domain has been marketed as a means of attracting network users to Web sites specializing in television and video content. Despite the fact that its use did not attach any legal status to a domain name, in early 1998 attempts were made at marketing the *.tm* domain as means of associating names with the international symbol for trademark—TM.

By the end of September 1999, the *.nu* domain had acquired approximately 50,000 registrations, and by May 2001 this figure exceeded 100,000.[15] The *.tv* domain was launched in April 2000 and obtained more than 350,000 registrations within its first year of operation.[16] The company that acts as the registry for the *.tm* domain, Netnames Ltd, began accepting registration requests in February 1998.[17] Shortly thereafter, however, it was forced to cease accepting registrations for this domain when it was discovered that names which were legally obscene in Turkmenistan had been accepted for registration. At the time of writing, the acceptance of any further registrations for this domain remained suspended pending the development and implementation of new registration policies.

When asked if they agreed that ccTLDs should not be marketed as substitutes for gTLDs, 58 percent of the participants answered yes, 21 percent disagreed, and 21 percent responded that they had no opinion on the matter. Attempts to discern whether any relationships existed between perceptions of support for, and opposition to, this use of ccTLDs and the commercial characteristics of the respondent organizations failed to yield any statistically significant results. Nevertheless, opinions regarding this matter encompass different conceptions of how the DNS should be administered and managed. More specifically, attempting to prevent the use of ccTLDs in this way would necessitate the implementation of new coordination measures that did not exist at the time, or at present. Support for limiting how this set of domains is utilized may be seen as being indicative of support for a more structured approach to how the domain names system was being managed and administered than was the case at the time the survey was conducted.

Protection of Trademark Rights Within the DNS?

The issue of trademark protection was, and continues to be, one of the most politically charged dimensions of the proceedings associated with attempts to reconfigure the Internet addressing regime. At issue here is the nature of domain names and the function they serve. Recall that, in contrast to numerically based Internet Protocol (IP) addresses, domain names are hierarchically structured character strings that allow users to remember network addresses relatively easily.[18] However, unlike the classification system for trademarks, which allows for the registration of identical marks for separate categories of products and services, the problematic feature of domain names is that identical character strings cannot be used within the same domain. Consequently, intellectual property problems have arisen with regard to the registration of domain names either matching, or closely reflecting, the character strings of established trademarks by "unauthorized" parties or cybersquatters.[19] Problems of reverse domain name hijackings where actors with sufficient legal and financial clout attempt to wrest control of potentially valuable names from legitimate name holders also have arisen (Mueller 1999a; Nathenson 1997; Oppedahl 1997). In many of these cases the holder of the domain name is a legitimate business, and in other instances the holder is a private party that has registered his or her surname or nickname.

When queried about their respective organization's view on whether trademarks should be protected within the context of the domain name system, 67 percent of 105 respondents[20] indicated support for this notion, 23 percent were opposed, and 10 percent claimed to have no opinion on the matter. In the light of the divisive nature of this issue, the subsequent failure to identify any statistically significant relationships between perceptions of this issue and the commercial characteristics of the respondent organizations had been anticipated.

As with the two other issues examined thus far, perceptions of the necessity of protecting trademark rights in the cyber-realm appear to be based primarily on individual convictions regarding how the Internet should evolve. That said, the fact that two-thirds of the respondents claimed to favor the protection of trademark rights in the cyber-realm serves to reinforce the view that, within the sample population at least, there was a high degree of support for a more structured approach to the coordination of the domain name system.

Direct Role for Registries and/or Registrars in Dispute Resolution?

The role that registries and/or registrars should play in the resolution of disputes between competing parties claiming a stronger right to register a specific domain name was another major issue underpinning debates about the restructuring of the Internet addressing regime throughout 1998. Much of the controversy regarding this particular aspect of domain naming policy was rooted in what was widely perceived as the five flawed dispute resolution policies[21] that were imposed by Network Solutions Inc. between July 1995 and February 1998.[22]

The bulk of the criticism levied against the dispute resolution policies implemented by Network Solutions Inc. focused on specific objectionable factors and the finer aspects of policy litigation (Maher 1996; Oppedahl 1997; Rony and Rony 1998; Shaw 1996). In essence, its approach to dispute resolution was widely criticized on the grounds that by seeking to focus on the "rights" attached to second-level domain name registration, trademark law was being grafted onto domain name registration in a manner that favored the rights of trademark holders over those of the registrant who registered a given domain name first, or who despite not holding a trademark may have a very legitimate claim to a particular name (i.e. when a family name corresponds with a company or brand name). The formation of ICANN and its implementation of its Uniform Dispute Resolution Policy has done little to diminish such allegations. In fact, Mueller (1998c, 2000) and Geist (2001) offer very compelling evidence that appears to substantiate such claims.

Bearing in mind that when the survey was conducted, ICANN had only very recently been created and the role of WIPO in resolving domain name disputes had not yet been clearly delineated, approximately 65 percent of the 106 respondents indicated that they felt that registries and/or registrars should play a direct role in resolving domain name disputes, with 24 percent opposed to the idea, and 11 percent indicating that they had no opinion on the matter. In line with this view, approximately half of the total respondents also indicated that their respective organizations exercised editorial control over the names they were willing to submit for registration on behalf of their clients.

Paralleling the findings about the three previous issues, a more detailed analysis of the data about this specific issue failed to identify any statistically significant relationships between support for, and opposition to, the direct involvement of registries and/or registrars in dispute resolution and the commercial characteristics of the respondent organizations.

Involvement of the World Intellectual Property Organization

In attempting to respond to concerns about the infringement of trademarks and intellectual property, each of the framework proposals put forth since 1996 regarding the technical management of Internet addressing proposed various strategies for dealing with this issue. Prior to the formation of ICANN a key avenue of controversy focused on whether the WIPO should play a role in resolving trademark disputes involving domain names. Early advocates of WIPO involvement in dispute resolution pointed to the necessity of establishing a uniform dispute resolution process to deal with domain name challenges in a manner that facilitated the avoidance of litigation (Gymer 1998), whereas opponents tended to view WIPO involvement as a means of establishing "an infrastructure for the exploitation of domain name data for regulatory purposes" (Mueller 1999a:19).

The data obtained from the questionnaire regarding the perceived desirability of WIPO involvement in dispute resolution was relatively ambiguous. In November 1998, only 43 percent of the 106 respondents supported such action, with 22 percent opposing it, and 35 percent indicating that they had no opinion on the matter. Further analysis of the data suggested that support for, and opposition to, WIPO involvement in dispute resolution was not related in a statistically significant manner to the commercial characteristics of the respondent organizations. The lack of registrar-based opposition to the incorporation of this international organization into the overall management of the domain name system seems to further reinforce the notion that the survey respondents' deep-structure perceptions appeared to favor a more formally structured approach to the administration and management of the domain name system than existed prior to November 1998.

Overall, the evidence regarding the five specific domain name-related issues examined above suggests that the respondents' positions vis-à-vis these issues were based primarily on convictions about how the Internet should evolve rather than on any distinguishing characteristics of the respondent organizations. This assertion is supported by the fact that no statistically significant relationships were found between the opinions expressed and organization size, core businesses, target clients, or average monthly registration volumes.

At the time the survey was conducted the majority of respondents supported expanding the number of available top-level domains, restricting the way in which country-code top-level domains were used, protecting trademark rights within the context of the domain name system, and registry/registrar-based dispute resolution. In addition, almost half of the respondents indicated support for the involvement of WIPO domain name-related dispute resolution. These findings suggest that within the United Kingdom, at least, there was relatively little support for the *laissez-faire* approach to Internet governance advocated by proponents of the decentralized, or libertarian, school of thought

We now turn our attention to the amount of influence the participants believed different actors exerted on the shaping of domain name policy in the autumn of 1998.

Actor Influence in Shaping Domain Name Policy

In order to obtain an indication of the reputational power of the various actors involved in the restructuring of the Internet addressing regime, the respondents were asked to rate the amount of influence they felt various entities exerted on shaping the evolution of domain naming policy. These ratings were based on a five point scale where: 1 = Very Influential; 2 = Influential; 3 = Moderately Influential;4 = Not Influential; and 5 = Don't Know. Figure 5.3 provides a summary of the overall rating of each of the actors listed in the questionnaire.

Figure 5.3: Actor Influence Ratings

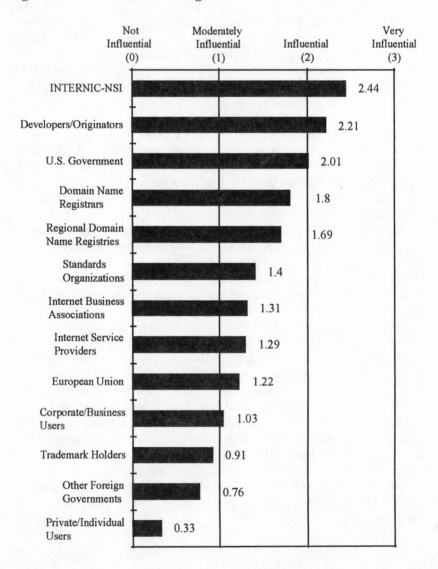

The participants ranked Network Solutions as the most influential player in the restructuring process. It obtained a rating of 2.44 out of a possible three. The developers/originators of the Internet (2.21 out of a possible three) and the United States government (2.01 out of a possible three) were rated as the second and third most influential actors. Given that at the time the survey was conducted, (i) Network Solutions Inc. had a monopoly over registering names at the gTLD level, (ii) the United States government White Paper had stipulated that the American government would adhere to a policy oversight role in this realm until a new management entity was established and operationally stable, and (iii) registrations within the *.com* domain continued to be dominated by United States-based registrants, the reputational ratings reported in figure 5.3 conformed to the expected findings.

There was, however, one very surprising feature regarding the information listed in figure 5.3. In spite of the criticisms levied regarding trademark and intellectual property interests exerting undue influence on the restructuring process, the survey results suggested that the respondents did not perceive this group of actors as being particularly influential (0.91 out of a possible three). Some of the factors that may underpin this finding are addressed in greater detail in the next section.

In line with the official response of the European Commission to the United States government Green Paper, *Reply of The European Community and Its Member States to the US Green Paper,* and the opinions put forth in a number of interviews with representatives of the British government and the U.K. Internet industry, these influence ratings also seemed to reflect what many regarded as an American domination of issues pertaining to the technical management of the Internet. This premise was exemplified by the fact that despite its continued involvement in the events leading up to the formation of ICANN, the influence of the European Union was ranked as being among the bottom third of actors (1.22 out of a possible three). Private/individual users were rated as being the least influential.

In summary, the respondents' overall deep-structure perceptions do not appear to have been related to the commercial characteristics of their respective organizations. Rather, they appear to be based on a series of personal convictions which:

1. Supported a more highly coordinated approach to the management and administration of the domain name system than was in place prior to November 1998;
2. Sought to reduce the amount of influence American-based actors were perceived as having over the administration and management of the domain name system.

In the next section, the focus of the discussion shifts toward the extent to which these deep-structure perceptions motivated U.K.-based providers of Internet services to monitor, and/or become involved with, the processes associated with the reconfiguration of the Internet addressing regime.

Participation in Surface-Level Politicking

Although the analysis presented in the previous section highlighted registrar perceptions about an assortment of domain name-related issues, whether the opinions expressed may or may not have motivated these entities to become involved directly in the restructuring process has not yet been addressed. In order to deal with this aspect of registrar activity, the participants in the survey were also queried about their respective organizations' level of involvement in the events leading up to the formation of ICANN.

Considering that more than three-quarters of the participants indicated that they viewed the provision of domain name registration services as an important dimension of their respective organization's overall competitiveness, it seems reasonable to infer that U.K.-based registrars would have been motivated to become involved, albeit in varying degrees, in these proceedings. However, the information gathered from interviews with representatives from the commercial and government sectors portrayed a different picture. When asked about the reasons for the relative inactivity of U.K.-based registrars in this realm, most of the individuals interviewed suggested that this lack of participation could be attributed to a general lack of interest in these matters.

One individual from the commercial sector noted that although some service providers were inclined to express politically based anxieties about such things as the perceived growth of U.S. dominance in the restructuring process, at the end of the day this was not really a critical concern.[23] This individual went on to claim that Internet service providers were, for the most part, completely indifferent to these events because, from a service provider perspective, the domain name system worked just fine as it was. In line with this view, another interviewee from the private sector stressed that domain names were primarily a niche area that was of relatively little direct concern for most Internet service providers given that the future growth of these organizations was dependent upon other aspects of the internetworking market. According to this person, most providers of Internet services had more immediate concerns to deal with, and consequently, they "could not care less" about domain naming until the controversies surrounding them were resolved.[24] This individual went on to stress the need for distinguishing between the political and commercial motives of registrars, asserting that in order to do business at this level, there was a very real need to check one's political beliefs at the door.

A similar view was also expressed by another person representing a micro service provider. This individual claimed that the controversies associated with the restructuring of the domain name system were "somewhat irrelevant" and had virtually no direct bearing on the day-to-day operations of service providers.[25] Pointing to another potential reason for the apparent disinterest of U.K.-based service providers, the managing director of one small organization asserted that for most ISPs domain names were seen only as an address, and offering registration services had relatively little impact on their overall profits.[26] Noting that the debates associated with the restructuring process were little more than a "bunch of political hot air" that would eventually calm down, the managing director of yet another company also expressed the view that there was no real reason for Internet service providers to care about the restructuring of the technical management of Internet addressing.[27] According to this person, domain name registrars would simply carry on as usual with their activities regardless of the outcome(s) of this process.

Evidence suggesting that the views expressed above were more than just an artifact of the interview sample was provided by the fact that these opinions coincided with the views expressed by the government officials from the U.K. Department of Trade and Industry. According to one official, the apparent disinterest of U.K.-based providers of Internet services was linked to the fact that the primary concerns of most Internet service providers simply focused on other dimensions of the Internet such as the monitoring of content and consumer protection.[28] Likewise, a second official suggested that the DNS wars amounted to "little more than a storm in a teacup."[29]

During the course of these interviews with public and private sector representatives two additional issues which could be perceived as further dissuading domestic domain name registrars from concerning themselves with the restructuring process were also raised. First, the registration activities of U.K.-based domain name registrars are dominated by requests for names in the *.uk* name space. Hence, these organizations might be seen as having relatively little incentive to become engaged directly in activities associated with the management of other top-level domains. The second factor relates to the liability, or more specifically, the lack of liability assumed by U.K.-based registrars. In the United Kingdom, the relationship between the registrant, registrar, and the registry is based on an agency contract model. That is, domain name registrars submit the name requests to the registry on behalf of registrants. However, once the request is processed, a contractual relationship is established between the registry and the registrant. Thereafter, the registrar plays no role in the relationship between these parties. Consequently, once a registration request is accepted, registrants must deal directly with the registry if any problems arise regarding the name that has been registered.

Overall, the views expressed by the interviewees suggested that U.K.-based domain name registrars were essentially indifferent to attempts to institutionalize a new global Internet addressing regime. In spite of these assertions most interviewees did note that some organizational actors might be drawn into these proceedings for reasons ranging from broad concerns about the future evolution of the Internet to more specific concerns about the quality of service provided to Internet users, to simply having an "axe to grind." In order to identify some of the specific factors that may have underpinned organizational interest in the restructuring process, the survey participants were presented with a series of statements reflecting potential reasons for their respective organization's interest in these events and asked to indicate which of them best represented their view (see table 5.1).

Contrary to the claims of the interviewees, only eight percent of the respondents indicated that their respective organization had no significant interest in domain name related issues. Approximately three-quarters of the respondents indicated that their respective organizations' interest in domain name-related issues was based on concern for the long-term stability of internetworking. Somewhat less than half noted that their interest was based on concern about the impact of the management and administration of domain names on their organizations' competitiveness. An equal proportion of respondents also expressed a desire for greater European representation in the development of domain name policies.

Table 5.1: Registrar Interest Domain Name Issues

Statements Presented (Responses not limited to only one statement)	% of Total Respondents	Total No. of Respondents
1. Concern for long-term stability of the Internet	74.5	79
2. Impact of the management and administration of domain names on my organization's competitiveness	48.1	51
3. Desire for greater European representation in the development of domain name policies	48.1	51
4. Desire to assist in protecting the intellectual property rights of our clients	42.5	45
5. Opposition to NSI's control over the .com, .org, and .net top-level domains	25.5	27
6. No significant interest in domain name related issues	7.6	8
7. Other	2.8	3

A more detailed statistical analysis of the information presented table 5.1 suggests that at the time the questionnaire was distributed, the reasons underpinning U.K.-based registrar interest domain name-related issues were not related in a statistically significant manner with the commercial characteristics of these organizations. Instead, interest in these matters tended to center around broad principles (i.e., network stability, impact on competition, and European representation) pertaining to how the Internet was managed and administered.

The open comments of one survey participant aptly summarized this view. In expressing his organization's position, this person wrote:

> From a business point of view (as a supplier to corporate clients) domain name issues are not highly critical to us. . . . Of more concern is the technical and organizational structure of the domain name system which, if badly controlled and managed, could severely impact the quality of Internet services worldwide.

In the light of the of views put forth by the interviewees, an attempt was also made at discovering if the so-called disinterest of U.K.-based service providers was related to their perceptions of the uncertainties surrounding the restructuring of the domain name system. To this end, it seemed plausible that if the uncertainties associated with these events were perceived as having a negative impact on the respondents' commercial operations, then interest in these matters would be heightened. Approximately 68 percent of the 106 respondents claimed that the restructuring process was not negatively affecting their organization. Of the remaining group of respondents, 18 percent indicated that domain name-related uncertainties were having a negative impact on their respective organization, and 14 percent claimed to have no opinion on the issue. No statistically significant relationships between these perceptions and the commercial characteristics of the respondent registrars were identified. Bearing in mind that for the majority of the organizations that participated in this survey the dominant domain for which they performed registrations was the *.uk* domain, these findings were not particularly surprising.

In order to assess further the reliability of the interviewees' assertions regarding service provider disinterest, the participants were also queried about the level of attention that their respective organizations paid to the debates associated with the reconfiguration of the domain name system. An analysis of the responses obtained from the questionnaire appeared to provide a limited degree of support for the interviewees claims, revealing that slightly more than half of the respondent organizations paid only marginal or no attention to the debates associated with attempts to establish a new addressing regime (see figure 5.4).

Figure 5.4: Attention Given to Domain Name Related Debates

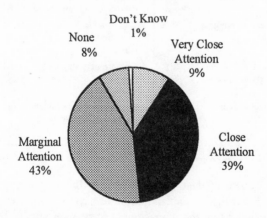

The amount of attention paid to the controversies associated with the reconfiguration of the domain name system was found to be independent of perceptions about whether or not uncertainties associated with the restructuring process were negatively affecting their organizations ($\chi^2=2.108$, df=1, p>.05). This finding is somewhat intriguing because it implies that respondents who felt that the uncertainties associated with the restructuring process were impacting negatively on their respective commercial operations were no more likely to pay attention to domain name-related issues than those who felt these events were not having a negative impact. Paralleling the conclusions regarding the reasons for registrar interest in the restructuring process, these results appear to suggest that the level of attention given to the events leading up to the formation of ICANN also were based on factors that transcended the commercial characteristics of the respondent organizations.

Ultimately, the only commercial factors that appeared to be related to the levels of attention given to domain name-related issues were the respondents' average monthly registration volumes (r(s) = 0.233, p<.05) and their perceptions of domain name registrations as being an important dimension of overall competitiveness (r(s) = 0.237, p<.05). Hence, and as would be expected, it appears that within the sample population those entities registering higher volumes of domain names and/or those that viewed domain name registration as an important dimension of overall competitiveness were likely to pay relatively high levels of attention to the restructuring process.

Table 5.2: Rationales for Varying Levels of Attention

Very Close Attention/ Close Attention (N=51)		Marginal Attention/No Attention (N=54)	
Reason:		Reason:	
1. High level of client interest in these matters.	14%	1. Little or no client interest in these matters.	28%
2. Organizational concern about long-term implications of how domain names are managed.	35%	2. Organization not concerned about long-term implications of how domain names are managed.	7%
3. Organization has resources required to monitor these issues.	10%	3. Organization does not have the resources required to monitor these issues.	33%
4. Organization believes that it should be directly involved in these matters.	16%	4. Organization does not believe that it should be directly involved in these matters.	17%
5. Organization has direct stake in outcome of these matters.	24%	5. Organization has no direct stake in outcome of these matters.	11%
6. Other	1%	6. Other	4%
Total	**100%**	**Total**	**100%**

The results presented in table 5.2 show that of the 48 percent of respondents who indicated that their organizations were paying a high level of attention to ongoing debates about the management of domain names, the primary rationales for such activity were a concern for the long-term implications of how domain names are managed and a view of themselves as having a direct stake in the outcome of these events. On the other hand, those organizations which indicated that little or no attention had been paid to these events most commonly cited as their rationales the lack of resources and a lack of client interest in these matters.

Although almost half of the participants purported to give a high level of attention to domain name-related issues, only nine percent of the 106 respondent organizations indicated that they had participated directly in the discussions and public meetings leading up to the creation of ICANN.[30] Mirroring the views expressed in the interviews, some respondents added in open comments to the questionnaire that their respective organization's lack of attention was related, in part, to a sense that the processes and controversies associated with the restructuring of the Internet addressing regime had been characterized by too much waffle, and too little action. One respondent wrote, "We're generally happy to 'go with the flow' but at the moment nobody seems to know what the flow *is*." Other respondents noted that the lack of attention given to these matters was attributable to the fact that domain names accounted for only a small portion of their organizations' financial returns. For example, one representative from a small service provider wrote,

> You may find that few ISPs are concerned about the current changes. The current US registration restructuring is unlikely to affect the UK as the new organization will still retain .com, .org, etc. So we will still have similar problems with "global identity" for clients. The current feeling is "let the courts sort it out"—The lack of profit margin in the industry means ISPs can't afford to get too involved. Also a domain name is no substitute for good PR and marketing, both online and off-line.

In summary, although the respondent organizations recognized generally the importance of the domain name system, their approach to the reconfiguration of the Internet addressing regime is perhaps best characterized as apathetic. The findings presented in this section suggest that

1. Organizational interest in domain name-related issues focused primarily on broad principles associated with the future evolution of internetworking;
2. There appeared to be relatively little incentive for many U.K.-based registrar organizations to pay high levels of attention to the restructuring process given a perceived lack of economic incentive to act otherwise, and the fact that the .*co.uk* domain accounts for the highest volume of name registrations submitted by these organizations;
3. Neither the levels of attention given to, nor the degree of participation in, the restructuring process by U.K.-based domain name registrars were related generally to any commercial characteristics of these organizations; and
4. Only a very small percentage of U.K. based registrars actually par-

ticipated directly in proceedings associated with the formation of ICANN.

In the final section of this chapter the nature of the relationship between perceptions of domain name-related issues and participation in events leading up to the formation of ICANN is examined.

Relationship between Deep-Structure Perceptions and Surface-Level Politicking

One of the central components of our power-oriented conceptual framework is the presence of a dynamic relationship between the tiers. Specifically, it was argued that events at one level of the model could influence, and be influenced by, what transpired in the other levels. In order to address this aspect of the model, the data obtained from the questionnaire were also analyzed to test for the presence of relationships between the respondents' deep-structure perceptions and the extent to which their respective organizations participated directly, and indirectly, in the events associated with the institutional reconfiguration of the domain name system.

Analysis of the data regarding participation in the discussions about the creation of a new self-regulatory organization to succeed the Internet Assigned Numbers Authority (IANA) and the respondents' deep-structure perspectives suggested that there were relatively few differences between the views of those organizations that participated directly in these events and those that did not. First, a comparison of the opinions expressed about specific domain name-related issues on the basis of whether or not organizations had participated directly in the restructuring process failed to identify any statistically significant differences of opinion between those that had participated directly and those that had not. No statistically significant correlation was found between the respondents' opinions about any of specific domain name-related issues examined earlier in this chapter and whether or not their respective organizations had participated directly in the restructuring process. This suggests that there was no discernible difference between the views of those organizations that participated directly in this process and those that did not.

A similar finding was observed when the reputational power ascribed to the actors listed in figure 5.3 was analyzed on the basis of whether or not the respondents had participated directly in the restructuring process. No statistically significant differences were identified between the actor influence ratings provided by those organizations that had participated directly in the restructuring process and those that had not. This suggests that the repuitional power ascribed to the various actors may not have been linked to their actual activities in this realm. Rather, perceptions of the relative influence of these actors may have been linked to biases in the beliefs and views held by the respondents. To this end, it seems plausible that these biases may have also played a role in influencing organizational decisions regarding the extent to which they become directly involved in the restructuring process.

Although direct participation in the events associated with the configuration of the management of the domain name system is the most obvious manifestation of surface-level politicking, indirect participation also comprises a salient dimension of attempts by social actors to exploit the rules of a given situation to their own advantage. To this end, the level of attention the respondents gave to domain name-related issues was seen as constituting an important component of surface level-politicking. In line with this view, the respondents' deep-structure perceptions of specific domain name issues were contrasted on the basis of the level of attention they gave to this matter. The results of a statistical analysis of the data suggested that opinions about only two of the issues examined were related to attention levels.

First, the correlation coefficient and the p-value obtained regarding the issue of whether trademark rights should be protected within the context of the domain name system, ($r(s)$= -0.203, $p<0.5$), suggests that those respondents claiming to have paid higher levels of attention to domain name-related issues tended to be opposed to the protection of these rights in the context of the domain name system. Second, and despite not being statistically significant, the relatively low p-value corresponding to the correlation coefficient for opinions about the marketing of country-code top-level domains as substitutes for generic top-level domains ($r(s)$= -0.191, $p=0.08$) suggests that there may have been a very weak relationship between views about this issue and attention levels. Specifically, an inverse correlation coefficient implies that those supporting the use of country-code top-level domains as substitutes for generic top-level domains tended to give higher levels of attention to domain name related issues than those who opposed such action. When taken together, these findings suggest that those entities claiming to pay higher levels of attention to domain name-related issues may have also been inclined to support a more decentralized approach to the management of domain names.

Further analysis of the data regarding the respondents' attention levels indicated that, for the most part, there was no relationship between the amount of attention the respondents claimed to have paid to the debates associated with the management of domain name and the degree of influence ascribed to the various actors associated with the restructuring process. The only influence rating found to be related to the attention levels was that of "other foreign governments." A statistically significant inverse correlation ($r(s)$= -0.296, $p<.05$) was identified between the degree of influence ascribed to this category of actors and the level of attention given to the restructuring process. In other words, those respondents claiming to pay lower levels of attention to these proceedings were more likely to ascribe higher levels of influence to foreign governments. It is unclear as to why the presence of a relationship between attention levels and reputational power was limited to the latter actors. The failure to identify any statistically significant relationships between attention levels and the influence ratings of other actors suggests that, as with opinions about specific domain name-related issues, assessments of the reputational power of the concerned actors appeared to be based on the individual convictions of the respondents.

In summary, the information presented in this section suggests that for U.K.-based domain name registrars, at least, there seem to have been relatively few links between their respective deep-structure perceptions and organizational decisions to participate in the restructuring process. More specifically, it seems that:

1. There were no statistically significant differences in the views of those entities that participated directly in the events associated with the formation of an organization to succeed IANA and those that did not.
2. The reputational power ascribed to individual groups of actors involved in the restructuring process was not linked to levels of participation in the restructuring process, nor to the level of attention given to domain name-related controversies.
3. Those entities that claimed to pay higher levels of attention to domain name-related controversies appeared to be more inclined to favor more decentralized approaches to the management of domain names.

Conclusions

This chapter has explored how U.K.-based providers of Internet services responded to the uncertainties fostered by the controversies associated with attempts to reconfigure the technical management and administration of the domain name system during the autumn of 1998. Although the survey participants generally recognized the importance of the domain name system, the uncertainties arising from these events were not a primary area of concern for most survey participants. In fact, the prevailing view of these events among most U.K.-based service providers can be best characterized as one of indifference. The apparent sense of apathy appears to have been related to the fact that (i) uncertainties about Internet addressing were not seen as having a negative effect on the commercial operations of Internet service providers; (ii) domain name registrations tended not to be regarded as a major revenue source; and (iii) the highest volume of name registrations for U.K.-based registrars was in the *.uk* domain.

The empirical evidence presented in this chapter suggests that organizational interest in domain name-related issues focused primarily on broad principles associated with the future evolution of internetworking. Specifically, analysis of the data obtained from the questionnaire implies that most U.K.-based registrars appeared to favor both a more highly coordinated approach to the management and administration of the domain name system than was in place prior to the formation of ICANN and a reduction in the amount of American influence over the development of domain naming policy. The analysis also demonstrated that, with very few exceptions, registrar perceptions of the restructuring process did not appear to be related to the commercial characteristics of the survey participants. Rather, it would seem that opinions about specific issues relating to the management of domain names and organizational decisions to participate in the events associated with attempts to institutionalize a new governance regime for Internet addressing were linked to individual convictions about how the Internet should evolve.

Additional evidence presented in this chapter suggested that although a majority of U.K.-based service provider organizations was concerned about maintaining the long-term stability of internetworking, this concern provided insufficient motivation for them to become directly involved in the proceedings associated with the institutional restructuring of the domain name system. In terms of developing a global regime for Internet addressing, this lack of participation on the part of domain name registrars is troubling and gives rise to two sets of concerns. First, the discourse associated with the reconfiguration of the technical management of Internet addressing placed, and continues to place, a strong emphasis on developing domain naming policies on the basis of consensus among *all* interested actors. However, the findings of this survey vis-à-vis the low levels of stakeholder participation in the events leading to the formation of ICANN is illustrative of the presence of a major discrepancy between discourse and practice.

Second, the evidence about the reputational power of the actors involved in the restructuring process suggests that some actors may have benefited from the presence of a positive influence cycle. That is, the influence of some actors who were perceived as being more influential may have been enhanced as a result of the fact that relatively few service providers participated directly or paid close attention to the restructuring process. As a result, those actors with high levels of reputational power may have been more influential in establishing domain naming policy than they otherwise would have been. Overall, the low levels of participation reported by the survey respondents point to the need for a questioning of *whose* interests are being considered in the drafting of global domain name policy. This issue is the focus of the next chapter.

Notes

1. Interview with the CEO of domain name registrar organization. Conducted by author on May 1, 1998.

2. See Paré (2000).

3. Prior to its distribution the questionnaire was piloted using four participants—two of which represented U.K.-based providers of Internet services, and two other individuals who were academics with previous experience in conducting surveys.

4. At the time of its mailing, the survey was the first known systematic attempt to address U.K.-based domain name registrar perceptions of the controversies associated with the restructuring of the DNS.

5. Information about these organizations was obtained from three sources: (i) Internet Business Magazine's *UK Internet Business Yearbook 1998*; (ii) *The List* guide of U.K.

Internet service providers: thelist.internet.com/country/code/44.html (last accessed April 7, 1998); and (iii) The Nominet members' referral page, www.nic.uk/members.html (last accessed April 7, 1998).

6. Of the 106 questionnaires returned, five contained no information about employee numbers.

7. The average number of employees per organization was 19.68. However, this figure is not very informative given that it is larger than both the median number of employees—seven—and the seventy-fifth quartile of the sample distribution—sixteen. This suggests that a select number of respondents, employing many more employees than the average, may be influencing this value disproportionately. If the four largest outliers are eliminated, the average number of employees drops to 11.7.

8. Nomination specializes in registering names under the *uk.com* domain. As of May 1999 a fifth company, Net Register UK.CO Ltd., began to accept registrations in the *uk.co* domain using the Colombian country-code top-level domain. In late 1999, Netnames was acquired by NetBenefit.

9. Both of these variables, perceived importance and organization size, were measured on an ordinal scale that allowed the responses to be ranked in two ordered series. Therefore, the Spearman rank order correlation coefficient was used to test for measures of association between these variables.

10. The average number of domain names registered per month by the respondent organizations was 50.45. However, the fact that this figure is larger than both the median—ten—and the seventy-fifth quartile—twenty—of the sample distribution suggests that a select number of service providers, registering many more names than the average, may be influencing this value disproportionately.

11. Cybersquatting and cyberpiracy refer to instances where entities knowingly register domain names comprising another party's trademark or company name and subsequently hold the mark, or name, hostage until a rightful owner of the mark, or name, pays a requested price for its release.

12. *Domain Name Supporting Organization Name Council Statement on new gTLDs*, www.dnso.org/dnso/notes/20000419.NCgtlds-statement.html (last accessed May 1, 2000). For the report submitted to the Name Council regarding this issue see *Report (Part 1) of Working Group-C of the Domain Name Support Organization Internet Corporation for Assigned Names and Numbers*, www.dnso.org/dnso/notes/20000321.NCwgc-report.html, and *Addendum to Working Group-C Consensus Report to the Names Council*, www.dnso.org/dnso/notes/20000417.NCwgc-addendum.html (last accessed May 1, 2000).

13. Among other things, each applicant was required to pay a non-refundable US$50,000 application fee to ICANN. An overview of the application process is available online at: www.icann.org/tlds/application-process-03aug00.htm (last accessed August 4, 2000).

14. The introduction of these TLDs is discussed in greater detail in chapter 6.

15. See www.nunames.nu (last accessed July 1, 2001).

16. See internet.tv (last accessed July 1, 2001).

17. See www.nic.tm (last accessed July 1, 2001).

18. For an elaboration on the legal dimensions of identifiers as well as the similarities and differences between domain names and identifiers such as telephone numbers see Burk (1995); Gigante (1996); Andeen and King (1997); and Loundy (1997).

19. On July 23, 1998, the English Court of Appeals decided that cybersquatting constituted both passing off and trademark infringement in a suit that was brought by five

well known U.K. companies—Marks & Spencer plc., Ladbrokes plc., J. Sainsbury plc., Virgin Enterprises plc., and British Telecommunications plc.—against a company called One in a Million. The directors of the latter company had registered as domain names the well known company names of the plaintiffs. In maintaining that cybersquatters were liable for trademark infringement, the Court of Appeals found that these registrations had been unfair and detrimental because the domain names were registered merely to take advantage of the distinctive character and repute of the plaintiffs' trademarks. The court also found that although the domain names could have been used in a nondeceptive manner, there was a danger that the domain names could have been used in a fraudulent way. A full text of the court's decision is available at: www.nic.uk/news/oiam-appeal-judgement.html (last accessed January 19, 1999).

20. One respondent did not complete this particular question.

21. The fifth iteration of Network Solutions' Dispute Resolution Policy, effective as of February 25, 1998, may be found at: www.networksolutions.com/legal/dispute-policy.html (last accessed January 6, 2000).

22. A discussion of the various versions of NSI's dispute resolution policy, as well as legal and economic consequences, may be found at: www.patents.com/nsi.sht (last accessed February 22, 1999).

23. Interview with the author conducted on March 30, 1998.

24. Interview with the author conducted on May 1, 1998.

25. Interview with the author conducted on September 9, 1998.

26. Interview with the author conducted on June 4, 1998.

27. Interview with the author conducted on April 29, 1998.

28. Interview with the author conducted on May 13, 1998.

29. Interview with the author conducted on September 22, 1998.

30. Within this group there were three organizations that could be categorized as being micro firms, one as small-sized, five as composites, and one for which the number of employees was not included in the returned questionnaire.

Chapter 6

The Politics of Internet Governance

Basically we're making everyone unhappy which ironically may mean that we've reached an equal compromise between wildly divergent points of view.
—Shaw (1998)

Up to this point the narrative has centered primarily on the mediation of interests between social actors that have participated in the institutional reconfiguration of domain naming at both the national and international levels. In this chapter, I use the power-oriented framework proposed in chapter 3 to organize and illuminate a discussion about the relationship between the politicization of Internet architectures and the emergent, or changing, structure of regulation in the electronic context. This discussion is divided into three sections. The first reexamines the sociopolitical processes associated with the formation of ICANN. It highlights the ways in which shifting constellations of power relations between social agents transformed the administration and management of the DNS from a matter of technical coordination into a regulatory issue.

In the second section ICANN's activities since the autumn of 1998 are examined. Special attention is given to the development and implementation of the Uniform Dispute Resolution Policy (UDRP) and to the events surrounding the introduction of new generic top-level domains. Examining the sociopolitical processes associated with each of these undertakings and their consequences draws attention to the ways in which the interests of particular groups of social actors have been able to influence the governance trajectory that ICANN has embarked upon. In the last section of the chapter the discussion centers on how the empirical evidence derived from the institutional reconfiguration of Internet addressing at the international level, and within the British context, may be used to gain a critical perspective on contemporary theories of Internet governance.

Politics and Power in the ICANN Formation Process

The empirical evidence derived from the previous chapters suggests that each phase of the domain name wars was marked by periods of closure and usurpation that were related to shifts in the constellation of power relations between social actors. The highly politicized nature of the sociopolitical processes associated with the formation of ICANN reflected different actors' perceptions of the goals of this entity and how those goals might best be achieved, as well as the international context within which these events manifested themselves. The intensity of the debate appears also to have been directly related to, if not indicative of, the perceived economic significance of Internet addressing. The following are some of the key summary points that represent the evidence to support this view:

1. Much of the negotiating associated with the events preceding the formation of ICANN centered on broader issues pertaining to the governance of people's behavior on the Internet and World Wide Web.
2. A significant part of the controversies associated with the formation process was related to differences in the deep-structure interests of the actors who perceived themselves as having a stake in how the domain name system is managed.
3. Suppliers of registrar services appear to have played a relatively limited role in delineating the parameters of the constraints that would be placed on their domain name registration activities.
4. Both the United States government and the European Commission appear to have influenced heavily the outcome of the reconfiguration process.
5. Those representing trademark and intellectual property interests also appear to have influenced heavily the outcome of the reconfiguration process.

Prior to the commercialization of internetworking in the mid-1990s, the administration and management of the Internet domain name system was not generally perceived as being linked to issues of public policy or regulation. While internetworking remained primarily in the education and research realms, the way in which this addressing architecture was coordinated reflected a state of closure in so far as there was virtually no controversy about how it was managed. Network Solutions Inc. enjoyed a monopoly over the registration of names in the generic top-level domains, and IANA maintained *de facto* authority for overseeing the technical coordination of the domain name system. By the end of 1995 the dramatic increase in demand for domain names helped to fuel three major controversies about the established social order. The first area of contention centered around Network Solutions Inc.'s *first come, first served* registration policy and its approach to the resolution of domain name disputes. The second realm of debate focused on Network Solutions Inc.'s introduction of fees for the registering of names. The third set of disputes was largely limited to members of the Internet technical community and representatives of the United States government. It focused on the attempt by Jon Postel to have IANA chartered by the Internet Society (ISOC).

Of the three controversies noted above, by far the most notable of these, in terms of fermenting seeds of discontent about the established social order, was the introduction of fees for name registrations. This action transformed Network Solutions Inc.'s narrow right to register domain names from a mere government-subsidized contract into an extremely lucrative monopoly.[1] Responding to this action, Jon Postel recommended to the ISOC Board of Trustees that in order to "encourage good service at low prices," the existing social order should be altered in a manner that fostered competition between registration service providers.[2] Throughout the period spanning from September 1995 to June 1996 Postel released two proposals in the form of Internet drafts that sought to introduce 150 new top-level domains into the root. These new domains were to be managed by competing proprietary registries that paid a fixed fee plus a small percentage of their gross income into a fund managed by ISOC. In June 1996, Postel's second proposal was endorsed by ISOC.

This management structure was premised on a desire to: (i) provide IANA's activities with the international legal and financial umbrella of ISOC and (ii) maintain informal administrative arrangements that adhered to the view that the domain name system "should provide for the needs of the many rather than protecting the privileges of the few" (Postel 1996a:5). The evidence suggests that IANA and ISOC approached the issue of overhauling the administration of the domain name system as a technical matter wherein the *de facto* control they had exerted over the domain name system would simply evolve into a form of control that was legally constituted. In seeking to garner support for the Postel plan, the primary deep-structure strategy employed by these two actors seems to have been premised on naturalization. That is, regarding existing structures as inviolate. However, adherence to the traditional norms and values of internetworking failed to grant this initiative much legitimacy in the eyes an internationally diverse assortment of Internet stakeholders who questioned both the efficacy of these procedural and operational norms and the desirability of introducing new top-level domains into the legacy root.

In essence, the opposition encountered by the Postel plan, and the constellation of power relations it would have perpetuated, may be seen as indicative of differences in the deep-structure interests of various actors with a perceived stake in how the domain name system was managed and administered. These deep-structure interests can be classified into five conflicting groups (see table 6.1).

Throughout the summer of 1996 opponents of the IANA/ISOC framework challenged its legitimacy by employing a number of strategies oriented toward the creation of an alternative configuration of power relations. The actors who opposed this framework may be divided into two groups. The first consisted of representatives of trademark interests and the International Telecommunication Union (ITU). Representatives of these actors questioned the efficacy of treating the expansion of the number of available of top-level domains as being primarily a technical matter. Collectively, the interpretative frames and cognitive maps of the actors comprising this group were premised on creating regulatory mechanisms to constrain what they perceived as the negative externalities associated with the technological capabilities of the domain name system. Accordingly, the deep-structure interests of these two groups of actors corresponded with the tenets of what was described in chapter 2 as the commons school of thought. That is, they advocated the establishment of stable rules vis-à-vis property rights (intellectual and physical), means of exchange, and the enforcement of order on the basis of hierarchy.

Table 6.1: Actor Deep-Structure Interests

Actors:	Deep-Structure Interests
1. Network Solutions Inc.	Maintaining its monopoly status and converting its government contract to administer the *.com, .org, .net* domains into a private property right.
2. IANA/ISOC	Acquire authority over the administration of the legacy root and IP address space, thereby controlling how expansion of the system proceeds.
3. Holders of Trademark and Intellectual Property	Prevent further expansion of top-level domains in order to reduce scope of trademark conflicts, name speculation, and dilution.
4. Prospective Start-Up Registries	Expand the number of top-level domains and challenge IANA's authority to assess fees for entering the registry market.
5. International Telecommunication Union	Limit expansion of IANA and ISOC role outside the traditional Internet technical community. Enhance the ITU's role in the administration of the domain name system.

In seeking to enhance their role in determining how the addressing infrastructure was administered, these actors relied heavily on "higher order explanatory devices" (Deetz 1985:127) to challenge the IANA/ISOC initiative. For example, one influential ITU staff member who was highly critical of the IANA/ISOC framework argued that "the Internet has become far too commercial and strategically important as a global communications tool to simply perpetuate the same informal arrangements that have kept it glued together until now" (Shaw 1996). Similarly, representatives of trademark interests challenged the IANA/ISOC framework on the grounds that any increase in the number of top-level domains would hamper their already strained efforts at policing their intellectual property rights in the cyber-realm, and that registrations in these new domains would amount to a dilution and/or passing-off of their marks.

The second group of interests that also opposed the Postel plan comprised the entrepreneurial actors who sought to establish start-up registries. The influence of these actors pushed in the opposite direction to the first group. Their primary interest was based on a desire to enter the registry market by offering Internet users access to alternative top-level domains. In contrast to the first group of opponents, the deep-structure interests of this group of actors corresponded with the tenets of what was defined in chapter 3 as the decentralized school of thought. These actors appeared to support the view that the institutional norms that had evolved in tandem with the evolution of internetworking precluded the need for any external regulation of the domain name system or the creation of additional protective measures for trademarks and intellectual property. Although the Postel plan concurred with their calls for the creation of new top-level domains to be managed by proprietary registries, these entrepreneurial actors challenged the legitimacy of IANA's and ISOC's authority to levy fees for entering a new market.

By October 1996, the deep-structure strategies and surface-level politicking of the opponents of the Postel plan succeeded in undermining the perceived legitimacy of IANA's and ISOC's authority to create and implement a new administrative framework for managing the introduction of new top-level domains. In response to the legal, political, and economic issues that had arisen as a product of the controversies associated with this initiative the president of ISOC, Donald Heath, announced that a new panel, the Internet International Ad Hoc Committee (IAHC), would be formed to deal with the restructuring issue. This committee represented the creation of a coalition between the ISOC and its most powerful critics, thus signifying a shift in the constellation of power relations underpinning the administration of Internet addressing. More specifically, it may be seen as providing evidence to support the claim that the tactics employed by opponents of the Postel plan succeeded in shifting the issue of managing Internet addressing from the technical realm into the regulatory domain.

Four months after its formation, the IAHC released a final report that delineated the parameters of a new regulatory framework for managing and administering the Internet domain name system. The overarching framework of the proposed regulatory agenda was set out in the Generic Top-Level Domain Memorandum of Understanding (gTLD-MoU). There were three key features that distinguished this framework from the Postel plan. First, whereas the Postel framework proposed the creation of 150 new top-level domains, the gTLD-MoU restricted the expansion of new top-level domains to seven.[3] Second, while Postel had envisaged the creation of multiple proprietary for-profit registries competing against one another and Network Solutions Inc., this new framework defined domain name space as "a public resource" that was "subject to the public trust" (International Ad Hoc Committee 1997). As a result, the IAHC plan proposed the creation of a single nonprofit monopoly registry with a consortium of competing for-profit registrars sharing access to the same top-level domains (i.e. the Council of Registrars [CORE]) Third, and in contrast to Postel's attempt to distance the administration of the domain name system from trademark related disputes, the gTLD-MoU linked the administration of the domain name system to WIPO-based arbitration procedures for protecting trademarks and intellectual property rights.

The differences between the Postel and IAHC frameworks outlined above was indicative of the extent to which the latter model was imbued with the deep-structure interests of the actors who had comprised the IAHC panel. The gTLD-MoU upheld both IANA's and ISOC's deep-structure interest in main-taining authority over the root by making them members of a Policy Oversight Committee (POC) that was to be assigned stewardship over this core compo-nent of the addressing infrastructure.[4] The deep-structure interests of trademark and intellectual property holders were addressed by limiting the number of new top-level domains introduced into the root and proposing the establishment of WIPO-based mandatory arbitration mechanisms to protect their intellectual property rights.[5] As for the deep-structure interests of the ITU, these were fur-thered by the proposed governance framework through the incorporation of Internet addressing as an additional component of its role in administering global telecommunication resources. In granting primacy to the interests of this particular group of actors, however, the gTLD-MoU isolated Network Solutions Inc. and marginalized the concerns of proprietary registry advocates and other Internet stakeholders.

That said, the gTLD-MoU framework appears to have corresponded, broadly, with the deep-structure interests of U.K.-based domain name regis-trars. That is, it (i) proposed the establishment of a more stable approach to the management and administration of domain names than had existed previously; (ii) seemed to limit the amount of U.S.-based influence over Internet addressing by having the domain name system coordinated by a consortium of registrars operating as a Switzerland-based nonprofit corporation; (iii) introduced only a limited number of new top-level domains; and (iv) proposed a means of pro-tecting trademarks in the cyber-realm. In spite of this apparent symmetry of interests, however, only eight U.K.-based providers of Internet services signed the Memorandum of Understanding, while nine other U.K.-based service pro-viders registered to become domain name registrars under the auspices CORE (see table 6.2). During the course of this study, five of the seventeen companies listed in table 6.2 were interviewed. When queried about their rationales for signing up to this agreement, only one company representative expressed sup-port for the plan, while the four other interviewees noted that despite being opposed to its substantive content, they believed their organizations would be able to derive some economic benefit by being associated with it. This suggests that the deep-structure interests of these organizations were linked to issues of economic gain, rather than to broad concerns about the type of administrative regime that was created to oversee the domain name system.

It is worth bearing in mind that although proponents of the gTLD-MoU initiative sought to present this initiative as a fait accompli representing an international consensus, there remained a very high level of uncertainty regarding its implementation. Much of this uncertainty hinged on two factors that served to undermine the political legitimacy of this framework. Despite having allowed a six-week period for public comment between the release of the draft and final reports, the members of the IAHC panel were not able to successfully overcome the widely held perception that this framework had been promulgated through a closed process that failed to sufficiently represent the diverse interests of Internet stakeholders. The second source of uncertainty was fostered by the response of national governments, and, in particular, the United States government, to the attempts by gTLD-MoU proponents to present this framework as an international agreement signed under the auspices of the ITU.[6]

Table 6.2: U.K.-based CORE Registrars and gTLD-MoU Signatories

U.K.-based CORE Registrars	U.K.-based gTLD-MoU Signatories
General Internet Corporation	Argo Interactive Ltd
Just Results plc.	DESIGN.NET
Virtual Internet	Imminus
Business Names Registration	NetSearchers
Corpex	Oyster Systems Ltd
Netlink	Rebel Net
Demon UK	Siraat Solutions
Netnames International	VBCNet GB Ltd
Network Web Design Service	

Ultimately, the constellation of power relations proposed by the gTLD-MoU established a basic policy/legal model that created a quasi-governmental role for IANA, ISOC, the ITU, and WIPO. In so doing, this private sector-dominated initiative raised the decision making authority of the latter organizations to an international level without having involved national governments in the process. In response, both the European Commission and the United States government entered into the domain name fray, challenging the proposed constellation of power relations. More specifically, and in spite of the fact that the United States government favored a private sector-based approach to resolving the issue of managing Internet addressing, the gTLD-MoU's affiliation with the ITU served to antagonize certain members of the United States government who viewed it as an attempt to incorporate the Internet into the ITU-based telecommunication regime.[7] The European Commission also failed to give its support to the gTLD-MoU on the grounds that there had been insufficient governmental involvement in its development, and insisted that further public debate about the management of domain names was required. In the light of the controversies revolving around this initiative, and the impending

expiration of the cooperative agreement between the National Science Foundation and Network Solutions Inc. in July 1997 the United States government
issued a Notice of Inquiry to solicit public comments on, "the current and future
system(s) for the registration of domain names" (United States Department of
Commerce 1997:35896).

Drawing from the more than 400 comments it received in response to its
request for comments in late January 1998, the U.S. Department of Commerce
released a proposal for transferring stewardship of the domain name system to a
private sector-based administrative regime. This document became known as
the Green Paper. In comparison to the gTLD-MoU model, the constellation of
power relations proposed by this document implied a major reduction in the
potential influence of those representing trademark and intellectual property
interests, the ITU, and WIPO, while simultaneously enhancing the role of the
United States government in Internet administration. This document proposed
that the functions IANA had hitherto been responsible for (i.e., allocation of IP
address space, overseeing the operation of the authoritative root server, determining circumstances under which new top-level domains would be added to
the root, and protocol parameter assignment) would be taken over by a new
private not-for-profit corporation, headquartered in the United States and incorporated under United States law. Second, it proposed that during the period
of transition to private sector administration, there should be some experimentation with the introduction of five new top-level domains to be administered by
five new competing registries, each administering a single top-level domain.
Third, this document stipulated that rather than creating a "a monolithic
trademark dispute resolution process" (United States Department of Commerce
1998b), registries should establish their own minimum dispute resolution procedures with regard to trademark considerations.

The constellation of power relations proposed by this document was perceived as presenting a direct challenge to the interests of Internet stakeholders
who opposed government intrusions into this realm, as well as those who favored the adoption of a regulatory model for dealing with domain name related
matters. It is not too surprising therefore that the proposals contained within
the Green Paper were widely condemned as lacking international accountability
and being overly U.S.-centric. The creators of the gTLD-MoU lamented the
Green Paper's failure to mention their efforts in this realm arguing that "it is
inconceivable that any attempt to deal with the issue of top-level domains
would ignore an effort such as that embodied in the MoU."[8] Although it did not
respond officially to the request for comments about the Green Paper proposals,
the U.K. government also opposed this model, in part because it favored WIPO
involvement in the arbitration of domain name disputes. To this end, the former head of the DTI International Communications Policy Section suggested
that the Green Paper's approach to trademark dispute resolution was akin to
"throwing out the baby with the bath water."[9] Similarly, the European Commission responded that "the US proposals do not bring about any significant
improvements to the current situation, in particular with regard to the guaran-

tees given to holders of trademark rights when registering domain names" and requested the "opportunity to enter into full consultations with the United States before certain features of these proposals are implemented" (Council of the European Union 1998).

Drawing on the more than 650 comments it received in response to the Green Paper, the United States government released its final plan, the White Paper, in early June 1998 (United States Department of Commerce 1998a). This policy statement outlined the United States government's strategy for privatizing the administration of the domain name system in accordance with the notion of "private sector leadership." Drawing from the Green Paper, it was noted in this new document that the four principles guiding the evolution of the domain name system should be stability, competition, private bottom-up coordination, and representation. In addition, this policy framework insisted that the private sector, rather than the United States government, would be responsible for creating a new nonprofit corporation (Newco) to administer the Internet's name and address space. Once formed, the U.S. Department of Commerce would then formally recognize this entity and, over a two year period, transfer to it the functions of IP address space allocation, root server management, domain name system management, and protocol parameter assignment. In contrast to the contents of the Green Paper, the White Paper gave greater recognition to the concerns of trademark and intellectual property interests in so far as it called upon WIPO to initiate a process leading to the development of recommendations for: (i) a uniform approach to trademark/domain name disputes, (ii) protecting famous trademarks in generic top-level domains, and (iii) evaluating the effects of introducing new generic top-level domains.

Although the principles that were supposed to guide the privatization of Internet addressing seemed to parallel the norms and values that traditionally had underpinned the evolution of internetworking, their ambiguous nature perpetuated a situation wherein most actors believed that their particular positions had been endorsed by the White Paper (Shaw 1998). For example, those actors who viewed this issue as a regulatory matter did not perceive any incongruities between the creation of a regulatory agenda for the administration of the domain name system and the principles of stability, competition, private bottom-up coordination, and representation. Likewise, those actors who opposed the linking of domain naming with a regulatory agenda concluded that the White Paper had sanctioned a process for creating a new corporation whose remit would be limited largely to technical coordination. Moreover, and as Mueller (1999b:498) has correctly observed, the rhetoric of "self-regulation" upon which these principles were premised served to further obscure the issue of "whether the *power* exercised by the institution [the new corporation] is governmental in nature and whether that power is adequately circumscribed by law, market forces, and internal checks and balances." Ultimately, this ambiguity manifested itself clearly in the way in which the White Paper's call for "private sector leadership" was approached by different actors during the final phase of the domain name wars.

The institutional formation process initiated by the release of the White Paper was characterized by two parallel streams of activity, each involving different groupings of social agents and alternative visions about how to proceed with the formation of the new corporation. The first stream comprised the activities of the International Forum on the White Paper (IFWP). This organization convened a series of public meetings, during July and August 1998, whose aim was to establish a consensus on the founding principles for the new corporation proposed in the White Paper.[10] Many of the actors who participated in these activities seemed to have interpreted this policy statement as entailing a call for Internet stakeholders to set aside past differences and make a fresh start at forging a consensus on the structure and powers of the new corporation.

Although the IFWP created an electronic discussion list focusing on issues pertaining to the formation of a new corporation and held one of its meetings in Geneva, relatively few of the participants were U.K.-based domain name registrars. This lack of participation, however, did not appear to be related to a lack of support for the IFWP's activities. Rather, both the interview and survey results presented in chapter 5 confirmed that it seems to have been related to a general sense among these organizations that the uncertainties associated with the regime formation process were of relatively little importance to their commercial activities. In addition, the analysis of the data collected regarding the reputational power of actors involved in the restructuring process implied that this relative lack of participation may also have been linked to the sense that U.K.-based registrars did not view themselves, or other IFWP participants, as having sufficient influence to effect change.

The second stream of activity sparked by the release of the White Paper involved a series of interactions involving actors who empathized, albeit in varying degrees, with various elements of the regulatory agenda propagated earlier through the gTLD-MoU. For example, despite expressing support for the principles of the White Paper, the European Commission continued to call for a creation of advisory roles vis-à-vis the new corporation for international organizations such as WIPO and the ITU on the grounds that "there will be certain policy issues where a self-regulatory body will in practice have to respect public policy" (Wilkinson 1998). Similarly, representatives of trademark interests also expressed support for the principles of the White Paper while maintaining that "problems arising out of the use of trade marks, trade names and other distinctive signs on the Internet, and potential conflicts with domain names ... should be addressed at an international level in a forum such as WIPO" (Gymer 1998). For their part, IANA and ISOC began to draft articles of incorporation and bylaws aimed at entrenching a hierarchical set of power relations, devolved from the two latter entities, into the core of the new corporation. Moreover, away from the public domain, and with input from the U.S. Department of Commerce, the European Commission, and IBM,[11] IANA and ISOC also began to contact prospective members of the new corporation's interim board of directors.

Lessig (1998c) offers the following synopsis of the differences between the

IANA and IFWP approaches to the process of corporation building:

> IANA thus proceeded as IFWP did to develop its own view in the way that it thought such views should be developed. IANA in a process of comments and drafts that it ultimately controlled; IFWP in an extraordinarily messy but public process, with meetings that its directors could not control. Both processes had a claim of legitimacy; but each represented the views of the net in a different way.

The differences between the IANA and IFWP processes to which Lessig alludes focus on the policy formation process itself. The approach of IANA toward the development of Internet-related policies was based on what Rony and Rony (1998:122) call "authority by announcement." Traditionally, IANA would issue a proposal and community feedback would be sought, with subsequent proposals incorporating the views expressed in earlier iterations. This process would then continue until it was felt that interested parties had reached a "rough consensus," at which point, the contents of the "consensus" proposal would be implemented as policy. The IFWP process, on the other hand, altered these norms. Now, interested parties were hashing out their ideas in a relatively unstructured manner in the hope of achieving a "rough consensus" that could be articulated in the form of a document at a later date.

By September 1998 it had become clear that no consensus existed between the deep-structure interests of the actors who had participated in these differing approaches to establishing a new addressing regime. On the one hand, the participants in the IFWP process had succeeded in establishing a rough consensus about the principles for the new corporation. Broadly speaking, these principles may be seen as paralleling the management structure of Nominet in so far as they called for the creation of a membership organization, and envisaged a separation of powers between its board of directors, and the management of the corporation. In contrast, the IANA and ISOC frameworks proposed the creation of a closed structure wherein there would be no members per se and very few checks placed on the power of the members of the board of directors.[12] Throughout the month of September, participants in the second stream succeeded in undermining the IFWP process by continuing to participate in behind-the-scenes negotiations with both some members of the IFWP steering committee and Network Solutions Inc. As a result of these negotiations, IANA and ISOC were able to subvert attempts by the IFWP to arrange a final wrap-up meeting aimed at transforming its international consensus into a framework for outlining the bylaws and articles of incorporation for the new corporation.

On October 2, 1998, IANA submitted its proposal for the new corporation, the Internet Corporation for Assigned Names and Numbers (ICANN), and its list of interim members of the board of directors, to the United States National Telecommunications and Information Administration (NTIA). Shortly thereafter, two additional proposals were submitted to the NTIA—one from the Open Root Server Confederation, a grouping of proprietary registry advocates who had the backing of Network Solutions Inc. and another from an informal grouping of ICANN critics calling themselves the Boston Working Group. In the light of the concerns raised in the latter two proposals about the account-ability (fiscal and representational) and structure of ICANN, the NTIA ordered the new corporation to address these issues by amending its bylaws. In subse-quent weeks ICANN made some minor changes to its bylaws, including a commitment to create an open membership structure. However, these altera-tions did little to assuage the concerns of those who were dismayed by the closed and secretive way in which this organization had been formed. Subse-quently, on November 25, 1998, the U.S. Department of Commerce officially sanctioned a new form of closure around the administration of Internet ad-dressing by recognizing ICANN as the entity it would work with to effect the transition to private sector administration of the domain name system. Com-menting on these events, one prominent observer characterized them as being "not a promising start for the process of self-governance on the Internet" be-cause "rather than something different, IANA gives us politics as usual: Insid-ers, in closed meetings, answering to ideas and arguments as only they think best" (Lessig 1998a).

The latter quote highlights succinctly the fact that ICANN was, in essence, the product of behind-the-scenes surface-level politicking between actors who shared a common deep-structure interest in asserting their influence over the structure and operation of a private sector-based Internet governance regime. That is, IANA and ISOC, the United States government, the European Com-mission, other national governments, multilateral organizations, as well as those representing trademark and intellectual property interests were able to align themselves in such a way as to ensure that the new corporation reflected their concerns about how the domain name system was managed and adminis-tered. However, this surface-level politicking failed to address many of the deep-structure concerns of other Internet stakeholders. Specifically, given the failure of participants in the IFWP and IANA camps to reach a deep-structure consensus about the organizational and administrative parameters of this entity, ICANN may be seen as embodying the deep-structure interests of a particular conglomeration of social actors. Consequently, the perceived legitimacy of its authority for managing and administering the domain name system remains tenuous (Clausing 1998a, 1998b; Froomkin 2000b; Lessig 1998b; Mueller 1999b; Post 1998; Weinberg 2000).

Ironically, both opponents and supporters of ICANN have drawn upon the IETF paradigm to engage in deep-structure strategies aimed at advancing their respective causes. On the one hand, some defenders of ICANN have used neu-tralization and legitimation strategies emphasizing the meritocratic nature of IETF standards making activities in attempting to enhance the credibility of this entity. For example, Shaw (1999) has argued that although terms like "private-sector," "bottom-up," and "self-governance" are often associated with the IETF, such rhetoric "reflects a deep and profound misunderstanding of the IETF" when it is simultaneously linked to the concept of democracy. Other supporters of ICANN have even attempted to promote the view that it did indeed reflect an international stakeholder-based consensus by claiming that it signified "an unprecedented effort by Internet business, technical, noncommercial and academic communities to create a globally representative nongovernmental policymaking entity" (Global Internet Project).

Critics of ICANN, on the other hand, have employed similar deep-structure tactics to emphasize the contrast between the open, consensus building aspects of the IETF paradigm and the way in which ICANN was initially created and currently oversees the administration of the DNS.[13] For instance, in pointing out the extent to which the remit of ICANN transcends the realm of technical coordination, Post (1999) asks, "Who decided that the bottom-up, decentralized, consensus based governance structures under which the Internet grew and flourished are incompatible with its continued growth and development?" Likewise, in a scathing review of ICANN's first year of operation, Mueller (1999b:520) concludes that "a fundamental untruth festers at ICANN's core" because "the rhetoric of market liberalism was cynically abused to gloss over the true nature of the transition."

Politics and Power in ICANN

At the time of this writing, ICANN has been overseeing the administration and management of the Internet domain name system for slightly more than two years. In that time there have been a number of important addressing-related development of which two, in particular, stand out because of their implications for the governance trajectory of internetworking. The first is the development and implementation of the Uniform Dispute Resolution Policy (UDRP). The second involves the decision to introduce seven new generic top-level domains into the root. The deep-structure and surface-level politicking associated with these actions and its influence on decision outcomes serves to illustrate the extent to which ICANN's activities have transcended an agenda of technical coordination to encompass the making and enforcement of regulatory policy for the Internet.

The WIPO, ICANN, and the UDRP

The relationship between domain names and trademarks has been, and remains, one of the most highly contentious aspects of the public Internet. In fact, the demands by intellectual property holders for greater protection from infringements of their rights in online environments has been a core driving force in the institutional reconfiguration of Internet addressing. During the latter half of the 1990s, Network Solutions Inc. consistently grappled with this issue but failed to find a satisfactory solution to this intractable problem. The IAHC, and its gTLD-MoU framework sought to address this issue by appointing the WIPO as the sole arbiter for dealing with any intellectual property-related disputes arising from conflicts between trademark holders and domain name registrants who may not have registered trademarks. Advocates of WIPO involvement in resolving trademark/domain name disputes primarily employed deep-structure strategies based on neutralization and legitimation to garner support for its participation in this forum. They drew on its linkage to the United Nations to advance the view that it was a neutral entity best suited to protecting the intellectual property related interests of Internet stakeholders throughout the world. Many of the actors who opposed the gTLD-MoU, on the other hand, rejected this view and questioned, among other things, whether the WIPO's mandate for protecting and promoting intellectual property would impede its ability to act as a neutral expert body for adjudicating trademark/domain name disputes. Given the divisive nature of the debates surrounding this issue, the WIPO quickly came to be identified by advocates of the rapid deployment of new generic top-level domains as being an entity that was acting in collusion with those who opposed the introduction of new top-level domains and who sought to expand the rights of existing trademark holders in the electronic realm.

Responding to the White Paper's call for the WIPO to develop recommendations for resolving problems arising from the intersection of domain names and trademarks, it initiated the *Internet Domain Name Process* in early July 1998. This process got under way with the release of RFC 1, a document which set out the issues that the WIPO proposed to seek to address, and a schedule for doing so.[14] Drawing on the sixty-six comments received in response to its call[15] and those of a panel of experts appointed to consult with WIPO staff on this matter, in September 1998 the WIPO issued its formal terms of reference for the *Internet Domain Name Process* in RFC 2. This document outlined that, the WIPO planned to make recommendations about: (1) dispute prevention; (2) dispute resolution; (3) a process for protecting famous and well-known marks in the generic top-level domains; and (4) the effects on intellectual property rights of new top-level domains (World Intellectual Property Organization (WIPO) 1998a:12).

Throughout the autumn of 1998, the WIPO consultation process involved a combination of eleven public meetings held in an internationally diverse range of cities, and online consultations.[16] The outcome of these meetings and online submissions served as the basis for *RFC 3—Interim Report of the WIPO Internet Domain Name Process.* Released on December 23, 1998, this report contained the first draft of the WIPO's proposed recommendations for "a uniform approach to resolving trademark/domain name disputes involving cyberpiracy" (United States Department of Commerce 1998a). Among the most noteworthy proposals contained in the Interim Report were recommendations to: (i) enhance and expand the veracity of the contact information provided by domain name registrants when registering names, thereby facilitating their identification by intellectual property owners who believe their rights are being infringed by registrants; (ii) require domain name applicants to agree to submit to a mandatory dispute resolution procedure administered by the WIPO when disputes over names arise; and (iii) introduce a mechanism allowing owners of famous or well-known marks to obtain an exclusion whose effect would prohibit third parties from registering the mark as a domain name. There was one other striking feature of this report. Namely, it offered no clear definition of cybersquatting, but rather equated it with the broad and ambiguous notion of "making the abusive registration of a domain name" (WIPO 1998b:244).

Following the release of the Interim Report, an additional series of public meetings were held in six cities. Expounding upon his experiences as a member of the WIPO's panel of experts during the consultation process, Michael Froomkin (2000a:11) writes,

[the] turnout at the meetings was not on the whole very impressive. The 11 regional consultations following RFC 2 averaged 77 persons, with a very uneven geographic distribution ranging from 30 in Cape Town to 160 in Asunción. The six meetings following RFC 3 averaged just under 70 people, ranging from 48 in Toronto to 117 in Dakar. I only attended one meeting in the first round and four of the final six meetings, but it was my strong impression that the very large majority of the speakers, and indeed the attendees, at those events were either intellectual property rights holders, their lawyers, their trade associations, or Internet Service Providers. There were a few representatives from user groups, *but only a few* [emphasis added].

In addition to the public meetings, interested parties were given until March 19, 1999[17] to electronically submit their comments about the Interim Report to the WIPO. The 196 comments received by the WIPO in response to this document expressed varying degrees of support for the proposed framework and/or specific aspects of it.[18] Although the report seemed to correspond, in principle, with the deep-structure interests of intellectual property holders, some trademark representatives argued that the proposed framework still did not offer them sufficient protection. Other actors, and in particular, those who had previously opposed the gTLD-MoU raised an assortment of objections about this framework and the constellation of power relations that it was likely to perpetuate. These concerns were, perhaps, most clearly summarized in Froomkin's (1999b) detailed critique of the draft proposals. In his response to the Interim Report he highlighted a number of factors which, collectively, suggested that RFC 3 was unfairly biased in favor of intellectual property holders. Included among the problematic issues were the proposed policy's broad scope, the failure to offer sufficient protection of free speech interests, the failure to balance the requirement that domain name registrants provide accurate detailed contact information with privacy protections, and the expansion of protections enjoyed by holders of famous or well-known marks.

The *Final Report on the WIPO Internet Domain Name Process* was released on April 30, 1999, and contained forty-four recommendations for dealing with intellectual property disputes concerning domain names (World Intellectual Property Organization (WIPO) 1999). By the time of its release, the WIPO had convened seventeen public meetings and had received in excess of 300 written submissions from professional associations, governments, intergovernmental organizations, corporations, and individuals. Nonetheless, Froomkin (2000a:17) cautions against reading too much into these numbers noting that "what the numbers do not tell you, however, is how much or little WIPO publicized the meetings and website, or to whom, and how lopsided (from my admittedly partisan perspective, of course) the participation in those meetings was—especially before a very small number of observers concerned about the process mounted a campaign to broaden awareness."

There were two main features that distinguished the Interim Report from the Final Report. First, whereas the Interim Report had not included a clear definition of cybersquatting, within the Final Report an attempt had been made to refine the notion of "abusive registrations" in a manner that was more in line with the definitions that have been emerging in case law throughout the world. Second, the scope of the types of cases for which the proposed dispute arbitration procedures would be applicable were narrower in the Final Report than in the Interim Report. However, and very controversially, the recommendations regarding the protection of famous or well-known marks remained essentially unchanged from that which had been proposed in the previous document.

The initial response to the Final Report was mixed and reflected the longstanding factional positions of the actors who were participating in these events. Many holders of intellectual property interests asserted that the new report was too limited in its scope and that its recommendations were not sufficiently extensive. In contrast, those actors who opposed the report in principle, and/or specific aspects thereof, expressed dismay both at the prospect of domain name registrants being subject to a process of mandatory arbitration and the fact that the controversial recommendations regarding the protection of famous or well-known marks remained. Expressing this concern, one prominent observer commented, "the prevailing assumption of the WIPO Report is that the Internet's raison d' être is e-commerce—a global marketplace dominated by trademarks and brands. . . . I suppose expecting a balanced report from an organization that exists to promote intellectual property rights is akin to asking a fox to guard the hen house" (Rony 1999).

The purpose of the WIPO's *Internet Domain Name Process* was to make advisory recommendations to Newco/ICANN about the interface between domain names and intellectual property rights. According to the terms of the White Paper, after further considerations ICANN would then be responsible for determining which aspects of the Final Report to implement and how. It is important to bear in mind, however, that the WIPO consultation process occurred concurrently with the events that led to the formal creation of ICANN and its supporting organizations. In fact, the Final Report was not made public until approximately six months after the establishment of ICANN and one month before the interim board of directors of the new corporation was scheduled to hold its third public meeting in Berlin.

The timing of the report's release gave rise to three major concerns among interested parties. The first focused on whether a period of one month provided both ICANN and other interested parties with sufficient time to carefully analyze the WIPO's recommendations and reach a consensus-based decision about whether or not to adopt its proposals. Second, during the period from November 1998 to May 1999 various actors had been involved with efforts to formalize the structures of ICANN's supporting organizations.[19] These structures were scheduled to be formally endorsed at the Berlin meeting. This meant that the yet-to-be constituted Domain Name Supporting Organization would not have time to review and comment upon the proposed WIPO framework. Third, and related to the latter issue, was the fact that the members of the interim board of directors who potentially would be making a decision about the WIPO plan had not been elected by the membership. For many observers and Internet stakeholders, the prospect of an unelected board deciding to adopt the WIPO framework, or elements of it, without having received prior input from members of ICANN's supporting organizations was antithetical to the principle of bottom-up decision making based on rough consensus.

Not too surprisingly, this state of affairs led to a proliferation of surface-level and deep-structure politicking among interested parties in the weeks leading up to the Berlin meeting. For example, in excess of seventy-five actors including service providers, scholars, technologists, Internet users, policy analysts, and four members of the WIPO's panel of experts submitted a petition to the ICANN board requesting that they defer from adopting any of the recommendations contained in the Final Report until the Domain Name Supporting Organization was constituted and an "accountable," elected board of directors was in place. Other actors, however, and in particular representatives of intellectual property interests, emphasized the need for the recommendations to be adopted as quickly as possible in order to avoid any further delay in moving forward with the development of protections for trademarks and intellectual property. At their core, these contrasting priorities paralleled the deep-structure tensions that had preceded the formation of ICANN and which continue to impact upon this organization's ability to convey legitimacy. At issue here is the conflict between the need to ensure that ICANN develops and implements policy in a timely manner and the need to ensure that its policy making procedures and structures adhere to the principle of representative, bottom-up, consensus-based decision making.

After a closed session held during the Berlin meeting, the members of interim board announced their endorsement of the principles of the WIPO Final Report, and in particular, the implementation of a uniform dispute resolution policy for all registrars that register names in the *.com, .net*, and *.org* top-level domains.[20] However, they deferred any final adoption of the report's specific recommendations until a public meeting scheduled for August 25-26, 1999, in Santiago, Chile. In addition, the structure of the Domain Name Supporting Organization (DNSO)[21] and six of its seven constituencies,[22] as well as the Protocol Supporting Organization (PSO)[23] were formally endorsed. Although the DNSO was still lacking a constituency representing individual and non-commercial domain name holders, the board asked the other constituents of the DNSO to use to the three months leading up to the Santiago meeting to develop proposals for moving forward with the specific recommendations contained in the WIPO report. In taking it upon themselves to endorse, in principle, the WIPO's Final Report before the DNSO was in place and its constituencies had had sufficient time to analyze its contents, the board essentially circumvented the deep-structure concerns of a large number of Internet stakeholders and violated the principle of bottom-up decision making based on the principle of rough consensus. As a consequence, the partisan positions of concerned actors became even further entrenched, assertions that ICANN was dominated by a particular group of interests gained further credence, and the complicated task of building trust and framing uncertainties in a manner that conveyed credibility to ICANN was further impeded.

A few weeks later, a working group comprised of various members of the DNSO's constituencies formed what was, in essence, a "restricted"[24] working group to examine the WIPO recommendations. At the end of July, the working group submitted its final report to the Names Council of the DNSO which approved this proposal and forwarded it to the ICANN board. However, the proposal was set aside by the board in favor of a different set of proposals voluntarily drafted by a group of domain name registrars. Based on these proposals, on August 26, 1999, the ICANN board resolved to adopt a uniform dispute resolution policy for accredited registrars in the *.com*, *.net*, and *.org* top-level domains, with the understanding that the documents concerning its implementation would be prepared by a "drafting committee" consisting of ICANN's counsel and select individuals chosen by the ICANN staff.[25] One month later ICANN released for public comment its draft Uniform Dispute Resolution Policy.[26] Despite the fact that a public meeting was scheduled for the first week of November in Los Angeles, on October 24, 1999, members of the interim board formally adopted the Uniform Domain Name Dispute Resolution Policy (UDRP) during a teleconference. In December 1999, the first trademark/domain name dispute was resolved under the new policy.

The primary objective of the UDRP is to provide a mechanism for resolving cybersquatting related trademark/domain name disputes in a timely and relatively inexpensive manner. Simply put, it seeks to offer a means for avoiding the high costs of litigation associated with seeking redress for wrongful online trademark infringements in national courts.[27] Under its terms domain name registrants are required to submit to a process of mandatory arbitration conducted when a complainant asserts that:

(i) The domain name is identical or confusingly similar to a trademark or service mark in which the complainant has rights; and
(ii) The domain name holder has no rights or legitimate interests in respect to the domain name; and
(iii) The domain name has been registered and is being used in bad faith (ICANN 1999: Article 4[a]).

The policy states explicitly that all three of the above elements must be present in order for a complainant to succeed and stipulates that evidence of "bad faith" includes:

(i) circumstances indicating that the registrant has registered or acquired the domain name primarily for the purpose of selling, renting, or otherwise transferring the domain name registration to the complainant who is the owner of the trademark or service mark or to a competitor of that complainant, for valuable consideration in excess of the registrant's out-of-pocket costs directly related to the domain name; or

(ii) the registrant has registered the domain name in order to prevent the owner of the trademark or service mark from reflecting the mark in a corresponding domain name, provided that the registrant has engaged in a pattern of such conduct; or

(iii) the registrant has registered the domain name primarily for the purpose of disrupting the business of a competitor; or

(iv) by using the domain name, the registrant has intentionally attempted to attract, for commercial gain, Internet users to the registrant's web site or other online location, by creating a likelihood of confusion with the complainant's mark as to the source, sponsorship, affiliation, or endorsement of the registrants web site or location or of a product or service on the registrant's web site or location (ICANN 1999: Article 4[b]).

In order to defend itself from the charge of bad faith, the registrant must be able to present evidence that:

(i) before any notice to the registrant of the dispute, the registrants use of, or demonstrable preparations to use, the domain name or a name corresponding to the domain name in connection with a bona fide offering of goods or services; or

(ii) the registrant (as an individual, business, or other organization) has been commonly known by the domain name, even if the registrant has acquired no trademark or service mark rights; or

(iii) the registrant is making a legitimate noncommercial or fair use of the domain name, without intent for commercial gain to misleadingly divert consumers or to tarnish the trademark or service mark at issue (ICANN 1999: Article 4[c]).

Perhaps the most controversial aspect of the UDRP is the right of complainants to select which arbitration provider will administer their dispute(s).[28] Initially, ICANN accredited three dispute resolution service providers on the premise that this would help to foster a competitive environment for dispute resolution. The first three service providers to be accredited were the World Intellectual Property Organization's Arbitration and Mediation Center, based in Switzerland; the National Arbitration Forum of the USA (NAF); and the eResolution consortium, based in Canada. In June 2000, ICANN accredited another U.S.-based company, the CPR Institute for Dispute Resolution. This was followed, in December 2001, with the accreditation of the Asian Domain Name

Dispute Resolution Center (ADNDRC).[29] Rather than fostering competition, however, the right of complainants to choose their arbitration provider has helped to perpetuate a phenomenon known as forum shopping. That is, the policy facilitates the ability of complainants to select service providers that tend to decide most frequently in their favor.

Given that trademark holders are invariably the complainants, critics of the UDRP assert that it is fundamentally biased in favor of intellectual property interests. Drawing on the data emerging from the more than 4000 disputes involving more than 7000 domain names,[30] since the UDRP was put into practice the results of two recent empirical studies provide compelling evidence to substantiate this claim. Mueller's (2000) study of the arbitration outcomes during the first year of the UDRP's operation identified a statistically significant positive correlation between the market share of service providers and their tendency to withdraw domain names from respondents. Consistent with this finding, Geist's (2001) study reveals that as of July 2001, and in spite of charging the highest fees, the WIPO had the largest share of the overall UDRP caseload and that complainants were winning the vast majority of the cases it deals with. In contrast, and despite charging the lowest fees, eResolutions,[31] a service provider that tended to be less complainant-friendly than the WIPO or the NAF in terms of win percentages, commanded only a minimal percentage of the UDRP caseload. Both Mueller and Geist argue that the lack of systemic fairness arising from forum shopping, the lack of transparency associated the arbitration processes, and the lack of predictable decision outcomes point to the need for reforming the UDRP in a way that strikes a better balance between the interests of intellectual property holders and other domain name registrants.

In undertaking this policy initiative ICANN clearly transcended an agenda of "technical coordination" and has entered into the realm of regulatory policy making, or global Internet policy (Post 1999). This is evidenced by the fact that the UDRP has created a small number of global online courts (i.e. the dispute resolution service providers) that are responsible for adjudicating disputes on the basis of a single set of rules implemented through a contractual arrangement between registrars and domain name registrants. The terms of the UDRP stipulate that domain name registrants in the *.com*, *.net*, and *.org* name spaces are subject to mandatory arbitration with one of ICANN's approved administrative dispute resolution service providers should a dispute arise with a trademark owner. However, in order to be accredited by ICANN, domain name registrars are required to include the terms of the UDRP in their registration contracts with their domain name customers.[32] Moreover, under the terms of article 3, sections A and C, of Network Solutions Inc. Registry Agreement with ICANN, Network Solutions Inc. cannot list registrations from any registrars that fail to include the UDRP in their registration contracts.[33] All told, this dimension of ICANN's activities plainly reflects the imposition of constraints on both the structure and users of the generic top-level domain name space in a top-down manner to achieve a regulatory end.

Introduction of New gTLDs

The notion of expanding the number of available generic top-level domains (gTLDs) is an issue that has been at the core of the deliberations associated with the institutional reconfiguration of Internet addressing. Shortly after Network Solutions Inc. began to levy fees for registering domain names, Jon Postel put forth a proposal for introducing 150 new top-level domains into the root, to be managed and administered by fifty competing proprietary registries. The level of controversy generated by his proposal revealed that despite its technological feasibility, many Internet stakeholders did not view the deployment of new gTLDs as being merely a technological matter. Whereas the advocates of expansion claimed that access to additional gTLDs would encourage competition and create alternate entry points to the gTLD name space, those opposed to this idea asserted that a number of social, political, and economic factors needed to be considered before any such action was implemented. These actors maintained that new gTLDs were likely to foster further trademark infringements, create confusion among users, and potentially undermine the stability of the Internet.

The gTLD-MoU framework also proposed the introduction new gTLDs, however, it sought to reduce the likelihood of any potentially negative consequences manifesting themselves by limiting the number of new gTLDs to seven, with competition taking place between registrars rather than registries. It was claimed that this, combined with its proposals for dealing with trademark/domain names disputes, would ensure "coherence, utility and efficient accessibility of the DNS name space to the constituency of the Internet" (International Ad Hoc Committee 1997:10). In contrast to the gTLD-MoU recommendations, the contents of the Green Paper indicated that the United States government favored experimentation with the introduction of five new top-level domains to be administered by five new competing registries, each overseeing a single gTLD. By the time the White Paper was released, the pendulum had shifted once again with the United States government declaring that responsibility for implementing any new gTLDs and for determining whether for-profit registries would be incorporated into the domain name system would be divested to the Newco.

In the weeks immediately following ICANN's Berlin meeting in May 1999, two DNSO-based working groups were established to formulate recommendations pertaining to the deployment of new gTLDs. The first of these was Working Group B. Focusing upon the recommendations set out in chapter four of the WIPO's Final Report, it was chartered to identify a consensus position about a mechanism for the granting exclusions to famous and well-known marks if and when new gTLDs were deployed. This working group was comprised of more than 120 participants, the majority of which were trademark attorneys and/or brand managers. The second entity was Working Group C. Its remit centered upon trying to identify a consensus position about whether there should be new gTLDs, and if so, the speed with which they should be added to the root. This working group was comprised of approximately 140 members, representing a much broader array of interests than was present in Working Group B.

Over the course of the next year the members of each working group participated in in-depth, and often heated, discussions about the introduction of new generic top-level domains.[34] In spite of the fact that it had been almost four years since the release of Postel's initial proposal, the deliberations regarding this matter had not, in essence, progressed very far in that time. Instead, the level of deep-structure and surface-level politicking that occurred between participants in these working groups was partisan in nature and reflected long standing factional divisions. Advocates of gTLD expansion continued to insist on the social, political, and economic desirability of creating new top-level name spaces. They maintained that the introduction of new gTLDs would foster competition, maximize user choice, and help to reduce trademark infringements because identical names could be distinguished on the basis of the gTLDs under which they were registered. Those actors opposed to the introduction of new gTLDs, on the other hand, asserted that the perceived need for new gTLDs was illusory, the commercial and social benefits of introducing new gTLDs were far from clear, and no new gTLDs should be deployed until functional safeguards were in place to protect the interests of intellectual property holders.

On March 21, 2000, Working Group C presented its final report to the DNSO Names Council.[35] This document stated that the participants had reached a rough consensus on two issues: (i) ICANN should add new gTLDs to the root;[36] and (ii) the initial deployment of new gTLDs should consist of six to ten new gTLDs followed by an evaluation period. In addition, the report noted that among both the supporters and opponents of the consensus call,[37] there appeared to exist a view that "ICANN's selection process should be procedurally regular and guided by pre-announced selection criteria" and the "name space should have room for both limited-purpose gTLDs (which have a charter that substantially limits who can register there) and open, general-purpose gTLDs." Approximately one month later, the DNSO Names Council passed a resolution recommending that the ICANN board adopt "a policy for the introduction of new gTLDs in a measured and responsible manner."[38]

On the day before the Names Council passed its resolution, it was presented with the Working Group B Formal Report.[39] This document stated that its participants also had reached consensus conclusions on two items. The members appeared to support the view that (i) there did not exist a need for creating a universally famous marks list at this point in time; and (ii) the protection afforded to trademark owners should be contingent upon the type of top-level domain (i.e. limited purpose versus general purpose). Aside from these conclusions, there were two additional elements of the report that are particularly noteworthy. In his concluding remarks, Michael Palage, the chairperson of Working Group B, indicated that some members of the group were concerned that the proposal to deploy six to ten new top-level domains was "overly ambitious considering we have failed to identify the specific safeguards designed to protect the trademark interests."

Second, on the day prior to the submission deadline for the report, representatives of the Intellectual Property Constituency had submitted a position paper to Palage. It recommended the creation of a sunrise period to be incorporated into the rollout of any new top-level domains. According to this proposal, owners of trademarks and service marks would be able to register their marks, as well as twenty variations of the mark, as domain names on a first-come, first-served basis in any new top-level domains prior to the new domain being opened to the general public. Although there had been insufficient time for all members of the working group to vet this proposal, the Formal Report concluded that the notion of establishing a sunrise period "has strong support in the registrar and IP communities."

Over the course of the next six weeks there was much heated discussion about this concept. While the supporters of the sunrise framework argued that it was a pragmatic solution to addressing the concerns of intellectual property holders, its critics claimed that it was technologically unfeasible, marked an expansion of intellectual property rights that was unfounded in law, and greatly expanded the scope of Working Group B's charter. By the time Working Group B's Final Report was presented to the Names Council, on May 15, 2000, no consensus had been reached on the type of protection mechanism that should be incorporated into the process of deploying new gTLDs.[40]

Perhaps the most striking feature of the statements emerging from both working groups was the breadth of their scope. This reflected the fact that participants in these two group simply could not reach any consensus on the specific policy issues raised by deploying new top-level domains (e.g. the principles for determining how new domains would be selected; whether the registries should be for-profit or not-for-profit). Given the diverse array of actors and interests with a perceived stake in the selection and deployment of new gTLDs, and the extent to which long standing partisan positions had become entrenched, this outcome was not particularly surprising. Commenting on these events Jonathan Weinberg (2001:323), the chairperson of Working Group C, points out that "the DNSO contribution left ICANN staff almost entirely free to craft its own proposal to the Board regarding the introduction of new gTLDs, and that is what staff did." This suggests that at this stage in the process the supposed decentralized decision making powers of the DNSO and Names Council were effectively transferred, by default, to the ICANN staff who subsequently assumed the role of purposeful agents.

One month before ICANN's July board meeting, in Yokohama, the ICANN staff prepared a document for public comment containing seventy-four questions to be addressed before new top-level domains were deployed.[41] Although this questionnaire was presented as a discussion document, its contents appeared to be tacitly proposing the creation of a particular configuration of power relations. For example, the authors of this document seemed to have assumed that some of the successful applicants would operate on a for-profit basis, thereby dispelling the notion that the new top-level domain name registries would be nonprofit ventures. Moreover, this document inferred that the process of deploying new top-level domains would proceed on the basis of ICANN selecting a very limited number of top-level domains according to the business, financial, and technical plans it received from prospective registry operators. This effectively prevented any possibility of first identifying potentially desirable top-level domain strings and subsequently soliciting tenders to manage and administer these domains (Weinberg 2001).

At the Yokohama meeting the board adopted a resolution supporting the introduction of new top-level domains and outlined a schedule for their deployment. This was followed by the announcement that at the beginning of August ICANN would issue a formal call for proposals for those seeking to sponsor or operate new top-level domains. When the call came, prospective registry operators were presented with an extremely detailed application form for which they were "urged to secure now the professional assistance of technical experts, financial and management consultants, and lawyers to assist in formulation of their proposals and preparation of their applications,"[42] and learned that they would need to pay a nonrefundable application fee of US$50,000 to ICANN. Although the prospect of deploying new gTLDs was generally welcomed by most interested parties, concerns were expressed about the costly application fee. For example, some representatives of nonprofit groups and small entrepreneurs argued that the amount being charged was beyond their reach and that it amounted to an entry barrier to becoming an operator of a top-level domain. By October 2, 2000, the deadline date for application submissions, ICANN had received forty-seven applications, many of which included more than one top-level domain string.[43]

The selection of the new top-level domains, and the registry operators that would manage and administer them, was scheduled to take place at a four-day meeting of the ICANN board in Los Angeles. On November 16, 2000, the twelve members of the board met to decide its selections during a single session. In contrast to Working Group C's earlier call for the selection process to be conducted in a procedurally regular manner according to a pre-announced selection criteria, the means by which new top-level domains were chosen was uncoordinated, subjective, and arbitrary. The board appeared to simply have no established framework or procedure for making their determinations.[44] This led one media observer to characterize their discussions as lurching and reeling "from sophomoric ramblings to vacuous platitudes to petty preferences and back again with disorienting rapidity" (Byfield 2000).

By the end of the day's session the board had agreed to commence negotiations with seven prospective registry operators. The new gTLDs that were selected and the organizations chosen to manage and administer them are listed below.

- *.aero*—Société Internationale de Télécommunications Aeronau-

tiques SC (SITA)
- *.biz*[45]—JVTeam, LLC[46]
- *.coop*—National Cooperative Business Association (NCBA)
- *.info*—Afilias, LLC
- *.museum*—Museum Domain Management Association (MDMA)
- *.name*—Global Name Registry, Ltd
- *.pro*—RegistryPro, Ltd.

Of the seven gTLDs selected, two—*.biz* and *.info*—are targeted at commercial enterprises as an alternative to the *.com* top-level domain. In contrast, *.pro* and *.name* are aimed at individuals. The remaining three top-level domains—*.aero*, *.coop*, and *.museum*—are restricted on the basis of business method, industry, or type of entity.

Following the announcement of the winning applicants, eleven organizations whose applications had been rejected launched unsuccessful appeals for reconsideration to ICANN. Citing concerns about the inconsistencies with the selection process and the potential for its outcome to thwart competition in the registration and assignment of domain names a congressional hearing was held in February 2001.[47] At the hearing, members of the congressional subcommittee on telecommunications criticized the selection process and recommended that ICANN develop a less arbitrary and more open process before deploying any additional top-level domains.[48]

The original schedule for the deployment of the new top-level domains had proposed that the new registries would be operational by the end of December 2000. However, ICANN's contract negotiations with the winning applicants extended far beyond the time frame that had initially been envisaged. By the end of 2001, all of the registry operators except RegistryPro Ltd had reached an agreement with ICANN,[49] and registrations were being accepted for the *.info*, *.biz*, and *.name* top-level domains.[50]

The introduction of new top-level domains into the root is a matter of technical coordination and clearly falls within ICANN's mandate. However, any attempt by this organization to address the broader social, political, and economic implications of selecting and deploying new gTLDs marks an increase in the scope of its authority, or mission creep, into the realm of public policy and regulation. Yet, the contractual terms that have been imposed upon the new gTLD registry operators reveal that this is what has happened. For example, these contracts[51] regulate, among other things, the privacy claims that domain name registrants can assert and the fees that the registries can charge for their services. In addition, they require the new registry operators to incorporate the UDRP into their contracts with their customers and to enact sunrise procedures designed to protect the interests of intellectual property holders. In exerting controls over these nontechnical aspects of domain naming policy, ICANN has embarked on a much more regulatory-oriented governance trajectory than that which characterized IANA's activities.

What is particularly significant about both the UDRP and the deployment of new gTLDs is that the means for achieving the regulatory ends associated with these initiatives were defined, adopted, and implemented by a private sector organization. This has further complicated ICANN's efforts at convincing Internet stakeholders of its legitimacy because many of the nontechnical issues it has addressed in this context have traditionally been the domain of public policy making. This has raised concerns about the extent to which ICANN has been exercising its legal authority in a manner that adheres to core democratic values because it is a private sector organization that, ultimately, is exerting global public authority over a key information and communication resource.

To date, ICANN's mission creep into the public policy domain seems to have undermined its social, political, and cognitive legitimacy among Internet stakeholders because appears to have used its *de jure* authority to put in place a regulatory architecture that appears to benefit the commercial interests of a particular group of actors at the expense of others, and has demonstrated the presence of a major disjuncture between the rhetoric of consensus based decision making and the actual manner in which policy is developed and implemented through its organizational structures.

Overall, the continued controversies surrounding ICANN are a reflection of a failure to resolve many of the deep-structure issues that underpinned the sociopolitical processes associated with its formation and which continue to manifest themselves in the various policy initiatives it has undertaken since 1998. This has impeded ICANN's ability to build trust and frame uncertainties in a manner that conveys its credibility. Consequently, its success remains a domain of intense speculation.

Understanding the Politics of Internet Governance

Before engaging in a discussion about how the findings of this study may help to address some of the analytical "blind spots" perpetuated by much of the literature about the Internet and its governance, it is beneficial to briefly review some of the key arguments put forth in these works. A major component of the discourse associated with the overhaul of the domain name system was the propagation of conflicting visions of the type of governance regime that should be created to oversee its management and administration. Reflecting many of the debates that took place over the four years of protracted discussions leading up to the formation of ICANN, the views of many authors writing in this context tended toward a prescriptive orientation and a focus on end results. Some authors advocated the creation of a governance regime premised on open bottom-up decision making processes, while others advocated more exclusionary top-down approaches to decision making. Given that much of the work emerging from proponents of these opposing schools of thought has focused primarily on optimal governance strategies, it is reasonable to conclude that it has not been intended to account for the emergent or changing policies and institutions that emerged in response to these disputes.

Although not centered specifically on domain naming controversies, a second corpus of Internet governance literature concerning itself with the procedures whereby outcomes are produced and the history out of which outcomes within the cyber-realm evolve has also emerged. The collective emphasis of these approaches rests on the processes by which rules are effectuated and on how specific attributes of internetworking technologies influence rule making processes.

Among the first of these approaches were David Post's and David Johnson's normative arguments opposing governmental regulation of the Internet and World Wide Web. Their perspective was rooted in the notion that the jurisdictional and substantive quandaries created by transnational electronic communication networks could be resolved by recognizing the cyber-realm as a nongeographical domain that is analogous to, but separate from, territorial space. Citing the fact that internetworking is oblivious to geographical constraints, they argued that the various dimensions of internetworking, including Internet addressing, could be governed by customary and privately produced default rules created by decentralized collective action at the local level. Accordingly, these authors speculate that such a process could lead to a new definition of "civic virtue" that is not linked to a replication of the traditional institutions of representative democracy in the cyber-realm. Under this scenario "civic virtue" would be related to the actions of those entities most intensely affected by, or with a marked interest in, a given issue(s) because they would be most likely to join and seek to influence relevant decision making forums that were perceived as having local significance (Post and Johnson 1997a, 1997b). In turn, the effectiveness of net governance,[52] would be judged on the extent to which, at a systems level, the outcome of these interactions between social agents managed to allow adequate levels of "pull and tug" among contending viewpoints such that "the overall matrix of complex, incompatible needs and desires makes steady progress towards a higher and higher aggregate level of utility" (Post and Johnson 1997a).

The empirical evidence presented in the previous chapters highlights a number of weaknesses in this perspective. Perhaps the most unsatisfactory aspect of Post's and Johnson's approach is the fact that their analysis fails to explain why potential stakeholders would forego control over, and protection of, their perceived interests. The evidence derived from the narratives about the Nominet and ICANN cases clearly demonstrates that in seeking to protect their perceived interests, most stakeholders simply made no distinction between the so-called cyberworld and the physical world. In the case of Nominet, it was precisely the perceived lack of congruity between the value constructs that a small group of social agents were seeking to uphold for the *.uk* name space and the commercial realities facing service providers that catalyzed demands for changing the existing registry architecture. Similarly, many of the key stakeholders who participated in the ICANN formation process and its policy making forum actively pursued an agenda oriented toward preventing the establishment of a regulatory regime premised on a distinction between the cyberworld and the physical world. For instance, representatives of trademark and intellectual property interests have consistently insisted on their need to uphold property rights in the cyber-realm that coincide with the rights they have under existing legislation and case law governing trademarks. In fact, Mueller (1998c, 2000) and Geist (2001) provide powerful evidence suggesting that representatives of these interests have successfully exploited the uncertainties associated with regulation in the cyber-domain "to claim property rights in Internet domain names that go far beyond the rights they have under existing legislation and case law" (Mueller 1998c:13). For their part, national governments also rejected, albeit to differing degrees, the idea that their public policy concerns should not be incorporated into a regulatory regime responsible for overseeing the administration and management of the domain name system.

The empirical evidence also appears to raise some questions about the efficacy of Post's and Johnson's postulations regarding the creation of a new form of civic virtue through the machinations of decentralized emergent law. According to their perspective, U.K.-based registrars perceived the issue of managing and administering the .*uk* name space as having local significance vis-à-vis their registration activities and, therefore, chose to participate in decision making forums that sought to establish a new addressing regime. However, the concept of "local significance" is ambiguous, and this theory provides little insight as to why social agents attach "significance" to particular issues, nor whether this sense of significance provides sufficient motivation to take action either in support of, or in opposition to, particular issues. The evidence regarding U.K.-based registrar participation in the ICANN formation process is illustrative of this point. Given that the way in which the domain name system is managed and controlled has implications for the quality of Internet services worldwide, it seems plausible that U.K.-based registrars would have perceived attempts at establishing a new addressing regime as having "local" significance. Nonetheless, only a very small number of these organizations were sufficiently motivated to participate in the proceedings associated with the formation of ICANN.

There is a third aspect of Post's and Johnson's perspective with which one may take issue. It concerns their lack of elaboration about how processes of net governance are judged. These authors assert simply that the legitimacy and efficacy of the workings of net governance are assessed on the basis of whether it permits an adequate level of "pull and tug" between contending interests leading toward higher aggregate levels of utility. The problem with this claim is that it provides no means of examining, and/or assessing, these processes of "pull and tug" between contending interests. Yet, as we have seen from the evidence presented in the two preceding chapters as well as in this chapter, the outcomes of such interactions between social agents are oriented toward the authoritative allocation of values, and, as such, are the locus of Internet politics. Moreover, Post's and Johnson's assertion assumes that all the actors involved in negotiating authoritative value allocations will judge the outcome of such events on the basis of a homogenous notion of legitimacy. Although the evidence pertaining to the formation of Nominet suggests that the primary concern of interested parties was the perceived degree of openness of this process of organizational change, this clearly has not been the case with the ICANN. In this instance, those actors whose interests have been upheld by the creation of ICANN and the policies it has implemented have tended to view the outcome of the "pull and tug" between contending interests as being a legitimate result of the negotiation process, whereas those who value openness and adherence to the norms and values that traditionally have underpinned the evolution of internetworking view ICANN as an illegitimate aberration that reflects the interests of a particular conglomeration of actors.

In contrast to Post's and Johnson's assertions about the futility of seeking to regulate the cyber-realm, Joel Reidenberg (1996, 1998) postulated that although internetworking was fostering a disintegration of territorial and substantive borders as key paradigms for regulatory governance, national governments could still influence the types of regulatory structures imposed within this domain. According to this perspective, the primary sources of default rule making in the cyber-realm are the technology developer(s) and the social processes through which customary uses of the technology evolve. Reidenberg postulated that although informal and formal standards setting forums, coupled with market forces, increasingly would serve as the critical sources of information policy, this would not necessarily entail a reduction of governmental activity in the regulatory domain. He concluded that since *Lex Informatica* could be seen as an important system of rules analogous to a legal regime, it was incumbent on policy makers to redirect their rule making activities away from direct regulation of the cyber-realm toward influencing changes in its architecture.

The evidence presented about the formation of both Nominet and ICANN appears to support Reidenberg's claims about the ability of national governments to influence the architectures of the electronic domain. In the Nominet case, the U.K. government was able to ensure that the structure and operations of this entity coincided with British public policy by maintaining the threat of sanction over its activities. Likewise, in the case of ICANN, both the United States government and the European Commission influenced the eventual structure of this entity by participating informally in the interim board selection process and by giving the WIPO a formal role in developing recommendations for addressing trademark/domain name disputes.

One of the problematic aspects of this theory in terms of contributing to an understanding of the Internet and its governance, however, is that in viewing technology developers as the primary sources of default rule making in the cyber-realm, it fails to account for the ability of other stakeholders to influence the impact of such rules.[53] In both cases of institutional formation examined in this book, the collective and individual actions of industry players, Internet and non-Internet organizations, governmental authorities, and specific individuals were important in determining the success or failure of the proposed rules. In terms of the Nominet case, stakeholders perpetuated a shift in the registry architecture by highlighting the incongruities between the name registration practices that the domain name system would support and the rules that certain member representatives of the Naming Committee sought to enforce. This transformation of the registry architecture did not require any alteration to the existing technology. Rather, it entailed the establishment of a new rule set that imposed fewer constraints on the way(s), and purposes, for which the addressing infrastructure was used.

The sociopolitical processes associated with the formation of ICANN appear to have pushed in the opposite direction. In this case, a particular group of interests actively sought to constrain the externalities made possible by the domain name system. More specifically, those representing trademark interests were threatened by the fact that the domain names were not intended to reflect trademarks, copyright, or other intellectual property. Consequently, these actors have actively promoted the placing of limitations on the way in which the domain name system is used and/or expanded. The fact that both of these cases illustrate the ability of social actors to alter the implications of the default rules of the addressing infrastructure highlights the importance of examining sociopolitical interactions of interested parties in order to foster a more precise understanding of governance in the cyber-realm.

The third, and final, process-oriented approach to Internet governance examined in chapter 3 was Lawrence Lessig's normative arguments about the need for government involvement in the development of Internet regulation. His starting premise expands on Reidenberg's concept of *Lex Informatica* by recognizing that the particular features of networking architectures, or code,[54] may perpetuate specific authoritative value allocations while constraining others. According to Lessig (1999a:6) cyberspace "demands a new understanding of how regulation works and of what regulates life there" because code may develop a degree of perfection of control that distinguishes it from the types of behavioral constraints imposed by law, social norms, and markets. In developing his argument, he suggests that although the freedom enhancing values originally embedded in code allow human liberty to flourish in the cyber-realm, there are no guarantees that such values will not be altered as as code becomes increasingly oriented toward facilitating better zoning (Lessig 1999a, 2001). He claims that restricting liberty in cyberspace may occur either by governmental encroachment into this realm or by a commercially based push toward "convergence on a uniform set of rules to govern network transactions" (Lessig 1999a:206).

It is the latter point which serves as the overarching premise underpinning Lessig's argument. He asserts that the architecture of cyberspace is "up for grabs and that, depending on who grabs it, there are several different ways it could turn out" (Lessig 1999a:219). In light of this view, he claims that there are choices to be made about the architecture of cyberspace and that many of these choices pertain to how we collectively experience this medium. His rationale for advocating government involvement in this realm rests on the notion that since the process of choosing among the values to be embedded in code entails collective choices about how this space will be ordered, this instance of decision making is *ipso facto* political in nature. It follows, therefore, that there is a need for greater governmental involvement in cyberspace because government is the vehicle through which democratic societies ensure that the process of collective decision making is fair and that its outcome is equitable.

There can be little doubt that Lessig's treatise on the significance of code is an indispensable contribution to the understanding of regulation in the cyber-realm. To this end, the narratives about Nominet and ICANN appear to substantiate his claim that since the mid-1990s political and commercial entities have sought to bring about control-orientated changes to the code of cyberspace. However, his argument does not address the dynamism of these processes of institutional change because it is premised on the notion that the drive toward uniformity in cyberspace is an inevitable consequence of the "invisible hand" of commerce.[55] This suggests that his argument is premised on a notion of power as the *ability* to produce intended effects, rather than a notion of power as the *capacity* to produce intended effects. The distinction is important here because when power is viewed as a capacity, this implies a recognition of power as a relational phenomenon rather than as something capable of being possessed.

One of the unfortunate consequences of adopting a "power as ability" perspective is that such an approach does not account for flux between relatively stable periods of coordinated administration and relatively unstable periods of transition that characterize institutional change. Moreover, despite recognizing the process of value allocation as being inherently political, Lessig's essentially linear view of change offers no means of interpreting how social actors involved in such processes make choices, or how they assess the legitimacy of emergent changes. Consequently, an analysis of the transformation of Internet addressing based on a "code is law" framework would not be able to account for the multiple reconfigurations of power relations that characterized the events preceding the incorporation of ICANN, nor the ways in which they influenced the policies implemented since its creation. Likewise, it would not be able to account for the fact that the outcome of the Nominet formation process corresponded with British public policy despite the relative lack of government involvement in these events.

The normative arguments emerging from the process-oriented perspectives discussed above appear to provide relatively little insight into the relationship between the negotiation processes associated with, and outcomes of, the two cases of institutional reconfiguration examined here. Simply put, although much of the process-oriented research work seeks to explain how the technical architecture of the Internet may influence regulatory procedures and the promulgation of certain types of social order, it cannot explain why particular changes manifest themselves, or why certain groups of actors may succeed in exerting greater influence than others over how the process of change is managed.

Conclusions

The Internet is comprised of the hardware and software that make internet-working possible and of the formal and informal organizational structures, or institutions, that are evolving around the technical infrastructure. Unfortunately, much of the current theorizing about the Internet and its governance appears to underestimate the importance of sociopolitical dynamics in influencing emergent policies and institutions that comprise a significant dimension of the architectural configurations.

This analysis of the transformation of the governance regimes for Internet addressing within both the domestic and international contexts suggests that specific features of the evolution of Internet governance can best be understood by examining the manner in which new configurations of power constellations are influencing the emergence of the policies and institutions responsible for managing and administering the Internet's core functions. In both of the instances of institutional reconfiguration examined in this book, the catalyst for establishing a new governance regime for Internet addressing was embedded in the power struggles over the techniques used for domain name allocation and administration. Change did not occur as a result of a specific plan. Instead, it was shaped by dynamic processes of cooperation and competition between participating social actors.

Focusing on the processes of interest mediation that characterize Internet politics has important implications for understanding the nature of regulation in the electronic domain. A key benefit of this approach is that it does not fall prey to ideologically motivated positions with respect to the appropriate roles of the private sector or the state. Second, it offers a means of coupling investigations of the determinants of the technical architecture of the Internet and the way the social and political interests of its designers and users become embedded in that architecture. Third, it offers a means of interpreting the way that the social, political, and cognitive legitimacy of Internet regulatory and coordinating bodies. organizations is being established in the cyber-realm.

Notes

1. At the end of the 1994 financial year Network Solutions reported a net revenue of approximately US$5 million. By the end of 1996, its net revenues had leaped to approximately US$19 million and were in the range of US$94 million by the end of the 1998 financial year.

2. Jon Postel email message to Internet Society Trustees (September 15, 1995). www.wia.org/pub/postel-iana-draft13.htm (last accessed January 5, 2000).

3. Recall that these were *.firm, .store, .web, .arts, .rec, .info,* and *.nom.*

4. Recall that the other members of the POC included representatives of the Internet Architecture Board (IAB), the ITU, WIPO, the International Trademark Association (INTA), and the Council of Registrars (CORE).

5. Despite these measures, some representatives of trademark interests were critical

of the International Trademark Association's participation in the development of this framework arguing that it should not have conceded to the introduction of any new domains into the domain name system.

6. The government of Albania was the only national government that signed up to the gTLD-MoU. www.itu.int/net-itu/gtld-mou/simple.htm (last accessed January 10, 2000).

7. On April 23, 1997, U.S. Secretary of State Madeleine Albright sent the Secretariat of the ITU a State Department cable in which she stated that the United States government "has concerns about the authority of the ITU Secretariat, without authorization of the member governments, both to hold a full meeting of member states and master members, and to commit to actions under the gTLD-MoU." She also noted that the "USG has not yet developed a position on any of the proposals to reform the Internet domain name system, including the gTLD-MoU, nor on the appropriate role, if any, of the ITU, WIPO, or other international organizations in the administration of the Internet." See Andy Sernovitz, "The US Govt is *not* Supportive of the gTLD-Mou." July 27, 1997. www.gtld-mou.org/gtld-discuss/mail-archive/04644.html. See also Margie Wylie, "U.S. concerned by ITU meeting" 29 April 1997. www.news.com/News/Item/0,4,10198,00.html (last accessed May 5, 1997).

8. www.ntia.doc.gov/ntiahome/domainname.130dftmail (last accessed April 15, 1998).

9. Interview with the author conducted on September 22, 1998.

10. Detailed archives of the consensus points emerging from these meetings are available at: cyber.law.harvard.edu/ifwp/consensuslist.asp (last accessed January 12, 2000). See also www.domainhandbook.com (last accessed January 12, 2000).

11. Working through the Global Internet Project, IBM became an active supporter of the White Paper on the grounds that it would be well-positioned within any private sector-led Internet governance regime. See www.gip.org (last accessed January 12, 2000). The Global Internet Project (GIP) is an international group of thirteen senior executives representing software and telecommunication segments of the Internet industry. It was founded by Dr. James Clark of the Netscape Communication Corporation, and its chairperson at the time of writing was IBM's vice president of Internet technology, John Patrick. The other companies comprising this group include: AT&T WorldNet Services, British Telecommunications plc., Deutsche Bank AG, Deutsche Telekom, Fujitsu Ltd, GTE Internetworking, MITAC, Solect Technology Group/Amdocs Ltd, Nokia Inc., MCI WorldCom, Sony Corporation, Teleglobe Communications Corporation, Telstra, and ITXC Corporation.

12. The proposed bylaws and articles of incorporation for the new corporation are available at: www.iana.org/bylaws-coop.html and www.iana.org/articles-coop.html respectively (last accessed January 12, 2000). A full listing of the initial board members, including biographies is available at: cyber.law.harvard.edu/ifwp/icannboard.html (last accessed January 12, 2000). Mike Roberts, an ISOC veteran and strong supporter of the gTLD-MoU, was appointed as the new chief executive officer of ICANN.

13. See www.icannwatch.org (last accessed January 12, 2002).

14. Reflecting the fact that the WIPO is a United Nations body responsible to all its member states, the terms of reference set out in this document were much broader in scope than those which had been outlined in the White Paper.

15. The comments received in response to RFC 1 are available at: wipo2.wipo.int/dns_comments/index.html (last accessed September 1, 2001).

16. The comments received in response to RFC 2 are available at: wipo2.wipo.int/dns_comments/rfc2/index.html (last accessed September 1, 2001).

17. The original deadline for submitting comments had been set for March 12, 1999. However, this deadline was extended by one week in the light of an upsurge in comment submissions shortly before that date.

18. The comments received in response to RFC 3 are available at: wipo2.wipo.int/dns_comments/rfc3/index.html (last accessed September 1, 2001).

19. Information about ICANN's organizational structure is available at: www.icann.org/general/icann-org-chart_frame.htm and www.icann.org/general/structure (last accessed November 30, 2001).

20. See www.icann.org/berlin/berlin-resolutions.html and www.icann.org/berlin/berlin-details.html (last accessed May 29, 1999).

21. The DNSO is primarily responsible for the development of policies relating to domain naming. It consists of two bodies: (i) the Names Council, which is the main policy making body; and (ii) the General Assembly, which is open to all individuals but which has no authority. The Names Council includes representatives from Network Solutions Inc. and three representatives from each of the constituencies.

22. The seven constituencies represent: (1) commercial and business entities; (2) intellectual property interests; (3) registrars for .com, .net, and .org top-level domains; (4) Internet service providers and connectivity providers; (5) country-code top-level domain registries; (6) a gTLD registries constituency for which Network Solutions Inc. is the sole member; and (7) noncommercial domain name holders. See www.dnso.org (last accessed May 1, 2001).

23. According to its bylaws, the PSO has jurisdiction over "the assignment of parameters for Internet protocols." See www.icann.org/pso/pso-mou.htm (last accessed October 1, 1999).

24. Although the chair of the working group allowed anyone to comment on the WIPO recommendations, numerous individuals who were known to be opponents of mandatory arbitration were denied the right to vote on the report (Froomkin 1999a).

25. *ICANN—Resolutions adopted in Santiago, August 26, 1999*. See www.icann.org/santiago/santiago-resolutions.htm (last accessed October 1, 1999)

26. *ICANN—Draft Uniform Domain Name Dispute Resolution Policy*. See www. ica nn.org udrp/udrp-policy-29sept99.htm (last accessed 1 October 1999).

27. The UDRP is not intended, nor designed, to deal with instances where two parties may have equally legitimate claims to a specific domain name.

28. The complainant also pays for the arbitration process, unless the respondent elects to nominate a panelist to the administration panel. If the complainant request either a one- or three-person panel they are responsible for paying the fees charged by the service provider. If the complainant requests a one-person panel while the respondent decides in favor of a three-person panel, the fees are split equally between the two parties.

29. This organization began accepting disputes in February 2002. See www.icann. org/ announcements/announcement-03dec01.htm (last accessed December 9, 2001).

30. See www.icann.org/udrp/proceedings-stat.htm (last accessed January 22, 2002).

31. Citing forum shopping and the "perception of bias" to which its "markedly lower complainant success rate" had given rise as the key factors for its negligible market share, on November 30, 2000, eResolutions announced that it was withdrawing its services as an ICANN UDRP provider. See www.eresolution.com/pr/30_11_01.htm (last accessed December 3, 2001).

32. Domain name registrars are required to include the UDRP in every registration contract with their customers. See *Registrar Accreditation Agreement*, www.icann.org/

nsi/icann-raa-04nov99.htm#llK (last accessed December 1, 1999).

33 See *NSI/ICANN Registry Agreement:* www.icann.org/nsi/nsi-registry-agreement-04nov99.htm (last accessed December 1, 1999).

34. The discussion list archives for Working Group B and Working Group C are available at www.dnso.org/wgroups/wg-b/Archives/maillist.html, www.dnso.org/wg roups/wg-c/Arc00/maillist.html and www.dnso.org/wgroups/wg-c/Arc01/maillist.html respectively (last accessed December 3, 2001). A complete list of the position papers submitted to Working Group B and Working Group C is available at: www.dnso.org/ wgroups/wg-b/Archives/msg00604.html and www.dnso.org/dnso/notes/19991023.NCwg c-report.html respectively (last accessed December 3, 2001).

35. *Report (Part One) of Working Group C of the Domain Name Supporting Organization Internet Corporation for Assigned Names and Numbers.* See www.dnso.org/dnso /notes/20000321.NCwgc-report.html and www.dnso.org/dnso/notes/20000417.NCwgc-a dden dum.html (last accessed May 3, 2000).

36. The final report noted that a consensus on this item had been reached in July 1999. By and large there appeared to be relatively little dissent, in principle, about this item but there were some members of the DNSO Intellectual Property Constituency that continued to oppose the introduction new gTLDs. For example, in Working Group C's interim report it was noted that representatives of AOL, British Telecom, Disney, the International Trademark Association, Nintendo of America, and Time Warner recommended delaying the deployment of new top-level domains until after the UDRP improved domain name registration procedures, and a system for protecting famous marks had been put in place.

37. Within both working groups points of consensus were determined on the basis of "consensus calls" where members were asked to vote on specific items, with a two-thirds margin constituting evidence of a rough consensus.

38. *DNSO Names Council Statement on new gTLDs (April 19, 2000).* See www.dnso .org/dnso/notes/20000419.NCgtlds-statement.html (last accessed April 20, 2000).

39. *Working Group B (WG-B) Report (March 21, 2000).* See www.dnso.org/dnso/not es/20000417.NCwgb-report.html (last accessed May 3, 2000).

40. *Working Group B (WG-B) Final Report (May 15, 2000).* See www.dnso.org/dnso /notes /20000515.NCwg-report.html (last accessed June 15, 2000).

41. *ICANN Yokohama Meeting Topic: Introduction of New Top-Level Domains (June 13, 2000).* See www.icann.org/yokohama/new-tld-topic.htm (last accessed June 17, 2000).

42. *New TLD Application Process Overview (August 3, 2000).* See www.icann.org/ tlds/application-process-03aug00.htm (last accessed September 3, 2000).

43. A full listing of the applicants and the proposed top-level domain strings is available at: www.icann.org/tlds/tld-applications-lodged-02oct00.htm (last accessed October 20, 2000).

44. Audio and text archives of this meeting are available at: cyber.law.harvard.edu/ic ann/la2000/archive (last accessed February 5, 2001).

45. The selection of this particular top-level domain was very contentious and highlights the subjective nature of the ICANN board's selection process. The application to operate a *.web* TLD was declined by the ICANN board on the grounds that it would conflict with a *.web* TLD that was being provided in alternative root servers by a company known as Image Online Design. However, despite the fact that the operators of a company known as the Atlantic Root Network, Inc. were already providing a *.biz* TLD in alternative root servers under systems operated by Open Root Server Confederated

Inc. permission to manage and administer a *.biz* TLD was allocated to NueLevel Inc.

46. This organization is now known as NeuLevel Inc.

47. In his testimony about the selection process to the House Energy and Commerce Subcommittee on Telecommunications Vint Cerf, ICANN's new chairperson, conceded that "the effort here was not to find the 'best' application, however that might be measured, but to ask the community to offer up a set of options from which ICANN could select a limited number that, taken in the aggregate, would satisfy the evaluation objectives of this proof of concept . . . this was never a process in which the absolute or relative merit of the particular application was determinative." See Dr. Vinton G. Cerf. Witness Prepared Testimony. House Energy and Commerce Subcommittee on Telecommunications Hearing—*Is ICANN's New Generation of Internet Domain Name Selection Process Thwarting Competition?* February 8, 2001. www.house.gov/commerce/ hearings/cerf.htm (last accessed December 22, 2001).

48. See Marsan (2001).

49. Once the registry operators are accredited by ICANN, they must subsequently be approved by the United States Department of Commerce before the top-level domains they are chartered to operate are added to the root.

50. *ICANN—New TLD Program* www.icann.org/tlds (last accessed December 31, 2001).

51. See www.icann.org/tlds/agreements/.

52. Recall that Post and Johnson defined a governance system as a set of institutions and mechanisms that enable inhabitants of an environment to solve ever present problem(s) of collective action.

53. For a discussion of the potential consequences of such influence on innovation see Lessig (2001).

54. Recall that according to Lessig, code refers to the design of the hardware and software elements constituting the cyber-realm, as well as to the protocols that permit these elements to interact with one another.

55. Post (2000) offers a similar critique of Lessig's argument on the grounds that, although his claim about the invisible hand of commerce somehow driving toward uniformity, may be correct, it is not *self evidently* correct.

Chapter 7

Conclusion

Railing away at ICANN because it doesn't meet some ideal model of democracy is likely to be about as effective as complaining that the US Congress is too dominated by the money of those who finance political campaigns. Everyone knows that, the question is how do you work from within the system to balance competing interests, many of which possess economic power?
—Mike Roberts (2000)

This book has explored the issue of regulation in the cyber-realm by focusing on the interactions between social actors involved in the transformation of Internet addressing at the domestic and international level. The starting point was a critical juxtaposition of contemporary perspectives about the Internet and its governance. To date, much of the literature about this topic has exhibited a propensity to emphasize the dichotomy between the perpetuation of a more libertarian-oriented paradigm and the creation of more regulatory- or control-oriented architectures. In the preceding chapters I have argued for the need to move beyond normative assertions about the nature of Internet governance toward a perspective that examines what social actors actually do, as opposed to prescriptive and/or ideologically laden speculation about what *should* be done.[1] In order to develop a less polemical and sociologically richer picture of Internet politics, a three-tiered framework that gives power relations and politicking pride of place was proposed. The intention was to lay the groundwork for an alternative, and in some ways complementary, approach which sheds greater light on the interactions between Internet architectures, social actors, and institutional outcomes.

The ethos that underpinned the creation and evolution of the Internet cultivated norms and values that stressed the importance of open participation, grassroots coordination, and consensus building. The informal and diffuse administrative structures that evolved from this ethos perpetuated a system of governance that was not legally constituted. In terms of the domain name system, responsibility for overseeing its coordination fell, essentially, on one person—Jon Postel. Up until his death on October 16, 1998, he managed, under the guise of IANA, the evolution of the domain name system on the basis of trust based leadership. Corresponding with the explosive growth of the Internet during 1995-1996, however, a diverse array of actors and interests with a perceived stake in the continued growth of the Internet and World Wide Web began to make demands for the creation of clearly defined administrative structures that would be legally constituted. Attempts to resolve the controversies arising from these competing social, economic, and political interests contributed, in important ways, to the design of the policies and institutions that emerged in response to these disputes. The differences between the Nominet and ICANN cases served to highlight the manner in which power relations helped to shape the parameters of these emergent administrative innovations and the social orders they have perpetuated.

The Case of Nominet

The narrative provided in chapter 4 illustrated that the transformation of the addressing regime for the *.uk* name space was marked by a period of closure and usurpation that was related to a shift in the constellation of power relations among social actors. Prior to the formation of Nominet, only representatives from a specific group of U.K. Internet service providers exercised authority for developing and implementing naming policies for the *.uk* domain. By the mid-1990s, domain name registrars and registrants began to express their dissatisfaction with various aspects of the organization responsible for managing and administering the *.uk* name space. The discontent expressed by Internet stakeholders at the existing state of affairs manifested itself in power struggles between U.K.-based domain name registrars over the techniques used to manage and administer this domain.

Although the transformation process was widely perceived as reflecting a conflict between large and small ISPs, at the core of these proceedings was a struggle between two conflicting value constructs. On the one hand, some actors sought to maintain a set of values mirroring their concerns about the technical and moral dimensions of both the *.uk* name space and the registry architecture. An alternative set of value constructs supported by other actors, pushed in the opposite direction and sought to eliminate the arbitrary and subjective procedures used by the Naming Committee to evaluate requests for domain name allocations. Hence, the issue here was not so much about how domain names were used per se. Rather, it centered on enhancing the efficiency and accountability of the name registration process and on establishing a legally constituted registry organization.

Responding to the growing problems arising from the practices and procedures of the U.K. Naming Committee, the responsible person for the *.uk* domain formally initiated a process of reform. In seeking to create a new entity to oversee the management and administration of the *.uk* domain, interested parties were invited to help develop coherent proposals for change. Through processes involving both cooperation and competition between social actors, participants in these proceedings were able to reach a consensus about the structural, technical, and funding parameters for a new organization. The administrative innovation that emerged from this period of flux, and the reconfiguration of power relations it entailed, resulted in a proposal for creating a shared registry architecture wherein all members would manage the registry in common.

The empirical evidence suggests that the relatively low degree of politicization associated with this process of institutional reconfiguration was linked to three factors. First, the reconfiguration of power relations within this context was limited to U.K. based domain name registrars because external actors (i.e. trademark interests, the U.K. government, individual and noncommercial users) did not become heavily involved in the restructuring process. Second, the transformation entailed a reconstitution of the administrative structures responsible for coordinating the *.uk* domain and did not modify, or alter, in any significant way the hardware and software responsible for the structuring and functioning of the *.uk* name space. Third, the proposal to establish a registry architecture in line with the principles of neutral service provision does not appear to have represented a threat to the deep-structure interests of the actors who chose to participate in these events. This resulted in a situation wherein most of the negotiations associated with this initiative occurred largely at the surface level and focused primarily on finding optimal strategies for ensuring the impartiality of the new organization. Consequently, the process of institutional formation was able to proceed on the basis of addressing a problem of technical coordination rather than entailing broader debates about how the *.uk* name space should be regulated.

Although being the "responsible person" appears to have given Dr. William Black *de jure* authority, his *de facto* authority over this segment of the Internet, as well as that of any emergent policies or organization, was dependent upon the support of interested parties forming the U.K. Internet industry. Recognizing this fact, he appears to have acted as a purposeful agent by taking a number of measures aimed at ensuring that interested parties perceived him as a neutral actor. Accordingly, the reconfiguration of power relations within this context was limited primarily to U.K.-based domain name registrars that sought to embed the emergent registry architecture with social, political, and economic values reflecting their deep-structure interests. Hence, the governance trajectory for administering the *.uk* domain was consolidated in a manner that enhanced the ability of suppliers of registrar services to determine for themselves the constraints placed upon their registration activities. This suggests that the emergent credibility of the Nominet initiative was rooted in trust-building strategies that enabled the unknown to be framed in a manner that made it credible to domestic ISPs, and Internet users, as well as the British government.

The strategies employed to make this possible manifested themselves at the deep-structure, surface, and technological levels. In terms of deep-structure politicking, the notion of establishing an independent legally constituted neutral entity that would not compete with existing registrars vis-à-vis the provision of registration services helped to nurture the view that this new organization would not threaten registrar interests. At the surface level, the manner in which the Nominet proposal was developed conformed with the established institutional norms and values that had evolved in tandem with the evolution of the Internet. That is, the business proposal for Nominet was developed through cooperative interactions between competing actors and no interested parties were restricted from participating in these proceedings. Furthermore, the architectural aspects of the new registry organization also enhanced the legitimacy of Nominet because it was seen as preventing the representatives of any particular group of interests from advancing their own interests at the expense of others. Once established, the continued legitimacy of Nominet was related to the technical efficacy of its operations and the maintenance of its neutrality.

The success of the Nominet initiative can be attributed to the inclusive strategies adopted to develop a proposal for change, the structural characteristics of the registry architecture that emerged, the minimization of its sphere of authority, and its continued neutrality in the policy making realm. Given that pioneering organizations cannot base trust building strategies purely on technological efficiency, the openness of the political dimensions of this period of flux combined with the observable and pragmatic efforts to put in place an neutral infrastructure that was representative of Internet stakeholders helped to foster a perception among interested parties that Nominet: (i) was inclusive; (ii) prevented the representatives of specific interests, or groups of interests, from exerting undue influence on the outcome of these events; and (iii) was not seeking to compete with other U.K.-based industry players. All told, one is left to conclude that the governance trajectory for administering the .*uk* domain was consolidated in a manner that basically corresponded with, and upheld, the traditional norms and values associated with internetworking.

The Case of ICANN

The narrative about the formation of ICANN presented in chapters 2 and 6, and the survey data presented in chapter 5, depicted the extent to which reconfiguration of the global Internet addressing regime also was marked by periods of closure and usurpation. The antecedents to the domain name wars paralleled the Nominet case in so far as they too were rooted in power struggles over the techniques used to allocate domain names and to administer the Internet domain name system. In addition, the change that occurred within this context did not result in the implementation of any significant modifications to the hardware and software upon which the domain name system rests. Instead, it centered on reconstituting the administrative structures and policies used to manage Internet addressing at the global level. In contrast to the Nominet case, however, a far greater number of external actors that perceived themselves as having a stake in how the domain name system was coordinated chose to become involved in this instance of institutional reconfiguration. This was in no small measure related to the international context within which these events were unfolding.

The primary struggles at the core of this period of flux appear to have been rooted in the conflicting deep-structure interests of technical, commercial, national, and supranational actors. IANA wanted its *de facto* authority for managing the domain name system to become legally constituted. Network Solutions Inc. aspired to convert its government contract to administer the *.com*, *.org*, and *.net* domains into a private right. Some commercial interests advocated the introduction of new top-level domains and the creation of proprietary registries, while others advocated competition at the registrar level. Trademark holders sought to limit any expansion in the number of available top-level domains and the implementation of enhanced measures for protecting their intellectual property interests in cyberspace. The ITU wanted to limit the expansion of IANA's and ISOC's role outside the traditional Internet technical community and to enhance its role in the administration of the domain name system. National governments wanted to ensure that any entity created to oversee the administration of the domain name system was internationally accountable. Given the growing economic, legal, and political significance of Internet addressing, all of the above actors began to jockey for position in order to promote their respective goals.

The conflicts between those with competing interests fostered new constellations of power relations that succeeded in transforming the issue of international domain name administration into a regulatory, rather than a technical-matter. The oscillations in power relations that characterized the period of the domain name wars led to the perpetuation of no less than three separate regulatory frameworks, each of which was developed with varying degrees of openness and reflected the deep-structure interests of the actors responsible for their creation. After four years of protracted debates, attempts at resolving the controversies associated with the administration of the domain name system culminated with the formation of ICANN.

The period immediately preceding the formation of this entity was characterized by two streams of activity. Each of these streams consisted of differing constellations of power relations that reflected alternative interpretations of the White Paper's call for the creation of a new corporation (Newco) to oversee the management of Internet addressing. The actors who participated in the International Forum on the White Paper (IFWP) stream engaged in a series of open meetings with the goal of establishing a "rough consensus" about the principles that would underpin how the new corporation was structured, and its operational bylaws. Although this process and the principles it propagated, appeared to embody the traditional values and norms of the Internet paradigm, it is worth noting that the policy formation process adopted by the IFWP deviated from the traditional RFC-based approach characteristic of the traditional Internet policy process.

A second stream of activity was characterized by the activities of IANA and the cooperative efforts of the U.S. Department of Commerce, the European Commission, IBM, ISOC, and gTLD-MoU adherents. In line with the way in which standards were developed traditionally in the Internet domain, IANA produced a series of documents pertaining to the structure of the new corporation that were posted on its Web site and distributed on electronic discussion lists to solicit comments. However, the corporate structure initially proposed in these documents did not embody the values of openness and grassroots coordination characteristic of such entities as the Internet Engineering Task Force (IETF). As the United States government's deadline for submissions about the new corporation approached, members of the IFWP invited IANA to a public wrap-up meeting aimed at producing a final draft comprising the work of both activity streams. However, IANA refused to participate in such a meeting and proceeded to engage in additional behind-the-scenes negotiations about the new corporation with select members of the IFWP and Network Solutions Inc.

When considering the case of ICANN, it appears that there were, and remain, several deep-structure, surface-level, and architectural issues that prevented the establishment of its authority for managing the domain name system from being framed in a manner that was credible to all interested parties. In the three years prior to its formation, issues relating to domain name management were extremely divisive, with stakeholders demonstrating a general unwillingness to cooperate or compromise when dealing with such matters. Despite the lack of any deep-structure consensus among stakeholders, the most substantive aspects of the initial ICANN framework emerged from behind-the-scenes negotiations involving a particular constellation of interests that sought to create a closed corporate structure. In terms of surface-level politicking, the behind-the-scenes manner in which the corporate structure of ICANN was developed and an interim board of directors selected, marked a major deviation from the established norms and values traditionally associated with the Internet paradigm.[2] Given that ICANN's initial corporate structure was that of a closed corporation with no members, and with only very limited checks on its power, the proposed architecture further undermined the ability of this organization to garner, from an early stage, the trust of stakeholders who felt that the entire formation process had been usurped by those with vested interests.

In the few years since its formation, ICANN and its supporters have attempted to establish its legitimacy by employing neutralization strategies such as espousing the view that it is merely a mechanism through which Internet stakeholders act to develop policies oriented toward the technical management of the Internet. The three-tiered model of interest group politics offers an analytical foundation for challenging this view. Focusing on the relationship between deep-structure interests, surface-level politicking, and technology draws attention to the fact that ICANN is not just a structure, but rather a purposive agent that has a direct influence over the governance trajectory of internetworking. The notion of consensus as a decision making tool refers to the desire to establish agreement among all participants with the expectation that the relevant authority will use the agreement as the basis for a policy decision (Coglianese 2001). The evidence regarding the events surrounding the evolution of the UDRP and the policy for deploying new top-level domains suggests that rhetoric of "consensus" notwithstanding, ICANN's policy making and implementation processes have no clear means for determining whether, or even if, a consensus has been reached. As a result, its consensus-based policy processes, outputs, and consequences often appear to run counter to the much lauded norms of openness, grassroots coordination, and representativeness.

In the light of these problems, and in spite of the fact that ICANN acquired a degree of legal legitimacy when the United States government officially recognized it as the entity the U.S. Department of Commerce would work with to effect private sector administration of the domain name system, this organization has yet to foster a broad sense of trustworthiness and credibility among Internet stakeholders. The evidence suggests that the crisis of legitimacy that ICANN has had to contend with can be attributed to the noninclusive strategies adopted to develop the most substantive elements of the original proposal for this organization, the fact that its original corporate structure restricted public input and lacked accountability, the remarkably diverse array of interests it must try to balance, and its subsequent ventures into the realm of regulatory policy making.[3] At the end of the day, one is left to conclude that the bulk of the criticism ICANN must contend with is rooted in the fact that it is a private organization which is exerting global public authority over a key information and communication resource in a manner that appears to be inconsistent with both the way in which decisions have traditionally been made in the public domain and the traditional norms and values associated with internetworking.

Reconsidering the Emergence of New Governance Trajectories

The early history of the Internet and its governance offers a striking example of successful informal governance. However, as this medium became increasingly commercialized during the mid- to late 1990s, the ambiguities fostered by the informal way in which the basic Internet related administrative arrangements traditionally had been propagated gave rise to, and perpetuated, numerous political, economic, and legal controversies. At their core, these conflicts reflected different actors' perceptions both of the goals of this information and communication resource and how these goals might best be achieved.

The design of policies and institutions that coordinate and regulate behavior in the electronic domain is part of a continuous struggle for control that is shaping the governance trajectory of interworking. At the start of this book, I expressed my hope that by understanding how the emergent and established Internet regulatory and coordinating bodies are constituted would enable us to hypothesize about their behavior and influence on this trajectory. This study has marked an attempt to address this ambition.

The benefit of the power-oriented framework presented here is that it reduces the likelihood that analyses of emergent governance trajectories will be influenced by ideologically motivated positions with respect to the appropriate role of the private sector or the state. It allows interested observers to engage, with a fresh perspective, in at least three of the debates coinciding with the emergence of new policies and institutions that coordinate and regulate behavior in the electronic domain. First, this framework bridges the gap between the libertarian and the "code is law" approaches to the Internet and its governance. The former is premised on the view of a coercive state making futile attempts to constrain the capabilities of the neutral facilitative technologies of internet-working, whereas the latter is rooted in the notion that the state can and should seek to ensure that certain values are upheld in this medium. The common theme emerging from these differing perspectives appears to be rooted in a somewhat technologically deterministic characterization of the architectures of cyberspace. In only looking at one facet of the governance equation, both of these perspectives disadvantage themselves in their arguments by underestimating the extent to which the emerging policies and institutions responsible for managing and administering the Internet's core functions are the product of complex sociopolitical processes that entail interactions between individuals, organizations, established norms and values, and technology.

Second, the power-oriented perspective proposed here provides a basis for treating both emergent and established Internet regulatory and coordinating bodies as autonomous sociopolitical actors. This presents a challenge to the pluralist, or rough consensus, ontologies prevalent in some of the most recent literature about the Internet and its governance.[4] Recognizing the importance of sociopolitical dynamics in establishing new architectural configurations highlights the fact that although code *may be* law, neither code nor law is developed in a vacuum. In short, just as the process of legislative review conditions the extent to which an emergent statute represents the initial aims of law makers, the emergent regulatory architectures of cyberspace are conditioned by the outcomes of the interactions between purposeful social actors. This suggests that the Internet's ability to facilitate regulatory arbitrage may not be as comprehensive as had once been suggested.

Third, focusing on power relations and politicking offers an alternative vantage point from which to assess the legitimacy of the emergent and established institutional bodies that coordinate and regulate various aspects of the cyber-realm. Specifically, it helps to illuminate the characteristics that make these agents authoritative as well as those that act to undermine their social, political, and cognitive legitimacy. Examining the influence of cultural values, beliefs, and practices provides a means of interpreting differences in the ability of certain actors to successfully impede changes they perceive as being detrimental and/or to promote agendas that are advantageous to their interests. Similarly, focusing on the day-to-day contests and struggles for collaboration between social actors offers a means of assessing the types of action orientated choices made by actors seeking to influence the parameters of emergent governance trajectories as well as the longer term implications of such activities.

Taken together, the outcome of this emphasis on power relations is a recognition that the narrow deep-structure interests of diverse actors with a perceived stake in how particular aspects of the network architecture are coordinated and regulated are better served by recognizing the mutual interests of all Internet stakeholders, than by perspectives that seek to give precedence to actors representing one particular set of interests.

By now I hope to have succeeded in persuading you that a detailed examination of sociopolitical interactions yields important insights both into how values are embedded within the emergent architectures of the Internet and how those values manifest themselves. Focusing on the nature of power relations and politicking offers an alternative, yet complementary, basis for thinking and theorizing about the Internet and its governance—one that focuses on how the collective and individual actions of industry players, Internet and non-Internet organizations, governmental authorities, and specific persons coalesce to help influence the success or failure of the emerging policies and institutions in the electronic domain. These processes of interest mediation are a quintessential dimension of the Internet governance equation.

Notes

1. Bearing in mind the relative novelty of the issue of Internet governance, this conclusion is in no small measure linked with the fact that, with a few exceptions, the majority of scholarly Internet governance-related theorizing has been dominated by work emerging from technologists and legal scholars.

2. On July 7, 2000, the United States General Accounting Office released a report in which it determined that the conduct of the Clinton administration was legal and proper during the period when private sector-based control of the domain name system was being established. See www.gao.gov/new.items/og00033r.pdf (last accessed July 9, 2000).

3. The most recent manifestation of ICANN's legitimacy problems occurred in early June 2000 when European country-code domain registries collectively refused to pay the fees that it sought to charge them for their registration activities in their respective domains. See Clausing (2000).

4. For a recent example of this perspective see Kleinwächter (2000, 2001).

Bibliography

Abbate, Janet. 1999. *Inventing the Internet*. Cambridge: MIT Press.

Aiken, Robert. 1995. Toplevel domain names—inquiring minds want to know—who owns them??????????. Email message to multiple discussion lists, March 17. www.wia.org/pub/postel-iana-draft5.htm (last accessed May 15, 2001).

Albitz, Paul, and Cricket Liu. 1997. *DNS and BIND*. 2nd ed. Sebastopol: O'Reilly & Associates.

Andeen, Ashley, and John Leslie King. 1997. Addressing and the future of communications competition: Lessons from telephony to the Internet. In *Coordinating the Internet*, edited by B. Kahin and J. Keller. Cambridge: MIT Press.

Arthur, Brian W. 1994. *Increasing returns and path dependence in the economy*. Ann Arbor: University of Michigan Press.

Bachrach, Peter, and Morton S. Baratz. 1962. Two faces of power. *American Political Science Review* 56: 947-952.

———. 1963. Decisions and nondecisions: An analytical framework. *American Political Science Review* 57: 641-651.

Barber, Anthony, and Guy Davies. 1995. Proposal for a United Kingdom network information centre (NIC). Cambridge: UnipalmPIPEX.

Barley, Stephen R., and Pamela S. Tolbert. 1997. Institutionalization and structuration: Studying the links between action and institution. *Organization Studies* 18 (1): 93-117.

Barlow, John Parry. 1996. A declaration of independence of cyberspace. www.eff.org/~barlow/library.html (last accessed February 27, 1997).

Barrett, Randy. 1999. Enough already! *ZDnet.com:* www.zdnet.com/intweek/stories /news /0,4164,2311649,00.html (last accessed August 11, 1999).

Beniger, James R. 1986. *The control revolution: Technological and economic origins of the information society*. Cambridge: Harvard University Press.

Benkler, Yochai. 2000. From consumers to users: Shifting the deeper structures of regulation toward sustainable commons and user access. *Federal Communications Law Journal* 52 (3): 561-579.

Berman, Harold J., and Colin Kaufman. 1978. The law of international commercial transactions (lex mercatoria). *Harvard International Law Journal* 19: 274-277.

Black, William. 1996. Business plan for the management of the .UK naming domain. Unpublished mimeo.

Blumenthal, Marjory S., and David D. Clark. 2000. Rethinking the design of the Internet: The end to end argument vs. the brave new world. *Working Paper*. MIT Lab for Computer Science.

Boyle, James. 1997. Foucault in cyberspace: surveillance, sovereignty, and hard-wired censors. *University of Cincinnati Law Review* 66: www.wcl.american.edu/pub /faculty /boyle/foucault.htm (last accessed May 30, 1999).

Bradner, Scott. 1996. The Internet standards process—revision 3, *RFC 2026*. www.ietf.org/rfc/rfc2026.txt (last accessed November 22, 1999).

Broersma, Matthew. 1998. New 'tm' domain makes debut. *ZDnet*, February 4. www.zdnet.com/zdnn/content/zdnn/0203/281758.html (last accessed September 27,

1999).

Burk, Dan L. 1995. Trademarks along the infobahn: A first look at the emerging law of cybermarks. *Richmond Journal of Law and Technology* 1 (1): www.richmond.edu/jolt/v1i1/burk.html (last accessed October 4, 1999).

Burr, Beckwith. 1998. Media advisory: Letter to ICANN. *National Telecommunication and Information Administration*, October 20. www.ntia.doc.gov/ntiahome/press/icann102098.htm (last accessed January 13, 2000).

Bush, Randy, Brian Carpenter, and Jon Postel. 1996. Delegation of international top level domains (iTLDs), *Internet Draft*. ftp://rg.net/pub/dnsind/relevant/draft-ymbk-itld-admin-00.txt (last accessed January 7, 2000).

Byfield, Ted. 2000. Ushering in banality. *Telepolis—magazin der netzkultur*, November 27. www.heise.de/tp/english/inhalt/te/4347/1.html (last accessed January 3, 2001).

Carbonneau, Thomas. 1990. *Lex mercatoria and arbitration*. Dobbs Ferry: Transnational Juris Publications.

Carpenter, Brian. 1996a. Architectural principles of the Internet, *RFC 1958*. www.ietf.org/rfc/rfc1958.txt (last accessed November 24, 1999).

——. 1996b. What does the IAB do, anyway? www.iab.org/connexions.html (last accessed December 12, 1999).

Castells, Manuel. 2001. *The Internet galaxy: Reflections on the Internet, business, and society*. Oxford: Oxford University Press.

Cerf, Vint. 1990a. The Internet activities board, *RFC 1160*. ftp://ftp.isi.edu/in-notes/rfc1160.txt (last accessed December 26, 1999).

——. 1990b. IAB recommended policy on distributing Internet identifier assignment and IAB recommended policy change to Internet "connected" status, *RFC 1174*. ftp://ftp.isi.edu/in-notes/rfc1174.txt (last accessed December 26, 1999).

——. 1995a. IANA authority. Email response to Robert Aiken, March 17. www.wia.org/pub/postel-iana-draft9.htm (last accessed May 15, 2001).

——. 1995b. IETF and ISOC. www.isoc.org/isoc/related/ietf/ (last accessed December 26, 1999).

Clausing, Jeri. 1998a. Internet governance board confronts a hostile public. *New York Times*, November 16. www.nytimes.com/library/tech/98/11/biztech/articles/16internet-admin.html (last accessed January 12, 2000).

——. 1998b. New Internet board hopes to build consensus. *New York Times*, November 1. www.nytimes.com/library/tech/98/11/cyber/articles/01domain.html (last accessed January 12, 2000).

——. 2000. European domain operators refuse to pay bills. *New York Times*, June 7. search1.nytimes.com/search/daily/fastweb?getdoc+cyber-lib+cyber-lib+11709+5+w AAA+%22ICANN%22 (last accessed June 9, 2001).

Coglianese, Cary. 2001. Is consensus an appropriate basis for regulatory policy? *John F. Kennedy School of Government Faculty Research Working Papers Series RWP01-012*. Harvard University, April.

Cook, Gordon. 1998. A shadow government: Clinton administration to establish public authority (new IANA Corp.) to run Internet. *The Cook Report*, November. www.cookreport.com/sellout.html (last accessed January 13, 2000).

Council of the European Union. 1998. Reply of the European Community and its member states to the US Green Paper, March 20. www.ispo.cec.be/eif/policy/govreply.html (last accessed May 25, 1999).

Crenson, Matthew A. 1971. *The un-politics of air pollution: A study of non-decisionmaking in the cities*. Baltimore: The Johns Hopkins University Press.

Crocker, Dave. 1993a. Making standards the IETF way. *StandardView* 1 (1). info.isoc
.org/papers/standards/crocker-on-standards.html (last accessed December 21,
1999).

———. 1993b. Evolving the system. In *Internet System Handbook*, edited by D. C. Lynch
and M. T. Rose. Reading: Addison-Wesley.

Daft, Richard L. 1978. A dual-core model of organisational innovation. *Academy of
Management Journal* 21: 193-210.

Dahl, Robert A. 1957. The concept of power. *Behavioural Science* 2: 201-215.

David, Paul A. 1985. Clio and the economics of QWERTY. *American Economic Review*
75 (2): 332-337.

———. 1995. Standardization policies for network technologies: The flux between freedom and order revisited. In *Standards, innovation, and competitiveness: The politics and economics of standards in national and technical environments*, edited by
R. Hawkins, R. Mansell and J. Skea. Aldershot: Edward Elgar.

———. 1997. Path dependence and the quest for historical economics: One more chorus
of the ballad of QWERTY. *Discussion Papers in Economic and Social History*,
November. www.nuff.ox.ac.uk/economics/history/paper20/david3.pdf (last accessed February 7, 2000).

———. 2001. The evolving accidental information super-highway. *Oxford Review of Economic Policy* 17 (2): 159-187.

David, Paul A., and Shane Greenstein. 1990. The economics of compatibility standards:
an introduction to recent research. *Economics of Innovation and New Technology* 1
(1/2): 3-41.

Deetz, Stanley. 1985. Critical-cultural research: New sensibilities and old realities.
Journal of Management 11 (2): 121-136.

Denis, Jean-Louis, Ann Langley, and Linda Cazale. 1996. Leadership and strategic
change under ambiguity. *Organization Studies* 17 (4): 673-699.

Dezalay, Yves, and Bryant Garth. 1995. Merchants of law as moral entrepreneurs: Con-
structing international justice from the competition for transnational business disputes. *Law and Society Review* 29 (1): 27-64.

Dueker, Kenneth Sutherlin. 1996. Trademark law lost in cyberspace: Trademark protection for Internet addresses. *Harvard Journal of Law and Technology* 9 (2).
law.harvard.edu/home/jolt/articles/v9n2p483.html (last accessed February 13,
1997).

Easton, David. 1965a. *A framework for political analysis*. Englewood Cliffs: Prentice-
Hall.

———. 1965b. *A systems analysis of political life*. New York: John Wiley & Sons.

Elg, Ulf, and Ulf Johansson. 1997. Decision making in inter-firm networks as a political
process. *Organization Studies* 18 (3): 361-384.

Ellickson, Robert C. 1991. *Order without law: How neighbors settle disputes*. Cambridge: Harvard University Press.

Engels, Friedrich. 1978. On authority. In *The Marx-Engels reader*, edited by R. Tucker.
New York: W. W. Norton.

Federal Networking Council. 1995. US government Internet domain names, *RFC 1816*.
ftp://ftp.isi.edu/in-notes/rfc1816.txt (last accessed December 15, 1999).

Finnemore, Martha, and Kathryn Sikkink. 1998. International norm dynamics and political change. *International Organization* 52 (4): 887-917.

Foster, William A. 1996. Registering the domain name system: An exercise in global
decision making. Paper read at Coordination and Administration of the Internet

Workshop, at Kennedy School of Government, Harvard University, September 8-10. ksgwww.harvard.edu/iip/cai/foster.html (last accessed June 2, 1997).

Foucault, Michel. 1977. *Discipline and punish: The birth of the prison.* London: Penguin Books.

———. 1978. *The history of sexuality, vol. 1: An introduction.* New York: Random House.

———. 1980. Two lectures. In *Power/knowledge: Selected interviews and other writings (1972-1977) by Michel Foucault*, edited by C. Gordon. Hemel Hempstead: The Harvester Press Ltd.

———. 1982. The subject and power. In *Michel Foucault: Beyond structuralism and hermeneutics*, edited by H. L. Dreyfus and P. Rabinow. Brighton: The Harvester Press Ltd.

Froomkin, Michael A. 1996. The Internet as a source of regulatory arbitrage. Paper read at Symposium on Information, National Policies, and International Infrastructure, at John F. Kennedy School of Government & Harvard Law School, September 8-10. www.law.miami.edu/~froomkin/articles/arbitr.htm (last accessed May 11, 1999).

———. 1999a. Consensus has not been established on dispute policy. www.icann watch.org/archive/essays/940255991.shtml (last accessed October 30, 1999).

———. 1999b. A critique of WIPO's RFC3. University of Miami School of Law. www.law.miami.edu/~amf/critique.htm (last accessed February 19, 1999).

———. 2000a. Semi-private international rulemaking: Lessons learned from the WIPO domain name process (version 2.0). University of Miami School of Law: www.law.miami.edu/~froomkin/articles/TPRC.pdf (last accessed January 9, 2002).

———. 2000b. Wrong turn in cyberspace: Using ICANN to route around the APA and the constitution. *Duke Law Journal* 50: 17-184. personal.law.miami.edu/~froomkin /articles/icann.pdf (last accessed September 1, 2001).

Frost, Peter J. 1989. Power, politics, and influence. In *Handbook of organizational communication: An interdisciplinary perspective*, edited by F. M. Jablin, L. L. Putnam, K. H. Roberts and L. W. Porter. London: Sage.

Frost, Peter J., and Carolyn P. Egri. 1990a. Influence of political action on innovation: Part 1. *Leadership and Organization Development Journal* 11 (1): 17-25.

———. 1990b. Influence of political action on innovation: Part II. *Leadership and Organization Development Journal* 11 (2): 4-12.

———. 1991. The political process of innovation. *Research in Organizational Behavior* 13: 229-295.

Gamson, William A. 1966. Reputation and resources in community politics. *American Journal of Sociology* 72 (2): 121-131.

Gandy, Oscar H. Jr. 1993. *The panoptic sort: A political economy of personal information.* Boulder: Westview Press.

Geist, Michael. 2001. Fair.com? An examination of the allegations of systemic unfairness in the ICANN UDRP. University of Ottawa, Faculty of Law. aix1.uottawa.ca/ ~geist/geistudrp.pdf (last accessed September 1, 2001).

Giddens, Anthony. 1995. *A contemporary critique of historical materialism.* Second ed. London: MacMillan Press, Ltd.

Gigante, Alexander. 1996. "Domain-ia": The growing tension between the DNS and trademark law. Paper read at The Self-Governing Internet: Coordination by Design, at Kennedy School of Government, Harvard University, September 8-10. ksgwww.harvard.edu/iip/cai/gigante.html (last accessed October 4, 1999).

Gillett, Sharon Eisner. 1998. Comments of Sharon Eisner Gillet. March 23. www.ntia

.doc.gov/ntiahome/domainname/130dftmail/03_23_98-3.htm (last accessed May 25, 1999).

Gillett, Sharon Eisner, and Mitchell Kapor. 1996. The self-governing Internet: Coordination by design. Paper read at Coordination and Administration of the Internet Workshop, at Kennedy School of Government, Harvard University, September 8-10. ccs.mit.edu/ccswp197.html (last accessed June 2, 1997).

Global Internet Project. 1999. Ensuring the stability of the Internet domain name system. September. www.gip.org/gipicann.htm (last accessed January 12, 2000).

Gould, Mark. 1996a. Governance of the Internet—a UK perspective. Paper read at Coordination and Administration of the Internet Workshop, at Kennedy School of Government, Harvard University, September 8-10. aranea.law.bris.ac.uk/Harvard Final.html (last accessed June 29, 1997).

——. 1996b. Rules in virtual society. *International Review of Law, Computers and Technology* 10 (2): 199-218.

——. 1997. An island in the Net: Domain naming and English administrative law. *John Marshall Journal of Computer and Information Law* 15 (3). aranea.law.bris.ac.uk/ JMLS (last accessed October 4, 1999).

——. 1999. Competing visions of standards and Internet governance. Paper read at Communications Regulation in the Global Information Society, at University of Warwick, June 3-5. aranea.law.bris.ac.uk/Warwick (last accessed October 4, 1999).

Gymer, Keith. 1998. Principles for an electronic commerce-friendly domain name system. Paper read at Internet Naming and Addressing: The Constitution of the New Self-Regulatory Organisation to Succeed IANA, at Brussels, Belgium. July 7, 1998.

Hadjilambrinos, Constantine. 1998. Technological regimes: An analytical framework for the evaluation of technological systems. *Technology in Society* 20 (2): 179-194.

Hafner, Katie, and Matthew Lyon. 1996. *Where wizards stay up late: The origins of the Internet*. New York: Touchstone.

Hanseth, Ole, Eric Monteiro, and Morten Hatling. 1996. Developing information infrastructure: The tension between standardization and flexibility. *Science, Technology, and Human Values* 21 (4): 407-426.

Hawkins, Richard, Robin Mansell, and Jim Skea, eds. 1995. *Standards, innovation, and competitiveness: The politics and economics of standards in national and technical environments*. Aldershot: Edward Elgar.

Helfer, Laurence R. 2001. International dispute settlement at the trademark-domain name interface. *Research Paper No. 2001-9*, Loyola Law School, Los Angeles. pap ers.ssrn.com/sol3/delivery.cfm/SSRN_ID265922_code010404630.pdf?abstractid=2 65922 (last accessed June 25, 2001).

Huigen, Jos. 1993. Information and communication technology in the context of policy networks. *Technology in Society* 15: 327-338.

Huitema, Christian, Jon Postel, and Steve Crocker. 1995. Not all RFCs are standards, *RFC 1796*. ftp://ftp.isi.edu/in-notes/rfc1796.txt (last accessed December 22, 1999).

Hunt, Courtney Shelton, and Howard E. Aldrich. 1998. The second ecology: Organizational communities. *Research in Organizational Behavior* 20: 267-301.

International Ad Hoc Committee. 1996. Draft specifications for administration and management of gTLDs. December 19. www.iahc.org/draft-iahc-gTLDspec-00.html (last accessed May 15, 2001).

——. 1997. Final report of the International Ad Hoc Committee: Recommendations for administration and management of gTLDs. www.gTLD-MoU.org/draft-iahc-recommend-00.html (last accessed February 2, 1997).

International Telecommunication Union. 1999. Internet ISO 3166-based top level domains survey. www.itu.int/net/cctlds (last accessed April 27, 1999).

Internet Architecture Board and Internet Engineering Steering Group. 1995. IPv6 address allocation management, *RFC 1881*. ftp://ftp.isi.edu/in-notes/rfc1881.txt (last accessed December 8, 1999).

Internet Corporation for Assigned Names and Numbers (ICANN). 1999. Uniform domain name dispute resolution policy. October 24. www.icann.org/udrp/udrp-policy-24oct99htm (last accessed December 5, 1999).

Internet Society. 1996. Blue ribbon international panel to examine enhancements to Internet domain name system (October 22). www.iahc.org/press/press1.html (last accessed May 15, 2001).

Johnson, David R., and David G. Post. 1996a. And how shall the Net be governed? A meditation on the relative virtues of decentralized, emergent law. Paper read at Coordination and Administration of the Internet Workshop, at Kennedy School of Government, Harvard University, September 8-10. www.cli.org/emdraft.html (last accessed June 2, 1997).

———. 1996b. Law and borders—the rise of law in cyberspace. *Stanford Law Review* 48. www.cli.org/X0025_LBFIN.html (last accessed May 10, 1999).

Kanter, Rosabeth M. 1985. *The change masters: Corporate entrepreneurs at work.* London: Unwin.

King, John Leslie, Rebecca E. Grinter, and Jeanne M. Pickering. 1997. The rise and fall of Netville: The saga of a cyberspace construction boomtown in the great divide. In *The culture of the Internet*, edited by S. Kiesler. Mahwah: Earlbaum.

Kleinwächter, Wolfgang. 2000. ICANN between technical mandate and political challenges. *Telecommunications Policy* 24 (6/7): 553-563.

———. 2001. Global governance in the information age: GBDe and ICANN as 'pilot projects' for co-regulation and a new trilateral policy? Centre for Internet Research, University of Aahus, Denmark. http://www.imv.au.dk/cfi/eng/pub/ (last accessed November 20, 2001).

Kornhauser, Lewis A. 1992. Are there cracks in the foundations of spontaneous order? *New York University Law Review* 67 (3): 647-673.

Krasner, Stephen D. 1983. Structural causes and regime consequences: regimes as intervening variables. In *International regimes*, edited by S. D. Krasner. Ithaca: Cornell University Press.

———. 1991. Global communications and national power: Life on the pareto frontier. *World Politics* 43 (4): 336-366.

Krol, Ed. 1989. The hitchhikers guide to the Internet, *RFC 1118*. ftp://ftp.isi.edu/in-notes/rfc.1118.txt (last accessed December 5, 1999).

Lasswell, Harold. D., and Abraham Kaplan. 1950. *Power and society: A framework for political inquiry.* New Haven: Yale University Press.

Leaffer, Marshall. 1998. Domain names, globalization, and Internet governance. *Indiana Journal of Global Legal Studies* 6 (1): 139-166. www.law.indiana.edu/glsj/vol6/no1/leaffer.html (last accessed May 10, 1999).

Leiner, Barry M., Vinton G. Cerf, David D. Clark, Robert E. Kahn, Leonard Kleinrock, Daniel C. Lynch, Jon Postel, Larry G. Roberts, and Stephen Wolff. 1998. A brief history of the Internet, version 3.1. www.isoc.org/internet-history/brief.html (last accessed August 8, 1999).

Lemley, Mark A., and Lawrence Lessig. 2000. The end of end-to-end: Preserving the architecture of the Internet in the broadband era. *Working Paper No. 207.* Stanford Law School, John M. Olin Program in Law and Economics. papers.ssrn.com/paper .taf?abstract_id=247737 (last accessed September 27, 2001).

Lessig, Lawrence. 1996a. Reading the constitution in cyberspace. *Emory Law Journal* 45 (summer). www.law.emory.edu/ELJ/volumes/sum96/lessig.html (last accessed June 3, 1999).

———. 1996b. The zones of cyberspace. *Stanford Law Reveiw* 48 (May): 1403-1411.

———. 1997. Tyranny in the infrastructure: The CDA was bad—but PICS may be worse. *Wired* 5.07 (July). www.wired.com/wired/5.07/cyber_rights.html (last accessed June 1, 1999).

———. 1998a. A bad turn for Net governance. *The Industry Standard*, September 18. www.thestandard.com/article/display/1,1151,1718,00.html (last accessed September 25, 1998).

———. 1998b. Comments to NTIA on ICANN DNS proposal, October 7. cyber.harvard .edu/works/lessig/c.pdf (last accessed June 21, 1999).

———. 1998c. Governance. Paper read at Computer Professionals for Social Responsibility (CPSR) Annual Meeting, One Planet, One Net: The Public Interest in Internet Governance, October 10, at Massachusetts Institute of Technology, Cambridge, Massachusetts. cyber.harvard.edu/works/lessig/Ny_q_d1.pdf (last accessed May 11, 1999).

———. 1998d. The laws of cyberspace. Paper read at Taiwan Net '98, March, at Taipei. cyber.harvard.edu/works/lessig/laws_cyberspace.pdf (last accessed May 11, 1999).

———. 1998e. The spam wars. *The Industry Standard*, September 18. www.thestandard .com/article/display/0,1151,3006,00.html (last accessed January 31, 2000).

———. 1999a. *Code and other laws of cyberspace.* New York: Basic Books.

———. 1999b. The law of the horse: What cyberlaw might teach. *Harvard Law Review* (Fall). cyber.harvard.edu/works/lessig/LNC_Q_D2.PDF (last accessed July 3, 1999).

———. 1999c. The limits of open code: Regulatory standards and the future of the Net. *Berkeley Technology Law Journal* 14: 759-769. cyber.harvard.edu/works/lessig/ Berk Pub.pdf (last accessed June 3, 1999).

———. 2001. *The future of ideas: The fate of the commons in a connected world.* New York: Random House.

Levitt, Barbara, and James G. March. 1988. Organisational learning. *Annual Review of Sociology* 14: 319-340.

Liu, Joseph P. 1999. Legitimacy and authority in Internet coordination: a domain name case study. *Indiana Law Journal* 74 (Spring): 587-626.

Loundy, David J. 1997. A primer on trademark law and Internet addressing. *John Marshall Journal of Computer and Information Law* 15. www.loudy.com/JMLS-Trade mark.html (last accessed May 10, 1999).

Lukes, Steven. 1974. *Power: A radical view.* London: MacMillan.

Maher, David. 1996. Trademarks on the Internet: Who's in charge? Paper read at CIX/ISOC Workshop, at Washington D.C. www.aldea.com/cix/maher.html (last accessed October 4, 1999).

Malkin, G. 1994. The tao of IETF—a guide for new attendees of the Internet Engineering Task Force, *RFC 1718.* www.ietf.org/rfc/rfc1718.txt (last accessed November 22, 1999).

Mansell, Robin, and Roger Silverstone, eds. 1996. *Communication by design: The politics of information and communication technologies.* Oxford: Oxford University

Press.

March, James G., and Johan P. Olsen. 1998. The institutional dynamics of international political orders. *International Organizations* 52 (4): 943-969.

Markoff, John. 2001. A plan to expand Internet addresses. *The New York Times*, May 14. www.nytimes.com/2001/05/14/technology/14CISC.html (last accessed May 15, 2001).

Marsan, Carolyn Duffy. 2001. ICANN under attack. *The Industry Standard*, February 8. www.thestandard.net/article/display/0,1151,22068,00.html (last accessed February 9, 2001).

Mathiason, John R., and Charles C. Kuhlman. 1998a. An international communication policy: The Internet, international regulation and new policy structures. Robert F Wagner Graduate School of Public Service: New York University. www.intlmgt.com/ITSpaper.html (last accessed May 26, 1998).

——. 1998b. International public regulation of the Internet: Who will give you your domain name. Paper read at The Internet in a Post-Westphalian Order, at Minneapolis, March 21. www.intlmgt.com/pastprojects/domain.html (last accessed May 26, 1998).

Meyer, John W., and Brian Rowan. 1977. Institutionalized organisations: formal structure as myth and ceremony. *American Journal of Sociology* 83 (2): 340-363.

Mills, D. L. 1981. Internet name domains, *RFC 799*. ftp://ftp.isi.edu/in-notes/rfc799.txt (last accessed December 15, 1999).

Minhas, Jag. 1995. UK Internet name service: A framework for the efficient management of the UK DNS. Hemel Hempstead: British Telecommunications plc.— Managed Network Services.

Mockapetris, Peter. 1983a. Domain names—Concepts and Facilities, *RFC 882*. ftp://ftp .isi.edu/in-notes/rfc882.txt (last accessed December 28, 1999).

——. 1983b. Domain names: implementation and specification, *RFC 883*. ftp://ftp.isi .edu/in-notes/rfc883.txt (last accessed December 28, 1999).

——. 1987a. Domain names—concepts and facilities, *RFC 1034*: ftp://ftp.isi.edu/in-notes/rfc1034.txt (last accessed January 15, 1999).

——. 1987b. Domain names: implementation and specification, *RFC 1035*. ftp//ftp.isi .edu/in-notes/rfc1035.txt (last accessed January 15, 1999).

Moody, Glyn. 2001. *Rebel code: Linux and the open source revolution*. London: Allen Lane The Penguin Press.

Mueller, Milton. 1997a. Comments of Dr. Milton L. Mueller. U.S. Department of Commerce. www.wia.org/pub/mueller-dnsnoi-comments.html (last accessed May 25, 1999).

——. 1997b. Internet domain names: Privatization, competition and freedom of expression. *Cato Institute Briefing Papers* 33. www.cato.org/pubs/briefs/bp-033es.html (last accessed December 3, 1997).

——. 1997c. Internet governance in crisis: The political economy of top-level domains. Paper read at INET '97, at Kuala Lampur, Malaysia. www.isoc.org/isoc/whatis/conferences/inet/97/proceedings/B5/B5_1.HTM (last accessed March 3, 1998).

——. 1998a. The battle over Internet domain names: Global or national TLDs. *Telecommunication Policy* 22 (2): 89-107.

——. 1998b. The 'governance' debacle: How the ideal of internetworking got buried by politics. Paper read at INET 98, at Geneva, Switzerland. www.isoc.org/inet98/proceedings/5a/5a_1.htm (last accessed August 15, 1998).

——. 1998c. Trademarks and domain names: Property rights and institutional evolution in cyberspace. School of Information Studies, Syracuse University. istweb.syr.edu/ ~mueller/study.html (last accessed June 29, 1998).

——. 1999a. Domain names and property rights: Investigating technology's ability to foment institutional change. Paper read at Second Berlin Internet Economics Workshop, at Berlin, May 28-29. istweb.syr.edu/~mueller/berlintoc.html (last accessed August 17, 1999).

——. 1999b. ICANN and internet governance: Sorting through the debris of 'self-regulation'. *Info* 1 (6): 497-520.

——. 2000. Rough justice: An analysis of ICANN's uniform dispute resolution policy. *The Information Society* 17 (3): 151-163.

Murai, Jun. 1999. Presentation to ICANN root server system advisory committee, May 26, at Berlin, Germany. cyber.law.harvard.edu/icann/berlin/archive/jun-murai-pres (last accessed December 14, 1999).

Murphy, Raymond. 1988. *Social closure: The theory of monopolisation and exclusion.* Oxford: Clarendon Press.

Murphy, Robin. 1997. From names to numbers: A brief overview of the domain name system. *InterNIC News*, April. www.superuser.net/manual/dns.html (last accessed May 11, 2001).

Nathenson, Ira S. 1997. Showdown at the domain name corrall: Property rights and personal jurisdiction over squatters, poachers and other parasites. *University of Pittsburgh Law Review* 58. www.pitt.edu/~lawrev/58-4/articles/domain.htm (last accessed October 4, 1999).

National Science Foundation. 1995. Cooperative Agreement No. NCR-9218742, Amendment No. 04. www.networksolutions.com/legal/internic/cooperative-agreement/amendment4.html (last accessed January 4, 2000).

National Science Foundation and Network Solutions Incorporated. 1993. Network information services manager(s) for NSFNET and the NREN: INTERNIC registration services cooperative agreement no. NCR-9218742. www.networksolutions.com /legal/internic/cooperative-agreement/agreement.html (last accessed December 14, 1999).

Naughton, John. 2000. *A brief history of the future: The origins of the Internet.* London: Phoenix.

Nelson, Richard R., and Sidney G. Winter. 1982. *An evolutionary theory of economic change.* Cambridge: The Belknap Press of Harvard University Press.

Network Solutions Inc. 1995. NSI domain dispute resolution policy statement. ftp://rs.internic.net/internic/policy/internic-domain-1.txt (last accessed January 6, 2000).

——. 1998. Annual report. www.netsol.com/nsi/annual98/NSAR98f.pdf (last accessed January 6, 2000).

Neuman, W. Russell, Lee McKnight, and Richard J. Solomon. 1998. *The gordian knot: Political gridlock on the information highway.* Cambridge: MIT Press.

Oliver, Christine. 1992. The antecedents of deinstitutionalization. *Organization Studies* 13 (4): 563-588.

Oppedahl, Carl. 1997. Remedies in domain name lawsuits: How is a domain name like a cow? *John Marshall Journal of Computer & Information Law* 15. www.patents .com/pubs/jmls.sht (last accessed January 19, 1999).

Paré, Daniel J. 2000. *Internet governance in transition: Just who is the master of this domain?* Doctoral dissertation, SPRU—Science and Technology Policy Research, University of Sussex, Falmer, Brighton.

——. 2002. Master of my domain: The politics of Internet governance. In *Inside the communications revolution: New patterns of social and technical interaction*, edited by R. Mansell. Oxford: Oxford University Press.

Parkin, Frank. 1979. *Marxism and class theory: A bourgeois critique.* London: Tavistock Publications.

Pierson, Paul. 2000a. Increasing returns, path dependence, and the study of politics. *American Political Science Review* 94 (2): 251-267.

——. 2000b. The limits of design: Explaining institutional origins and change. *Governance: An International Journal of Policy and Administration* 13 (4): 475-499.

Pinchot, J. III. 1985. *Intrapreneuring.* New York: Harper and Row.

Post, David G. 1995. Anarchy, state, and the Internet: An essay on law-making in cyberspace. *Journal of Online Law.* www.cli.org/DPost/X0023_ANARCHY.html (last accessed February 2, 1997).

——. 1998. Cyberspace's constitutional moment. *The American Lawyer,* November. www.temple.edu/lawschool/dpost/DNSGovernance.htm (last accessed June 9, 1999).

——. 1999. Governing cyberspace, or where is James Madison when we need him? www.temple.edu/lawschool/dpost/icann/comment1.html (last accessed June 7, 1999).

——. 2000. What Larry doesn't get: A libertarian response to *Code and Other Laws of Cyberspace.* January 5. www.temple.edu/lawschool/dpost/Code.html (last accessed January 28, 2000).

Post, David G., and David R. Johnson. 1997a. Borders, spillovers, and complexity: Rule-making processes in cyberspace (and elsewhere). Paper read at Olin Law and Economics Symposium on International Economic Regulation, at Georgetown University Law Centre, April 5. Unpublished manuscript—copies available on request from the authors.

——. 1997b. The new civic virtue of the Net: A complex systems model for the governance of cyberspace. Paper read at Annual Review of the "Internet as a Platform," at The Aspen Institute, Aspen Colorado. www.cli.org/paper4.htm (last accessed March 7, 1997).

Postel, Jon. 1972. Proposed standard socket numbers, *RFC 349.* ftp://ftp.isi.edu/in-notes/rfc349.txt (last accessed December 28, 1999).

——. 1979. IEN 116: Internet name server, *IEN 116.* www.cis.ohio-state.edu/ien/ien-116.txt (last accessed December 28, 1999).

——. 1982. Computer mail meeting notes, *RFC 805.* ftp://ftp.isi.edu/in-notes/rfc805.txt (last accessed December 28, 1999).

——. 1994. Domain name system structure and delegation, *RFC 1591.* ftp://ftp.isi.edu/in-notes/rfc1591.txt (last accessed November 5, 1999).

——. 1995. ISOC statement on domain name fees. Email to ISOC Trustees, September 15. www.wia.org/pub/postel-iana-draft13.htm (last accessed May 15, 2001).

——. 1996a. New registries and the delegation of international top level domains, June. www.newdom.com/archive/draft-postel-iana-itld-admin-01.txt (last accessed November 22, 1999).

——. 1996b. New registries and the delegation of international top level domains, Version 2, August. www.newdom.com/archive/draft-postel-iana-itld-admin-02.txt (last accessed November 22, 1999).

——. 1996c. US DOD [Internet] assigned numbers [authority]*, network information centers (NICs), contractors, and activities. www.wia.org/pub/iana.html (last accessed April 1, 1999).

Postel, Jon, and Joyce Reynolds. 1984. Domain requirements, *RFC 920.* ftp://ftp.isi.edu /in-notes/rfc920.txt (last accessed December 28, 1999).

Quintas, Paul. 1996. Software by design. In *Communication by design: The politics of information and communication technologies,* edited by R. Mansell and R. Silverstone. Oxford: Oxford University Press.

Reidenberg, Joel R. 1996. Governing networks and cyberspace rule—making. *Emory Law Journal* 45. www.law.emory.edu/ELJ/volumes/sum96/reiden.html (last accessed May 10, 1999).

———. 1998. Lex informatica: The formulation of information policy rules through technology. *Texas Law Review* 76 (3). www.epic.org/misc/gulc/materials/reidenberg2 .html (last accessed May 10, 1999).

Reynolds, Joyce, and Jon Postel. 1994. Assigned numbers, *RFC 1700.* ftp://ftp.isi.edu /in-notes/rfc1700.txt (last accessed December 22, 1999).

Rhodes, R. A. W. 1996. The new governance: Governing without government. *Political Studies* XLIV: 652-667.

Roberts, Michael M. 2000. Comments on the civil society statement, July 30. Computer Professionals for Social Responsibility. www.cpsr.org/internetdemocracy/Statement _July-13_Comments.html (last accessed September 3, 2000).

Robins, Kevin and Frank Webster. 2001. *Times of technoculture.* London: Routledge.

Romano, S., and M. Stahl. 1987. Internet numbers, *RFC 1020.* ftp://ftp.isi.edu/in-notes/rfc1118.txt (last accessed December 17, 1999).

Rony, Ellen. 1999. Re: WIPO final report flops. Email message to <DOMAIN-POLICY@LISTS.INTERNIC.NET> (May 1, 1999).

Rony, Ellen, and Peter Rony. 1998. *The domain name handbook: High stakes and strategies in cyberspace.* Lawrence: R&D Books.

Rosenau, James N. 1990. *Turbulence in world politics: A theory of change and continuity.* Princeton: Princeton University Press.

———. 1992. Governance, order, and change in world politics. In *Governance without government: Order and change in world politics,* edited by J. N. Rosenau and E.O. Czempiel. Cambridge: Cambridge University Press.

Ruggie, John Gerard. 1975. International responses to technology: concepts and trends. *International Organization* 29 (summer): 557-583.

Rutkowski, Anthony M. 1997a. Comments of Anthony M. Rutkowski. August 18. www.wia.org/pub/amr-dnsnoi-comments.html (last accessed May 26, 1999).

———. 1997b. The Internet DNS historical timeline. World Internet Alliance. www.wia.org/pub/timeline.txt (last accessed December 17, 1999).

———. 1998a. Factors shaping Internet self-governance. World Internet Alliance. www.wia.org/pub/limits.html (last accessed May 26, 1999).

———. 1998b. The Internet: governance for grabs? World Internet Alliance. www.wia.org/pub/forgrabs.html (last accessed May 24, 1999).

———. 1998c. ITU models and the quest for the Internet. World Internet Alliance. www.wia.org/pub/ITU-MoU.html (last accessed 24 May 1999).

———. 1999. Regulate the Internet? Try if you can. *Communications Week International* 10, April 26.

Samarajiva, Rohan, and Peter Shields. 1990. Macro and micro theoretical frameworks for the new information-communication technologies. Paper read at 40th Annual Conference of the International Communication Association, at Dublin, Ireland, June 24-29.

------. 1992. Emergent institutions of the 'intelligent network': Toward a theoretical understanding. *Media, Culture, and Society* 14: 397-419.

Semeria, Chuck. 1999. Understanding IP addressing: Everything you ever wanted to know. 3Com Corporation, Santa Clara, California. www.3com.com/nsc/501302 .html (last accessed November 22, 1999).

Shaw, Robert. 1996. Internet domain names: Whose domain is this? Paper read at Coordination and Administration of the Internet Workshop, at Kennedy School of Government, Harvard University, September 8-10. www.itu.ch/intreg/dns.html (last accessed February 28, 1997).

------. 1998. Internet governance: Herding cats and sacred cows. Paper read at INET 98, at Geneva, Switzerland. July 22. people.itu.int/~shaw/docs/int-gov.html (last accessed January 10, 2000).

------. 1999. Reflections on governments, governance and sovereignty in the Internet age. Paper read at ICANN Governmental Advisory Committee Meeting, at Santiago, Chile. August 24. people.itu.int/~shaw/docs/reflections-on-ggs.htm (last accessed January 10, 2000).

Simon, Craig. 1998. The technical construction of globalism: Internet governance and the DNS crisis. School of International Studies, University of Miami. www.flywheel.com/ircw/dnsdraft.html (last accessed December 28, 1999).

Slappendel, Carol. 1996. Perspectives on innovation in organizations. *Organization Studies* 17 (1): 107-129.

Smythe, Dallas W. 1972. The "orbital parking slot" syndrome and radio frequency management. *Quarterly Review of Economics and Business* (summer): 7-17.

------. 1977. Communications: Blindspot of western marxism. *Canadian Journal of Political and Social Theory* 1 (3): 1-28.

Stahl, M. 1987. Domain administrators guide, *RFC 1032*. ftp://ftp.isi.edu/in-notes /rfc1032.txt (last accessed January 25, 1999).

Su, Zaw-Sing. 1982. A distributed system for Internet name service, *RFC 830*. ftp://ftp.isi.edu/in-notes/rfc830.txt (last accessed December 28, 1999).

Su, Zaw-Sing, and Jon Postel. 1982. The domain naming convention for Internet user applications, *RFC 819*. ftp://ftp.isi.edu/in-notes/rfc819.txt (last accessed January 19, 1999).

Tang, Puay. 1995. Institutional instability, governance and telematics. *Review of International Political Economy* 2 (4): 567-599.

Tribe, Laurence H. 1972. Policy science: Analysis or ideology. *Philosophy and Public Affairs* 2 (1): 66-110.

United States Department of Commerce. 1997. Request for comments on the registration and administration of Internet domain names. No. 970613137-7137-01, July 2. *Federal Register* 62 (127): 35895-35897. www.ntia.doc.gov/ntiahome/domainname .DN5NOTIC.htm (last accessed May 5, 2000).

------. 1998a. Management of Internet Names and Addresses, June 5. www.ntia.doc.gov /ntiahome/domainname/6_5_98dns.htm (last accessed October 3, 1999).

------. 1998b. A Proposal to Improve Technical Management of Internet Domain Names and Address. National Telecommunications and Information Administration, Washington D.C., January 30. www.ntia.doc.gov/ntiahome/domainname/dns draft .htm (last accessed October 2, 1999).

------. 1998c. Special Award Conditions, NCR-9218742, Amendment No. 11, October 7. www.ntia.doc.gov/ntiahome/domainname/proposals/docnsi100698.htm (last accessed October 10, 1998).

Wallis, Joe, and Brian Dollery. 1997. Autonomous policy leadership: Steering a policy process in the direction of a policy quest. *Governance* 10 (1): 1-22.

Walton, John. 1966a. Discipline, method, and community power: A note on the sociology of knowledge. *American Sociological Review* 31: 684-689.

———. 1966b. Substance and artifact: The current status of research on community power structure. *American Journal of Sociology* 71: 430-438.

Weber, Max. 1978. *Economy and society.* Translated by G. Roth and C. Wittich. Berkeley: University of California Press.

Webster, Frank, and Kevin Robins. 1986. *Information technology: A luddite analysis.* Norwood: Ablex Publishing Corporation.

Weinberg, Jonathan. 2000. ICANN and the problem of legitimacy. *Duke Law Journal* 50: 187-260. www.law.wayne.edu/weinberg/legitimacy.PDF (last accessed September 1, 2001).

———. 2001. Geeks and Greeks. *Info* 3 (4): 313-332.

Wendt, Alexander E. 1987. The agent-structure problem in international relations theory. *International Organization* 41 (3): 335-370.

———. 1998. Constitution and causation in international relations. *Review of International Studies* 24 (4): 101-117.

Wendt, Alexander E., and Raymond Duvall. 1989. Institutions and international order. In *Global changes and theoretical challenges: Approaches to world politics for the 1990s,* edited by E.O. Czempiel and J. N. Rosenau. Lexington: Lexington Books.

Wilkinson, Christopher. 1998. Internet—the next steps. Paper read at Internet Naming and Addressing: The Constitution of the New Self-Regulatory Organisation to Succeed IANA, at Brussels, July 7. www.ispo.cec.be/eif/dns/cw020798.html (last accessed June 24, 2000).

Wilske, Stephan, and Teresa Schiller. 1997. International jurisdiction in cyberspace: Which states may regulate the Internet? *Federal Communications Law Journal* 50 (1). www.law.indiana.edu/fclj/pubs/v50/no1/wilske.html (last accessed June 1, 1999).

Winner, Langdon. 1977. *Autonomous technology: Technics-out-of-control as a theme in political thought.* Cambridge: The MIT Press.

———. 1986. *The whale and the reactor: A search for limits in an age of high technology.* Chicago: University of Chicago Press.

———. 1993. Upon opening the black box and finding it empty: Social constuctivism and the philosophy of technology. *Science, Technology, & Human Values* 18 (3): 362-378.

Woolgar, Steve. 1991. The turn to technology in social studies of science. *Science, Technology, & Human Values* 16: 20-50.

World Intellectual Property Organization (WIPO). 1998a. RFC 1: Request for comments on terms of reference, procedures and timetable for the WIPO Internet domain name process, July 9. ecommerce.wipo.int/domains/process/eng/rfc.html (last accessed July 12, 1998).

———. 1998b. RFC 3: Interim report of the WIPO Internet domain name process, December 23. ecommerce.wipo.int/domains/process/eng.consult.html (last accessed December 28, 1998).

———. 1999. Final report on the WIPO Internet domain name process, April 30. wipo2.wipo.int/process/eng/final_report.html (last accessed May 5, 1999).

Wu, Timothy. 1997. Cyberspace sovereignty? The Internet and the international system. *Harvard Journal of Law and Technology* 10 (3): 647.

——. 1999. Application-centered Internet analysis. *Virginia Law Review* 85: 1163-1203. www.student.virginia.edu/~lawrev/WuPDF.pdf (last accessed October 29, 2001).

Zittrain, Jonathan, and David Clark. 1997. On the issue of domain names. Transcript of Dialogue. Harvard Law School, Cambridge, Massachusetts. October 1. cyber.harva rd.edu /fallsem97/trans/clark/. (last accessed April 1, 1999).

Index

About the Author

Dr. Daniel Paré has a research background in political science and and in science, technology and innovation studies. He completed his DPhil at SPRU—Science and Technology Policy Research, University of Sussex in November 2000 and is now employed as a research fellow in Media@LSE, London School of Economics and Political Science. His research interests focus on the transformative influence of information and communication technologies on sociopolitical networks, standards and regulatory regimes, intellectual property rights, and e-democracy.